PostgreSQL Server Programming
Second Edition

Extend PostgreSQL using PostgreSQL server
programming to create, test, debug, and optimize
a range of user-defined functions in your favorite
programming language

Usama Dar

Hannu Krosing

Jim Mlodgenski

Kirk Roybal

[PACKT] open source ✳
PUBLISHING community experience distilled

BIRMINGHAM - MUMBAI

PostgreSQL Server Programming
Second Edition

First published: June 2013

Second edition: February 2015

Production reference: 1210215

Published by Packt Publishing Ltd.
Livery Place
35 Livery Street
Birmingham B3 2PB, UK.

ISBN 978-1-78398-058-1

www.packtpub.com

Credits

Authors
Usama Dar
Hannu Krosing
Jim Mlodgenski
Kirk Roybal

Reviewers
Stephen Frost
Rick van Hattem
Vibhor Kumar
Jeff Lawson
Mariano Reingart
Julien Tachoires

Commissioning Editor
Usha Iyer

Acquisition Editors
Antony Lowe
Meeta Rajani
Sam Wood

Content Development Editor
Adrian Raposo

Technical Editors
Mrunmayee Patil
Chinmay Puranik

Copy Editors
Dipti Kapadia
Aarti Saldanha

Project Coordinator
Kinjal Bari

Proofreaders
Maria Gould
Linda Morris

Indexer
Monica Ajmera Mehta

Production Coordinator
Nitesh Thakur

Cover Work
Nitesh Thakur

About the Authors

Usama Dar is a seasoned software developer and architect. During his 14 years' career, he has worked extensively with PostgreSQL and other database technologies. He worked on PostgreSQL internals extensively while he was working for EnterpriseDB. Currently, he lives in Munich where he works for Huawei's European Research Center. He designs the next generation of high-performance database systems based on open source technologies, such as PostgreSQL, which are used under high workloads and strict performance requirements.

Hannu Krosing was a PostgreSQL user before it was rewritten to use SQL as its main query language in 1995. Therefore, he has both the historic perspective of its development, as well as almost 20 years of experience in using it to solve various real-life problems.

He was the first database administrator and database architect at Skype, where he invented the sharding language PL/Proxy that allows you to scale the user database in order to work with billions of users.

After he left Skype at the end of 2006 — about a year after it was bought by eBay — he has been working as a PostgreSQL consultant with 2ndQuadrant, the premier PostgreSQL consultancy with a global reach and local presence in most parts of the world.

He has coauthored *PostgreSQL 9 Administration Cookbook*, *Packt Publishing*, together with one of the main PostgreSQL developers, Simon Riggs.

I want to sincerely thank my wife, Evelyn, for her support while writing this book.

Jim Mlodgenski is the CTO of OpenSCG, a professional services company focused on leveraging open source technologies for strategic advantage. He was formerly the CEO of StormDB, a database cloud company focused on horizontal scalability. Prior to StormDB, he has held highly technical roles at Cirrus Technology, Inc., EnterpriseDB, and Fusion Technologies.

Jim is also a fervent advocate of PostgreSQL. He is on the board of the United States PostgreSQL Association as well as a part of the organizing teams of the New York PostgreSQL User Group and Philadelphia PostgreSQL User Group.

Kirk Roybal has been an active member of the PostgreSQL community since 1998. He has helped organize user groups in Houston, Dallas, and Bloomington, IL. He has mentored many junior database administrators and provided cross-training to senior database engineers. He has provided solutions using PostgreSQL for reporting, business intelligence, data warehousing, applications, and development support.

He saw the scope of PostgreSQL when his first small-scale business customer asked for a web application. At that time, competitive database products were either extremely immature or cost prohibitive.

Kirk has stood by his choice of PostgreSQL for many years now. His expertise is founded on keeping up with features and capabilities as they become available.

Writing a book has been a unique experience for me. Many people fantasize about it, few start one, and even fewer get to publication. I am proud to be part of a team that actually made it to the book shelf (which itself is a diminishing breed). Thanks to Sarah Cullington from Packt Publishing for giving me a chance to participate in the project. I believe that the PostgreSQL community will be better served by this information, and I hope that they receive this as a reward for the time that they have invested in me over the years.

A book only has the value that the readers give it. Thank you to the PostgreSQL community for all the technical, personal, and professional development help you have provided. The PostgreSQL community is a great bunch of people, and I have enjoyed the company of many of them. I hope to contribute more to this project in the future, and I hope you find my contributions as valuable as I find yours.

Thank you to my family for giving me a reason to succeed and for listening to the gobbledygook and nodding appreciatively.

Have you ever had your family ask you what you were doing and answered them with a function? Try it. No, then again, don't try it. They may just have you involuntarily checked in somewhere.

About the Reviewers

Stephen Frost is a major contributor and committer to PostgreSQL, who has been involved with PostgreSQL since 2002, and has developed features such as the role system and column-level privileges.

He is the chief technology officer at Crunchy Data Solutions, Inc., the PostgreSQL company for Secure Enterprises. He is involved in the advancement of PostgreSQL's capabilities, particularly in the area of security in order to support the needs of government and financial institutions who have strict security and regulatory requirements.

Rick van Hattem is an entrepreneur with a computer science background and a long-time open source developer with vast experience in the C, C++, Python, and Java languages. Additionally, he has worked with most large database servers such as Oracle, MS SQL, and MySQL, but he has been focusing on PostgreSQL since Version 7.4.

He is one of the founders of the Fashiolista.com social network, and until recently, he was the CTO. Here, he used PostgreSQL to scale the feeds for millions of users to show that PostgreSQL can hold up to NoSQL solutions, given some tuning and additional tools. After Fashiolista, he worked as a freelance consultant for several companies, including 2ndQuadrant.

He is currently the founder of PGMon.com, a monitoring service that analyzes your databases, indexes, and queries to keep them running at peak performance. In addition to analyzing your database settings, the system actively monitors your queries and gives you recommendations to enhance performance.

He is also the creator and maintainer of a large number of open source projects, such as pg_query_analyser, pg_cascade_timestamp, QtQuery, Python-Statsd, and Django-Statsd.

Vibhor Kumar is a principal system architect at EnterpriseDB who specializes in assisting Fortune 100 companies to deploy, manage, and optimize Postgres databases. He joined EnterpriseDB in 2008 to work with Postgres after several years of working with Oracle systems. He has worked in team leadership roles at IBM Global Services and BMC Software as well as an Oracle database administrator at CMC Ltd. for several years. He has developed expertise in Oracle, DB2, and MongoDB and holds certifications in them. He has experience working with MS SQL Server, MySQL, and data warehousing. He holds a bachelor's degree in computer science from the University of Lucknow and a master's degree in computer science from the Army Institute of Management, Kolkata. He is a certified PostgreSQL trainer and holds a professional certification in Postgres Plus Advanced Server from EnterpriseDB.

Jeff Lawson has been a fan and user of PostgreSQL since the time he discovered it in 2001. Over the years, he has also developed and deployed applications for IBM DB2, Oracle, MySQL, Microsoft SQL Server, Sybase, and others, but he always prefers PostgreSQL for its balance of features and openness. Much of his experience involves developing for Internet-facing websites/projects that require highly scalable databases with high availability or with provisions for disaster recovery.

He currently works as the director of software development for FlightAware, which is an airplane-tracking website that uses PostgreSQL and other open source software to store and analyze the positions of the thousands of flights that are operated worldwide every day. He has extensive experience in software architecture, data security, and network protocol design from the software engineering positions he has held at Univa / United Devices, Microsoft, NASA's Jet Propulsion Laboratory, and WolfeTech. He is a founder of distributed.net, which pioneered distributed computing in the 1990s, and he continues to serve as the chief of operations and as a member of the board there. He earned a BSc degree in computer science from Harvey Mudd College.

He is fond of cattle, holds an FAA private pilot certificate, and owns an airplane based in Houston, Texas.

Mariano Reingart lives in Buenos Aires, Argentina, and is a specialist in the software development of applications and libraries (web services, PDF, GUI, replication, and so on) with more than 10 years of experience. Currently, he is the PostgreSQL regional contact for Argentina and a Python Software Foundation member.

He is a major contributor to the web2py Python web framework, and now he's working on the wxWidgets multiplatform GUI toolkit (specifically in the Qt port and Android mobile areas). Also, he has contributed to more than a dozen open source projects, including an interface for Free Electronic Invoice web services (PyAfipWs) and Pythonic replication for PostgreSQL (PyReplica).

He has a bachelor's degree in computer systems analysis, and currently, he's a master's candidate for the MSc in free software degree at the Open University of Catalonia.

He works on his own funded entrepreneurial venture formed by an open group of independent professionals, dedicated to software development, training, and technical support, focusing on open source tools (GNU/Linux, Python, PostgreSQL, and web2py/wxPython).

He has worked for local Python-based companies in large business applications (ERP, SCM, and CRM) and mission critical systems (election counting, electronic voting, and 911 emergency events support). He has contributed to books such as *web2py Enterprise Web Framework, Third Edition,* and *web2py Application Development Cookbook, Packt Publishing*, and several Spanish translations of the PostgreSQL official documentation.

His full resume is available at http://reingart.blogspot.com/p/resume.html.

Julien Tachoires is a PostgreSQL specialist, who works as consultant for the French PostgreSQL company Dalibo. He is the main developer of pg_activity, a top-end software dedicated to follow the PostgreSQL incoming traffic in real time, which is written in Python.

> I want to thank my employer Dalibo; my wife, Camille; and my son, Arthur.

www.PacktPub.com

Support files, eBooks, discount offers, and more

For support files and downloads related to your book, please visit
www.PacktPub.com.

Did you know that Packt offers eBook versions of every book published, with PDF
and ePub files available? You can upgrade to the eBook version at www.PacktPub.com
and as a print book customer, you are entitled to a discount on the eBook copy. Get in
touch with us at service@packtpub.com for more details.

At www.PacktPub.com, you can also read a collection of free technical articles,
sign up for a range of free newsletters and receive exclusive discounts and offers
on Packt books and eBooks.

https://www2.packtpub.com/books/subscription/packtlib

Do you need instant solutions to your IT questions? PacktLib is Packt's online digital
book library. Here, you can search, access, and read Packt's entire library of books.

Why subscribe?

- Fully searchable across every book published by Packt
- Copy and paste, print, and bookmark content
- On demand and accessible via a web browser

Free access for Packt account holders

If you have an account with Packt at www.PacktPub.com, you can use this to access
PacktLib today and view 9 entirely free books. Simply use your login credentials for
immediate access.

Table of Contents

Preface

This fascinating guide to server programming will take your skills of PostgreSQL to a whole new level. A step-by-step approach with illuminating examples will educate you about the full range of possibilities. You will understand the extension framework of PostgreSQL and leverage it in ways you haven't even invented yet. You will learn how to write functions and create your own data types, all in your favorite programming language. It is a step-by-step tutorial, with plenty of tips and tricks to kick-start server programming.

What this book covers

Chapter 1, What Is a PostgreSQL Server?, introduces you to the PostgreSQL server and will set the tone for the rest of the book. It introduces you to the ways in which a PostgreSQL server is extendible, and shows you that it can be treated as a complete software development framework instead of just a database server.

Chapter 2, Server Programming Environments, elaborates that PostgreSQL is built to handle user needs, but more importantly, it is built not to change underneath users in the future. It will touch upon the environments and will highlight some of the important things to be kept in mind when programming on the server in PostgreSQL.

Chapter 3, Your First PL/pgSQL Function, builds the foundations by demonstrating how to write simple PL/pgSQL functions.

Chapter 4, Returning Structured Data, builds on the knowledge of writing PL/pgSQL functions and demonstrates how to write functions that return a set of values such as rows, arrays, and cursors.

Chapter 5, PL/pgSQL Trigger Functions, discusses how to write PL/pgSQL functions that are used to write trigger logic. It also discusses the various types of triggers available in PostgreSQL and the options that a database developer has when writing such functions.

Chapter 6, PostgreSQL Event Triggers, discusses PostgreSQL's event trigger functionality. Event triggers are fired when running a DDL operation on a table. This chapter discusses the various possibilities and options of creating event triggers and their limitations in PostgreSQL.

Chapter 7, Debugging PL/pgSQL, elaborates on how to debug PL/pgSQL's stored procedures and functions in PostgreSQL. This chapter explains how to install the debugger plugin and use the pgAdmin debugger console.

Chapter 8, Using Unrestricted Languages, explains the differences between restricted and unrestricted PostgreSQL languages. This chapter uses PL/Python as an example and demonstrates the examples of both restricted and unrestricted functions in PL/Python.

Chapter 9, Writing Advanced Functions in C, explains how to extend PostgreSQL by writing user-defined functions (UDFs) in C.

Chapter 10, Scaling Your Database with PL/Proxy, explains the use of a special programming language in PostgreSQL called PL/Proxy and how to use it in order to partition and shard your database.

Chapter 11, PL/Perl – Perl Procedural Language, discusses a popular PL language in PostgreSQL called PL/Perl. This chapter uses some simple examples to demonstrate how you can use Perl to write database functions.

Chapter 12, PL/Tcl – Tcl Procedural Language, discusses Tcl as a language of choice when writing database functions. It discusses the pros and cons of using Tcl in the database.

Chapter 13, Publishing Your Code as PostgreSQL Extensions, discusses how to package and distribute the PostgreSQL extensions. Well-packaged extensions can be easily distributed and installed by other users. This chapter also introduces you to the PostgreSQL Extension Network (PGXN) and shows you how to use it to get the extensions published by other developers.

Chapter 14, PostgreSQL as an Extensible RDBMS, discusses more extensibility options in PostgreSQL, such as creating new data types, operators, and index methods.

What you need for this book

In order to follow this book, you need the following software:

- PostgreSQL Database Server 9.4
- Linux/Unix Operating System
- Python 2, Perl, and Tcl

Who this book is for

This book is for moderate to advanced level PostgreSQL database professionals. To get a better understanding of this book, you should have a general experience in writing SQL, a basic idea of query tuning, and some coding experience in a language of your choice.

Conventions

In this book, you will find a number of text styles that distinguish between different kinds of information. Here are some examples of these styles and an explanation of their meaning.

Code words in text, database table names, folder names, filenames, file extensions, pathnames, dummy URLs, user input, and Twitter handles are shown as follows: "If any of the checks fail, you should do ROLLBACK instead of COMMIT."

A block of code is set as follows:

```
CREATE TABLE accounts(owner text, balance numeric, amount
    numeric);
INSERT INTO accounts VALUES ('Bob',100);
INSERT INTO accounts VALUES ('Mary',200);
```

When we wish to draw your attention to a particular part of a code block, the relevant lines or items are set in bold:

```
CREATE OR REPLACE FUNCTION fibonacci_seq(num integer)
  RETURNS SETOF integer AS $$
DECLARE
  a int := 0;
  b int := 1;
BEGIN
  IF (num <= 0)
    THEN RETURN;
```

```
    END IF;

    RETURN NEXT a;
    LOOP
       EXIT WHEN num <= 1;
       RETURN NEXT b;

          num = num - 1;
          SELECT b, a + b INTO a, b;
    END LOOP;
  END;
  $$ LANGUAGE plpgsql;
```

Any command-line input or output is written as follows:

```
$ psql -c "SELECT 1 AS test"
```

New terms and **important words** are shown in bold. Words that you see on the screen, for example, in menus or dialog boxes, appear in the text like this: "Enter some values into the columns, as seen in the preceding screenshot, and click on the **Debug** button."

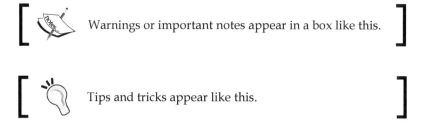

Warnings or important notes appear in a box like this.

Tips and tricks appear like this.

Reader feedback

Feedback from our readers is always welcome. Let us know what you think about this book—what you liked or disliked. Reader feedback is important for us as it helps us develop titles that you will really get the most out of.

To send us general feedback, simply e-mail feedback@packtpub.com, and mention the book's title in the subject of your message.

If there is a topic that you have expertise in and you are interested in either writing or contributing to a book, see our author guide at www.packtpub.com/authors.

Customer support

Now that you are the proud owner of a Packt book, we have a number of things to help you to get the most from your purchase.

Downloading the example code

You can download the example code files from your account at `http://www.packtpub.com` for all the Packt Publishing books you have purchased. If you purchased this book elsewhere, you can visit `http://www.packtpub.com/support` and register to have the files e-mailed directly to you.

Errata

Although we have taken every care to ensure the accuracy of our content, mistakes do happen. If you find a mistake in one of our books—maybe a mistake in the text or the code—we would be grateful if you could report this to us. By doing so, you can save other readers from frustration and help us improve subsequent versions of this book. If you find any errata, please report them by visiting `http://www.packtpub.com/submit-errata`, selecting your book, clicking on the **Errata Submission Form** link, and entering the details of your errata. Once your errata are verified, your submission will be accepted and the errata will be uploaded to our website or added to any list of existing errata under the Errata section of that title.

To view the previously submitted errata, go to `https://www.packtpub.com/books/content/support` and enter the name of the book in the search field. The required information will appear under the **Errata** section.

Piracy

Piracy of copyrighted material on the Internet is an ongoing problem across all media. At Packt, we take the protection of our copyright and licenses very seriously. If you come across any illegal copies of our works in any form on the Internet, please provide us with the location address or website name immediately so that we can pursue a remedy.

Please contact us at `copyright@packtpub.com` with a link to the suspected pirated material.

We appreciate your help in protecting our authors and our ability to bring you valuable content.

Questions

If you have a problem with any aspect of this book, you can contact us at questions@packtpub.com, and we will do our best to address the problem.

1
What Is a PostgreSQL Server?

If you think that a PostgreSQL Server is just a storage system and the only way to communicate with it is by executing SQL statements, you are limiting yourself tremendously. That is, you are using just a tiny part of the database's features.

A PostgreSQL Server is a powerful framework that can be used for all kinds of data processing, and even some non-data server tasks. It is a server platform that allows you to easily mix and match functions and libraries from several popular languages.

Consider this complicated, multilanguage sequence of work:

- Call a string parsing function in Perl
- Convert the string to XSLT and process the result using JavaScript
- Ask for a secure stamp from an external timestamping service, such as http://guardtime.com/, using their SDK for C
- Write a Python function to digitally sign the result

This multilanguage sequence of work can be implemented as a series of simple function calls using several of the available server programming languages. The developer who needs to accomplish all this work can just call a single PostgreSQL function without the need to be aware of how the data is being passed between languages and libraries:

```
SELECT convert_to_xslt_and_sign(raw_data_string);
```

In this book, we will discuss several facets of PostgreSQL Server programming. PostgreSQL has all of the native server-side programming features available in most larger database systems such as triggers, which are automated actions invoked automatically each time data is changed. However, it has uniquely deep abilities to override the built-in behavior down to very basic operators. This unique PostgreSQL ability comes from its catalog-driven design, which stores information about data types, functions, and access methods. The ability of PostgreSQL to load user-defined functions via dynamic loading makes it rapidly changeable without having to recompile the database itself. There are several things you can do with this flexibility of customization. Some examples of this customization include the following:

- Writing **user-defined functions (UDF)** to carry out complex computations
- Adding complicated constraints to make sure that the data in the server meets guidelines
- Creating triggers in many languages to make related changes to other tables, audit changes, forbid the action from taking place if it does not meet certain criteria, prevent changes to the database, enforce and execute business rules, or replicate data
- Defining new data types and operators in the database
- Using the geography types defined in the PostGIS package
- Adding your own index access methods for either the existing or new data types, making some queries much more efficient

What sort of things can you do with these features? There are limitless possibilities, such as the ones listed here:

- Write data extractor functions to get just the interesting parts from structured data, such as XML or JSON, without needing to ship the whole, possibly huge, document to the client application.
- Process events asynchronously, such as sending mails without slowing down the main application. You can create a mail queue for changes to user information, populated by a trigger. A separate mail-sending process can consume this data whenever it is notified by an application process.
- Implement a new data type to custom hash the passwords.
- Write functions, which provide inside information about the server, for example, cache contents, table-wise lock information, or the SSL certificate information of a client connection for a monitoring dashboard.

The rest of this chapter is presented as a series of descriptions of common data management tasks, showing how they can be solved in a robust and elegant way via server programming.

> The samples in this chapter are all tested to work, but they come with minimal commentary. They are used here just to show you various things that server programming can accomplish. The techniques that are described will be explained thoroughly in later chapters.

Why program in the server?

Developers program their code in a number of different languages, and it can be designed to run just about anywhere. When writing an application, some people follow the philosophy that as much of the logic as possible for the application should be pushed to the client. We see this in the explosion of applications leveraging JavaScript inside browsers. Others like to push the logic into the middle tier, with an application server handling the business rules. These are all valid ways to design an application, so why will you want to program in the database server?

Let's start with a simple example. Many applications include a list of customers who have a balance in their account. We'll use this sample schema and data:

```
CREATE TABLE accounts(owner text, balance numeric, amount
    numeric);
INSERT INTO accounts VALUES ('Bob',100);
INSERT INTO accounts VALUES ('Mary',200);
```

Downloading the example code

You can download the example code files for all the Packt books you have purchased from your account at http://www.packtpub.com. If you purchased this book elsewhere, you can visit http://www.packtpub.com/support and register to have the files e-mailed directly to you.

When using a database, the most common way to interact with it, is to use SQL queries. If you want to move 14 dollars from Bob's account to Mary's account with simple SQL, you can do so using the following:

```
UPDATE accounts SET balance = balance - 14.00 WHERE owner = 'Bob';
UPDATE accounts SET balance = balance + 14.00 WHERE owner = 'Mary';
```

However, you also have to make sure that Bob actually has enough money (or credit) in his account. Note that if anything fails, then none of the transactions will happen. In an application program, this is how the preceding code snippet will be modified:

```
BEGIN;
SELECT amount FROM accounts WHERE owner = 'Bob' FOR UPDATE;
-- now in the application check that the amount is actually bigger
-- than 14
UPDATE accounts SET amount = amount - 14.00 WHERE owner = 'Bob';
UPDATE accounts SET amount = amount + 14.00 WHERE owner = 'Mary';
COMMIT;
```

Did Mary actually have an account? If she did not, the last UPDATE command will succeed by updating zero rows. If any of the checks fail, you should do ROLLBACK instead of COMMIT. Once you have done all this for all the clients that transfer money, a new requirement will invariably arrive. Perhaps, the minimum amount that can be transferred is now 5.00. You will need to revisit the code in all your clients again.

So, what can you do to make all of this more manageable, secure, and robust? This is where server programming, executing code on the database server itself, can help. You can move the computations, checks, and data manipulations entirely into a UDF on the server. This not only ensures that you have only one copy of operation logic to manage, but also makes things faster by not requiring several round trips between the client and the server. If required, you can also make sure that only the essential information is given out from the database. For example, there is no business for most client applications to know how much money Bob has in his account. Mostly, they only need to know whether there is enough money to make the transfer, or to be more specific, whether the transaction succeeded.

Using PL/pgSQL for integrity checks

PostgreSQL includes its own programming language named PL/pgSQL that is aimed to integrate easily with SQL commands. PL stands for procedural language, and this is just one of the many languages available for writing server code. pgSQL is the shorthand for PostgreSQL.

Unlike basic SQL, PL/pgSQL includes procedural elements, such as the ability to use the if/then/else statements and loops. You can easily execute SQL statements, or even loop over the result of a SQL statement in the language.

The integrity checks needed for the application can be done in a PL/pgSQL function that takes three arguments: names of the payer and the recipient and the amount to be paid. This sample also returns the status of the payment:

```
CREATE OR REPLACE FUNCTION transfer(
            i_payer text,
            i_recipient text,
            i_amount numeric(15,2))
RETURNS text
AS
$$
DECLARE
  payer_bal numeric;
BEGIN
  SELECT balance INTO payer_bal
     FROM accounts
  WHERE owner = i_payer FOR UPDATE;
  IF NOT FOUND THEN
    RETURN 'Payer account not found';
  END IF;
  IF payer_bal < i_amount THEN
    RETURN 'Not enough funds';
  END IF;

  UPDATE accounts
      SET balance = balance + i_amount
    WHERE owner = i_recipient;
  IF NOT FOUND THEN
    RETURN 'Recipient does not exist';
  END IF;

  UPDATE accounts
      SET balance = balance - i_amount
    WHERE owner = i_payer;
  RETURN 'OK';
END;
$$ LANGUAGE plpgsql;
```

Here are a few examples of the usage of this function, assuming that you haven't executed the previously proposed UPDATE statements yet:

```
postgres=# SELECT * FROM accounts;
 owner | balance
-------+---------
 Bob   |     100
 Mary  |     200
(2 rows)

postgres=# SELECT transfer('Bob','Mary',14.00);
 transfer
----------
 OK
(1 row)

postgres=# SELECT * FROM accounts;
 owner | balance
-------+---------
 Mary  |  214.00
 Bob   |   86.00
(2 rows)
```

Your application will need to check the return code and decide how to handle these errors. As long as it is written to reject any unexpected value, you can extend this function to do more checking, such as the minimum transferrable amount, and you can be sure it will be prevented. The following three errors can be returned:

```
postgres=# SELECT * FROM transfer('Fred','Mary',14.00);
         transfer
-------------------------
 Payer account not found
(1 row)

postgres=# SELECT * FROM transfer('Bob','Fred',14.00);
         transfer
-------------------------
 Recipient does not exist
(1 row)

postgres=# SELECT * FROM transfer('Bob','Mary',500.00);
       transfer
-------------------
 Not enough funds
(1 row)
```

For these checks to always work, you will need to make all the transfer operations go through the function, rather than manually changing the values with SQL statements. One way to achieve this, is by revoking update privileges from users and from a user with higher privileges that define the transfer function with SECURITY DEFINER. This will allow the restricted users to run the function as if they have higher privileges similar to the function's creator.

About this book's code examples

The sample output shown here has been created with the psql utility of PostgreSQL, usually running on a Linux system. Most of the code will work the same way if you are using a GUI utility such as pgAdmin3 to access the server instead. Take an example of the following line of code:

```
postgres=# SELECT 1;
```

The postgres=# part is the prompt shown by the psql command.

The examples in this book have been tested using PostgreSQL 9.3. They will probably work on PostgreSQL Version 8.3 and later. There haven't been many major changes to how server programming happens in the last few versions of PostgreSQL. The syntax has become stricter over time to reduce the possibility of mistakes in the server programming code. Due to the nature of these changes, most code from newer versions will still run on the older ones, unless it uses very new features. However, the older code can easily fail to run due to one of the newly enforced restrictions.

Switching to the expanded display

When using the psql utility to execute a query, PostgreSQL normally outputs the result using vertically aligned columns:

```
$ psql -c "SELECT 1 AS test"
 test
------
    1
(1 row)


$ psql
psql (9.3.2)
```

```
Type "help" for help.


  postgres=# SELECT 1 AS test;
   test
  ------
      1
  (1 row)
```

You can tell when you're seeing a regular output because it will end up showing the number of rows.

This type of output is hard to fit into the text of a book such as this. It's easier to print the output from what the program calls the expanded display, which breaks each column into a separate line. You can switch to the expanded display using either the -x command-line switch or by sending \x to the psql program. Here's an example of using each of these:

```
$ psql -x -c "SELECT 1 AS test"
-[ RECORD 1 ]
test | 1


$ psql
psql (9.3.2)
Type "help" for help.
postgres=# \x
Expanded display is on.
postgres=# SELECT 1 AS test;
-[ RECORD 1 ]
test | 1
```

Notice how the expanded output doesn't show the row count and numbers each output row. To save space, not all of the examples in the book will show the expanded output being turned on. You can normally tell which type you can see, by differences such as whether you're seeing rows or RECORD. The expanded mode will normally be preferred when the output of the query is too wide to fit into the available width of the book. It is a good idea to set the expanded mode to auto. This will automatically switch to expanded mode for tables with a lot of columns. You can turn on the expanded mode using \x auto:

```
  postgres=# \x auto
  Expanded display is used automatically.
```

Moving beyond simple functions

Server programming can mean a lot of different things. Server programming is not just about writing server functions. There are many other things you can do in the server, which can be considered as programming.

Data comparisons using operators

For more complex tasks, you can define your own types, operators, and casts from one type to another, letting you actually compare apples and oranges.

As shown in the next example, you can define the type fruit_qty for fruit-with -quantity and then teach PostgreSQL to compare apples and oranges, say to make one orange to be worth 1.5 apples, in order to convert apples to oranges:

```
postgres=# CREATE TYPE FRUIT_QTY as (name text, qty int);

postgres=# SELECT '("APPLE", 3)'::FRUIT_QTY;
 fruit_qty
----------------
 (APPLE,3)
(1 row)

CREATE FUNCTION fruit_qty_larger_than(left_fruit FRUIT_QTY,
    right_fruit FRUIT_QTY)
RETURNS BOOL
AS $$
BEGIN
    IF (left_fruit.name = 'APPLE' AND right_fruit.name = 'ORANGE')
    THEN
        RETURN left_fruit.qty > (1.5 * right_fruit.qty);
    END IF;
    IF (left_fruit.name = 'ORANGE' AND
      right_fruit.name = 'APPLE' )
    THEN
        RETURN (1.5 * left_fruit.qty) > right_fruit.qty;
    END IF;
    RETURN  left_fruit.qty > right_fruit.qty;
END;
$$
LANGUAGE plpgsql;

postgres=# SELECT fruit_qty_larger_than('("APPLE",
            3)'::FRUIT_QTY,'("ORANGE", 2)'::FRUIT_QTY);
```

```
   fruit_qty_larger_than
 -----------------------
  f
(1 row)

postgres=# SELECT fruit_qty_larger_than('("APPLE",
            4)'::FRUIT_QTY,'("ORANGE", 2)'::FRUIT_QTY);
   fruit_qty_larger_than
 -----------------------
  t
(1 row)

CREATE OPERATOR > (
    leftarg = FRUIT_QTY,
    rightarg = FRUIT_QTY,
    procedure = fruit_qty_larger_than,
    commutator = >
);

 postgres=# SELECT '("ORANGE", 2)'::FRUIT_QTY > '("APPLE",
            2)'::FRUIT_QTY;
 ?column?
 ----------
  t
(1 row)

postgres=# SELECT '("ORANGE", 2)'::FRUIT_QTY > '("APPLE",
            3)'::FRUIT_QTY;
 ?column?
 ----------
  f
(1 row)
```

Managing related data with triggers

Server programming can also mean setting up automated actions (triggers), so that some operations in the database cause some other things to happen as well. For example, you can set up a process where making an offer on some items is automatically reserved to them being in the stock table.

So, let's create a fruit stock table, as shown here:

```
CREATE TABLE fruits_in_stock (
    name text PRIMARY KEY,
```

```
    in_stock integer NOT NULL,
    reserved integer NOT NULL DEFAULT 0,
    CHECK (in_stock between 0 and 1000 ),
    CHECK (reserved <= in_stock)
);
```

The CHECK constraints make sure that some basic rules are followed: you can't have more than 1000 fruits in stock (they'll probably go bad), you can't have a negative stock, and you can't reserve more than what you have. The fruit_offer table will contain the fruits from stock which are on offer. When we insert a row in the fruit_offer table. The offered amount will be reserved in the stock table as shown:

```
CREATE TABLE fruit_offer (
    offer_id serial PRIMARY KEY,
    recipient_name text,
    offer_date timestamp default current_timestamp,
    fruit_name text REFERENCES fruits_in_stock,
    offered_amount integer
);
```

The offer table has an ID for the offer (so you can distinguish between offers later), recipient, date, offered fruit name, and offered amount.

In order to automate the reservation management, you first need a TRIGGER function, which implements the management logic:

```
CREATE OR REPLACE FUNCTION reserve_stock_on_offer () RETURNS trigger
AS $$
    BEGIN
        IF TG_OP = 'INSERT' THEN
            UPDATE fruits_in_stock
          SET reserved = reserved + NEW.offered_amount
        WHERE name = NEW.fruit_name;
    ELSIF TG_OP = 'UPDATE' THEN
        UPDATE fruits_in_stock
          SET reserved = reserved - OLD.offered_amount
                                  + NEW.offered_amount
        WHERE name = NEW.fruit_name;
    ELSIF TG_OP = 'DELETE' THEN
      UPDATE fruits_in_stock
          SET reserved = reserved - OLD.offered_amount
        WHERE name = OLD.fruit_name;
        END IF;
        RETURN NEW;
    END;
$$ LANGUAGE plpgsql;
```

You have to tell PostgreSQL to call this function each and every time the offer row is changed:

```
CREATE TRIGGER manage_reserve_stock_on_offer_change
AFTER INSERT OR UPDATE OR DELETE ON fruit_offer
    FOR EACH ROW EXECUTE PROCEDURE reserve_stock_on_offer();
```

After this, we are ready to test the functionality. First, we will add some fruits to our stock:

```
INSERT INTO fruits_in_stock VALUES('APPLE',500);
INSERT INTO fruits_in_stock VALUES('ORANGE',500);
```

Then, we will check the stock (using the expanded display):

```
postgres=# \x
Expanded display is on.
postgres=# SELECT * FROM fruits_in_stock;
-[ RECORD 1 ]----
name     | APPLE
in_stock | 500
reserved | 0
-[ RECORD 2 ]----
name     | ORANGE
in_stock | 500
reserved | 0
```

Next, let's make an offer of 100 apples to Bob:

```
postgres=# INSERT INTO
           fruit_offer(recipient_name,fruit_name,offered_amount
           ) VALUES('Bob','APPLE',100);
INSERT 0 1
postgres=# SELECT * FROM fruit_offer;
-[ RECORD 1 ]--+---------------------------
offer_id       | 1
recipient_name | Bob
offer_date     | 2013-01-25 15:21:15.281579
fruit_name     | APPLE
offered_amount | 100
```

On checking the stock, we see that indeed 100 apples are reserved, as shown in the following code snippet:

```
postgres=# SELECT * FROM fruits_in_stock;
-[ RECORD 1 ]----
name       | ORANGE
```

```
in_stock | 500
reserved | 0
-[ RECORD 2 ]----
name     | APPLE
in_stock | 500
reserved | 100
```

If we change the offered amount, the reserved amount also changes:

```
postgres=# UPDATE fruit_offer SET offered_amount = 115
           WHERE offer_id = 1;
UPDATE 1
postgres=# SELECT * FROM fruits_in_stock;
-[ RECORD 1 ]----
name     | ORANGE
in_stock | 500
reserved | 0
-[ RECORD 2 ]----
name     | APPLE
in_stock | 500
reserved | 115
```

We also get some extra benefits. First, because of the constraint on the stock table, you can't sell the reserved apples:

```
postgres=# UPDATE fruits_in_stock SET in_stock = 100
           WHERE name = 'APPLE';
ERROR:  new row for relation "fruits_in_stock" violates check
constraint "fruits_in_stock_check"
DETAIL:  Failing row contains (APPLE, 100, 115).
```

More interestingly, you also can't reserve more than you have, even though the constraints are on another table:

```
postgres=# UPDATE fruit_offer SET offered_amount = 1100
           WHERE offer_id = 1;
ERROR:  new row for relation "fruits_in_stock" violates check
constraint "fruits_in_stock_check"
DETAIL:  Failing row contains (APPLE, 500, 1100).
CONTEXT:  SQL statement "UPDATE fruits_in_stock
        SET reserved = reserved - OLD.offered_amount
                                + NEW.offered_amount
      WHERE name = NEW.fruit_name"
PL/pgSQL function reserve_stock_on_offer() line 8 at SQL statement
```

When you finally delete the offer, the reservation is released:

```
postgres=# DELETE FROM fruit_offer WHERE offer_id = 1;
DELETE 1
postgres=# SELECT * FROM fruits_in_stock;
-[ RECORD 1 ]----
name     | ORANGE
in_stock | 500
reserved | 0
-[ RECORD 2 ]----
name     | APPLE
in_stock | 500
reserved | 0
```

In a real system, you probably will archive the old offer before deleting it.

Auditing changes

If you need to know who did what to the data and when it was done, one way to find out is to log every action that is performed in an important table. In PostgreSQL 9.3, you can also audit the **data definition language** (**DDL**) changes to the database using event triggers. We will learn more about this in the later chapters.

There are at least two equally valid ways to perform data auditing:

- Using auditing triggers
- Allowing tables to be accessed only through functions and auditing inside these functions

Here, we will take a look at a minimal number of examples for both the approaches.

First, let's create the tables:

```
CREATE TABLE salaries(
    emp_name text PRIMARY KEY,
    salary integer NOT NULL
);

CREATE TABLE salary_change_log(
    changed_by text DEFAULT CURRENT_USER,
    changed_at timestamp DEFAULT CURRENT_TIMESTAMP,
    salary_op text,
    emp_name text,
    old_salary integer,
```

```
      new_salary integer
);
REVOKE ALL ON salary_change_log FROM PUBLIC;
GRANT ALL ON salary_change_log TO managers;
```

You don't generally want your users to be able to change audit logs, so only grant the managers the right to access these. If you plan to let users access the salary table directly, you should put a trigger on it for auditing:

```
CREATE OR REPLACE FUNCTION log_salary_change () RETURNS trigger AS $$
    BEGIN
        IF TG_OP = 'INSERT' THEN
       INSERT INTO salary_change_log(salary_op,emp_name,new_salary)
      VALUES (TG_OP,NEW.emp_name,NEW.salary);
   ELSIF TG_OP = 'UPDATE' THEN
INSERT INTO salary_change_log(salary_op,emp_name,old_salary,new_
salary)
        VALUES (TG_OP,NEW.emp_name,OLD.salary,NEW.salary);
   ELSIF TG_OP = 'DELETE' THEN
        INSERT INTO salary_change_log(salary_op,emp_name,old_salary)
        VALUES (TG_OP,NEW.emp_name,OLD.salary);
          END IF;
          RETURN NEW;
    END;
$$ LANGUAGE plpgsql SECURITY DEFINER;

CREATE TRIGGER audit_salary_change
AFTER INSERT OR UPDATE OR DELETE ON salaries
     FOR EACH ROW EXECUTE PROCEDURE log_salary_change ();
```

Now, let's test out some salary management:

```
postgres=# INSERT INTO salaries values('Bob',1000);
INSERT 0 1
postgres=# UPDATE salaries SET salary = 1100
           WHERE emp_name = 'Bob';
UPDATE 1
postgres=# INSERT INTO salaries VALUES('Mary',1000);
INSERT 0 1
postgres=# UPDATE salaries SET salary = salary + 200;
UPDATE 2
postgres=# SELECT * FROM salaries;
-[ RECORD 1 ]--
emp_name | Bob
salary   | 1300
```

```
-[ RECORD 2 ]--
emp_name | Mary
salary   | 1200
```

Each one of these changes is saved into the salary change log table for auditing purposes:

```
postgres=# SELECT * FROM salary_change_log;
-[ RECORD 1 ]-------------------------
changed_by | frank
changed_at | 2012-01-25 15:44:43.311299
salary_op  | INSERT
emp_name   | Bob
old_salary |
new_salary | 1000
-[ RECORD 2 ]-------------------------
changed_by | frank
changed_at | 2012-01-25 15:44:43.313405
salary_op  | UPDATE
emp_name   | Bob
old_salary | 1000
new_salary | 1100
-[ RECORD 3 ]-------------------------
changed_by | frank
changed_at | 2012-01-25 15:44:43.314208
salary_op  | INSERT
emp_name   | Mary
old_salary |
new_salary | 1000
-[ RECORD 4 ]-------------------------
changed_by | frank
changed_at | 2012-01-25 15:44:43.314903
salary_op  | UPDATE
emp_name   | Bob
old_salary | 1100
new_salary | 1300
-[ RECORD 5 ]-------------------------
changed_by | frank
changed_at | 2012-01-25 15:44:43.314903
salary_op  | UPDATE
emp_name   | Mary
old_salary | 1000
new_salary | 1200
```

On the other hand, you may not want anybody to have direct access to the salary table, in which case you can perform the REVOKE command. The following command will revoke all privileges from PUBLIC:

```
REVOKE ALL ON salaries FROM PUBLIC;
```

Also, give users access to only two functions: the first function is for any user taking a look at salaries and the other function can be used to change salaries, which is available only to managers.

The functions will have all the access to the underlying tables because they are declared as SECURITY DEFINER, which means that they run with the privileges of the user who created them.

This is how the salary lookup function will look:

```
CREATE OR REPLACE FUNCTION get_salary(text)
RETURNS integer
AS $$
    -- if you look at other people's salaries, it gets logged
    INSERT INTO salary_change_log(salary_op,emp_name,new_salary)
    SELECT 'SELECT',emp_name,salary
      FROM salaries
     WHERE upper(emp_name) = upper($1)
       AND upper(emp_name) != upper(CURRENT_USER);
    -- don't log select of own salary
    -- return the requested salary
    SELECT salary FROM salaries WHERE upper(emp_name) = upper($1);
$$ LANGUAGE SQL SECURITY DEFINER;
```

Notice that we implemented a **soft-security** approach, where you can look up other people's salaries, but you have to do it responsibly, that is, only when you need to, as your manager will know that you have checked.

The set_salary() function abstracts away the need to check whether the user exists; if the user does not exist, it is created. Setting someone's salary to 0 will remove him or her from the salary table. Thus, the interface is simplified to a large extent, and the client application of these functions needs to know, and do, less:

```
CREATE OR REPLACE FUNCTION set_salary(i_emp_name text, i_salary int)
RETURNS TEXT AS $$
DECLARE
    old_salary integer;
BEGIN
    SELECT salary INTO old_salary
      FROM salaries
```

```
            WHERE upper(emp_name) = upper(i_emp_name);
        IF NOT FOUND THEN
            INSERT INTO salaries VALUES(i_emp_name, i_salary);
      INSERT INTO salary_change_log(salary_op,emp_name,new_salary)
          VALUES ('INSERT',i_emp_name,i_salary);
            RETURN 'INSERTED USER ' || i_emp_name;
        ELSIF i_salary > 0 THEN
            UPDATE salaries
        SET salary = i_salary
      WHERE upper(emp_name) = upper(i_emp_name);
      INSERT INTO salary_change_log
                    (salary_op,emp_name,old_salary,new_salary)
          VALUES ('UPDATE',i_emp_name,old_salary,i_salary);
            RETURN 'UPDATED USER ' || i_emp_name;
        ELSE -- salary set to 0
            DELETE FROM salaries WHERE upper(emp_name) = upper(i_emp_
name);
      INSERT INTO salary_change_log(salary_op,emp_name,old_salary)
          VALUES ('DELETE',i_emp_name,old_salary);
            RETURN 'DELETED USER ' || i_emp_name;
        END IF;
  END;
  $$ LANGUAGE plpgsql SECURITY DEFINER;
```

Now, drop the audit trigger (otherwise the changes will be logged twice) and test the new functionality:

```
postgres=# DROP TRIGGER audit_salary_change ON salaries;
DROP TRIGGER
postgres=#
postgres=# SELECT set_salary('Fred',750);
-[ RECORD 1 ]------------------
set_salary | INSERTED USER Fred

postgres=# SELECT set_salary('frank',100);
-[ RECORD 1 ]------------------
set_salary | INSERTED USER frank

postgres=# SELECT * FROM salaries ;
-[ RECORD 1 ]---
emp_name | Bob
salary   | 1300
-[ RECORD 2 ]---
emp_name | Mary
salary   | 1200
```

```
-[ RECORD 3 ]---
emp_name | Fred
salary   | 750
-[ RECORD 4 ]---
emp_name | frank
salary   | 100

postgres=# SELECT set_salary('mary',0);
-[ RECORD 1 ]----------------
set_salary | DELETED USER mary

postgres=# SELECT * FROM salaries ;
-[ RECORD 1 ]---
emp_name | Bob
salary   | 1300
-[ RECORD 2 ]---
emp_name | Fred
salary   | 750
-[ RECORD 3 ]---
emp_name | frank
salary   | 100

postgres=# SELECT * FROM salary_change_log ;
...
-[ RECORD 6 ]-------------------------
changed_by | gsmith
changed_at | 2013-01-25 15:57:49.057592
salary_op  | INSERT
emp_name   | Fred
old_salary |
new_salary | 750
-[ RECORD 7 ]-------------------------
changed_by | gsmith
changed_at | 2013-01-25 15:57:49.062456
salary_op  | INSERT
emp_name   | frank
old_salary |
new_salary | 100
-[ RECORD 8 ]-------------------------
changed_by | gsmith
changed_at | 2013-01-25 15:57:49.064337
salary_op  | DELETE
emp_name   | mary
old_salary | 1200
new_salary |
```

Data cleaning

In the preceding code, we notice that employee names don't have consistent cases. It will be easy to enforce consistency by adding a constraint, as shown here:

```
CHECK (emp_name = upper(emp_name))
```

However, it is even better to just make sure that the name is stored as uppercase, and the simplest way to do this is by using `trigger`:

```
CREATE OR REPLACE FUNCTION uppercase_name ()
  RETURNS trigger AS $$
    BEGIN
        NEW.emp_name = upper(NEW.emp_name);
        RETURN NEW;
    END;
$$ LANGUAGE plpgsql;

CREATE TRIGGER uppercase_emp_name
BEFORE INSERT OR UPDATE OR DELETE ON salaries
    FOR EACH ROW EXECUTE PROCEDURE uppercase_name ();
```

The next `set_salary()` call for a new employee will now insert `emp_name` in uppercase:

```
postgres=# SELECT set_salary('arnold',80);
-[ RECORD 1 ]-------------------
set_salary | INSERTED USER arnold
```

As the uppercasing happens inside a trigger, the function's response still shows a lowercase name, but in the database, it is uppercased:

```
postgres=# SELECT * FROM salaries;
-[ RECORD 1 ]---
emp_name | Bob
salary   | 1300
-[ RECORD 2 ]---
emp_name | Fred
salary   | 750
-[ RECORD 3 ]---
emp_name | Frank
salary   | 100
-[ RECORD 4 ]---
emp_name |  ARNOLD
salary   | 80
```

After fixing the existing mixed-case employee names, we can make sure that all employee names will be uppercased in the future by adding a constraint:

```
postgres=# update salaries set emp_name = upper(emp_name)
             where not emp_name = upper(emp_name);
UPDATE 3
postgres=# alter table salaries add constraint
             emp_name_must_be_uppercasepostgres CHECK (
             emp_name = upper(emp_name));
ALTER TABLE
```

If this behavior is needed in more places, it will make sense to define a new type – say u_text, which is always stored as uppercase. You will learn more about this approach in *Chapter 14, PostgreSQL as Extensible RDBMS*.

Custom sort orders

The last example in this chapter, is about using functions for different ways of sorting.

Say we are given a task to sort words by their vowels only, and in addition to this, to make the last vowel the most significant one when sorting. While this task may seem really complicated at first, it can be easily solved with functions:

```
CREATE OR REPLACE FUNCTION reversed_vowels(word text)
    RETURNS text AS $$
  vowels = [c for c in word.lower() if c in 'aeiou']
  vowels.reverse()
  return ''.join(vowels)
$$ LANGUAGE plpythonu IMMUTABLE;

postgres=# select word,reversed_vowels(word) from words order by
             reversed_vowels(word);
    word      | reversed_vowels
--------------+------------------
 Abracadabra  | aaaaa
 Great        | ae
 Barter       | ea
 Revolver     | eoe
(4 rows)
```

 Before performing this code, please make sure you have Python 2.x installed. We will discuss PL/Python in much detail in the later chapters of this book.

The best part is that you can use your new function in an index definition:

```
postgres=# CREATE INDEX reversed_vowels_index ON words (reversed_
vowels(word));
CREATE INDEX
```

The system will automatically use this index whenever the `reversed_vowels(word)` function is used in the WHERE or ORDER BY clause.

Programming best practices

Developing application software is complicated. Some of the approaches that help manage this complexity are so popular that they have been given simple acronyms that can be remembered. Next, we'll introduce some of these principles and show you how server programming helps make them easier to follow.

KISS – keep it simple stupid

One of the main techniques to successful programming is writing simple code. That is, writing code that you can easily understand 3 years from now and that others can understand as well. It is not always achievable, but it almost always makes sense to write your code in the simplest way possible. You can rewrite parts of it later for various reasons such as speed, code compactness, to show off how clever you are, and so on. However, always write the code in a simple way first, so that you can be absolutely sure that it does what you want. Not only do you get working on the code quickly, but you also have something to compare to when you try more advanced ways to do the same thing.

Remember, debugging is harder than writing code; so, if you write the code in the most complex way you can, you will have a really hard time debugging it.

It is often easier to write a set returning function instead of a complex query. Yes, it will probably run slower than the same thing implemented as a single complex query, due to the fact that the optimizer can do very little to the code written as functions, but the speed may be sufficient for your needs. If more speed is required, it's very likely to refactor the code piece by piece, joining parts of the function into larger queries where the optimizer has a better chance of discovering better query plans until the performance is acceptable again.

Remember that most of the time, you don't need the absolutely fastest code. For your clients or bosses, the best code is the one that does the job well and arrives on time.

DRY – don't repeat yourself

This principle means you should implement any piece of business logic just once and put the code for doing it in the right place.

This may be hard sometimes; for example, you want to do some checks on your web forms in the browser, but still do the final checks in the database. However, as a general guideline, it is very much valid.

Server programming helps a lot here. If your data manipulation code is in the database near the data, all the data users have easy access to it, and you will not need to manage a similar code in a C++ Windows program, two PHP websites, and a bunch of Python scripts doing nightly management tasks. If any of them need to do this thing to a customer's table, they just call:

```
SELECT * FROM do_this_thing_to_customers(arg1, arg2, arg3);
```

That's it!

If the logic behind the function needs to be changed, you just change the function with no downtime and no complicated orchestration of pushing database query updates to several clients. Once the function is changed in the database, it is changed for all the users.

YAGNI – you ain't gonna need it

In other words, don't do more than you absolutely need to.

If you have a creepy feeling that your client is not yet well aware of how the final database will look or what it will do, it's helpful to resist the urge to design *everything* into the database. A much better way is to do a minimal implementation that satisfies the current specifications, but do it with extensibility in mind. It is very easy to "paint yourself into a corner" when implementing a big specification with large imaginary parts.

If you organize your access to the database through functions, it is often possible to do even large rewrites of business logic without touching the frontend application code. Your application still performs SELECT * FROM do_this_thing_to_ customers(arg1, arg2, arg3), even after you have rewritten the function five times and changed the whole table structure twice.

SOA – service-oriented architecture

Usually, when you hear the acronym SOA, it will be from enterprise software people trying to sell you a complex set of SOAP services. But the essence of SOA is to organize your software platform as a set of services that clients, and other services, call in order to perform certain well-defined atomic tasks, as follows:

- Checking a user's password and credentials
- Presenting him/her with a list of his/her favorite websites
- Selling him/her a new red dog collar with a complementary membership in the red-collared dog club

These services can be implemented as SOAP calls with corresponding WSDL definitions and Java servers with servlet containers, as well as a complex management infrastructure. They can also be a set of PostgreSQL functions, taking a set of arguments and returning a set of values. If the arguments or return values are complex, they can be passed as XML or JSON, but a simple set of standard PostgreSQL data types is often enough. In *Chapter 10*, *Scaling Your Database with PL/Proxy*, you will learn how to make such a PostgreSQL-based SOA service infinitely scalable.

Type extensibility

Some of the preceding techniques are available in other databases, but PostgreSQL's extensibility does not stop here. In PostgreSQL, you can just write UDFs in any of the most popular scripting languages. You can also define your own types, not just domains, which are standard types with some extra constraints attached, and new full-fledged types too.

For example, a Dutch company, MGRID, has developed a **value with unit** set of data types, so that you can divide 10 km by 0.2 hours and get the result in 50 km/h. Of course, you can also cast the same result to meters per second or any other unit of speed. And yes, you can get this as a fraction of **c** — the speed of light.

This kind of functionality needs both the types and overloaded operands, which know that if you divide distance by time, then the result is speed. You will also need user-defined casts, which are automatically or manually-invoked conversion functions between types.

MGRID developed this for use in medical applications, where the cost of an error can be high—the difference between 10 ml and 10 cc can be vital. However, using a similar system might also have averted many other disasters, where wrong units ended up producing bad computation results. If the amount is always accompanied by the unit, the possibility for these kinds of errors is diminished. You can also add your own index method if you have some programming skills and your problem domain is not well served by the existing indexes. There is already a respectable set of index types included in the core PostgreSQL, as well as several others that are developed outside the core.

The latest index method that became officially included in PostgreSQL is **k nearest neighbor (KNN)**—a clever index, which can return K rows ordered by their distance from the desired search target. One use of KNN is in fuzzy text search, where this can be used to rank full-text search results by how well they match the search terms. Before KNN, this kind of thing was done by querying all the rows which matched even slightly, then sorting all these by the distance function, and returning K top rows as the final step.

If done using the KNN index, the index access can start returning the rows in the desired order; so, a simple `LIMIT K` function will return the K top matches.

The KNN index can also be used for real distances, for example, answering the request "Give me the 10 nearest pizza places to Central Station."

As you saw, index types are different from the data types they index. Another example, is the same **General Inverted Index (GIN)** can be used for full-text searches (together with stemmers, thesauri, and other text-processing stuff), as well as for indexing elements of integer arrays.

Caching

Yet another place where server-side programming can be used is to cache values, which are expensive to compute. The following is the basic pattern here:

1. Check whether the value is cached.

2. If it isn't, or the value is too old, compute and cache it.

3. Return the cached value.

For example, calculating the sales for a company is the perfect item to cache. Perhaps, a large retail company has 1,000 stores with potentially millions of individual sales' transactions per day. If the corporate headquarters is looking for sales' trends, it is much more efficient if the daily sales numbers are precalculated at the store level instead of summing up millions of daily transactions.

If the value is simple, such as looking up a user's information from a single table based on the user ID, you don't need to do anything. The value gets cached in PostgreSQL's internal page cache, and all lookups to it are so fast that even on a very fast network, most of the time is spent doing the lookups in the network and not in the actual lookup. In such a case, getting data from a PostgreSQL database is as fast as getting it from any other in-memory cache (such as memcached) but without any extra overhead in managing the cache.

Another use case of caching is to implement materialized views. These are views that are precomputed only when required, not every time one selects data from the view. Some SQL databases have materialized views as separate database objects, but in the PostgreSQL versions prior to 9.3, you have to do it yourself using other database features to automate the whole process.

Wrapping up – why program in the server?

The main advantages of doing most data manipulation code on the server-side are stated in the following sections.

Performance

Doing the computation near the data is almost always a performance win, as the latencies to get the data are minimal. In a typical data-intensive computation, most of the time is spent in getting the data. Therefore, making data access inside the computation faster is the best way to make the whole thing fast. On my laptop, it takes 2.2 ms to query one random row from a 1,000,000-row database into the client, but it takes only 0.12 ms to get the data inside the database. This is 20 times faster and inside the same machine over Unix sockets. The difference can be bigger if there is a network connection between the client and the server.

A small real-word story:

A friend of mine was called to help a large company (I'm sure all of you know it, but I can't tell you which one) in order to make its e-mail sending application faster. They had implemented their e-mail generation system with all the latest Java EE technologies: first, getting the data from the database, passing the data around between services, and serializing and deserializing it several times before finally doing XSLT transformation on the data to produce the e-mail text. The end result being that it produced only a few hundred e-mails per second, and they were falling behind with their responses.

When he rewrote the process to use a PL/Perl function inside the database to format the data and the query returned already fully-formatted e-mails, it suddenly started spewing out tens of thousands of e-mails per second and they had to add a second copy of the sent mail to actually be able to send them out.

Ease of maintenance

If all the data manipulation code is in a database, either as database functions or views, the actual upgrade process becomes very easy. All that is needed is to run a DDL script that redefines the functions; all the clients automatically use the new code with no downtime and no complicated coordination between several frontend systems and teams.

Improved productivity

Server-side functions are perhaps the best way to achieve code reuse. Any client application written in any language or framework can make use of the server-side functions, ensuring maximum reuse in all environments.

Simple ways to tighten security

If all the access for some possibly insecure servers goes through functions, the database user of these servers can only be granted access to the needed functions and nothing else. They can't see the table data or even the fact that these tables exist. So, even if the server is compromised, all it can do is continue to call the same functions. Also, there is no possibility of stealing passwords, e-mails, or other sensitive information by issuing its own queries such as SELECT * FROM users; and getting all the data there is in the database.

Also, the most important thing is that programming in a server is fun!

Summary

Programming inside the database server is not always the first thing that comes to mind to many developers, but its unique placement inside the application stack gives it some powerful advantages. Your application can be faster, more secure, and more maintainable by pushing logic into the database. With server-side programming in PostgreSQL, you can secure your data using functions, audit access to your data and structural changes using triggers, and improve productivity by achieving code reuse. Also, you can enrich your data using custom data types, analyze your data using custom operators, and extend the capabilities of the database by dynamically loading new functions.

This is just the start of what you can do inside PostgreSQL. Throughout the rest of this book, you will learn many other ways to write powerful applications by programming inside PostgreSQL.

2
Server Programming Environments

You've had a chance to get acquainted with the general idea of using PostgreSQL, but now we are going to answer the question of why anyone will choose PostgreSQL as a development platform. As much as I'd like to believe that it's an easy decision for everyone, it's not.

For starters, let's get rid of the optimistic idea that you choose a database platform for technical reasons. Sure, we all like to think that we are objective, and we base our decisions on a preponderance of the technical evidence. This preponderance of evidence then indicates which features are available and relevant to our application. We will then proceed to make a weighted choice in favor of the most advantageous platform, and use a balance of the evidences to create workarounds and alternatives where our choice falls short. The fact is that we don't really understand all the requirements of the application until we are halfway through the development cycle. Here are some reasons why:

- We don't know how the application will evolve over time. Many start-ups pivot from their initial idea as the market tells them to change.

- We don't know how many users there will *really* be until we have some registrations and can begin to measure the curve.

- We don't realize how important a particular feature can be until we get user feedback. The truth is, that we don't really know much about the long-term needs of the application until we're writing version 2 or maybe even version 3.

That is, unless you're one of the fortunate few who has a Research and Development department that writes the alpha version, throws it out the window, and then asks you to write the next version based on the lessons learned. Even then, you really don't know what the usage patterns are going to be once the application is deployed.

What we generally see in the PostgreSQL community — when new users start asking questions — is people not looking to make a decision, but rather people who have already made a decision. In most cases, they are looking for technical justification for an existing plan of action. The decision has already been passed. What I am going to write about in this chapter is not a TPC benchmark, nor is it about the relative merits of PostgreSQL functions versus stored procedures. Frankly, nobody really cares about these things until they have already made a choice and want to justify it.

This chapter contains the guide that I wish someone had written for me when I chose to use PostgreSQL back in 1998.

Cost of acquisition

One of biggest the factors that decides which technology is used in the application stack is the cost of acquisition. I've seen many application architectures drawn on a whiteboard where the technical team was embarrassed to show them, but they justified the design by trying to keep software licensing costs down. When it comes to the database environment, the usual suspects are Oracle, SQL Server, MySQL, and PostgreSQL. Oracle, the dominant player in the database space, is also the most costly. At the low end, Oracle does have reasonably priced offerings and even a free Express Edition, but they are limited. Most people have needs beyond the low-priced offerings and fall into the enterprise sales machine of Oracle. This usually results in a high-price quote that makes your CFO fall out of his/her chair, and you're back to designing your solution in order to keep your licensing costs down.

Then comes Microsoft SQL Server. This is your first reasonably viable option. The pricing is listed on the Microsoft website. I will not reproduce it here because the pricing schedule is too volatile for a book that will remain in print for a longer time. Nonetheless, an experienced thumb value of the purchase cost for SQL Server will get you running with a web-capable model for about $5,000. This does not include a service contract. In the grand scheme of development costs, this is reasonable and not too high of a barrier to enter.

Then, we have the open source offerings such as MySQL and PostgreSQL. They cost nothing and the service contracts cost — wait for it — nothing. This is a very hard cost of acquisition to beat.

Remember, in the beginning of the chapter, when I was talking about all the things that you don't know when the project starts? Here's where the real win comes in. You can afford to fail.

There, I said it!

Low cost of acquisition is a synonym for *low cost of failure*. When we add up all of the unknowns for the project, we find out that we have a fairly good chance that the first iteration will not meet the market needs, and we need to find a way to jettison it quickly without long-term contracts and the additional costs of spinning up a new project.

This allows the project manager to move on to the next version using lessons learned from the consumer after the first version. Hopefully, this lesson in user acceptance will come at a very low cost and the project will then begin to thrive in the following versions. Don't let the success of the project hang on getting the first version perfect. You won't!

Availability of developers

This has been one of the most hilarious parts of my development life. I recently recommended a local company to use PostgreSQL for a reporting system. The company in question wanted to know that if they chose PostgreSQL, would anyone on staff be able to maintain it. So, I began to interview the developers to find out about their experiences with PostgreSQL.

Me: Do you have any experience with PostgreSQL?

Developer 1: Yes, I used it at the last job for a product fulfillment project, but I don't think many people have that experience. We should probably stick to using MySQL.

Me: Do you have any experience with PostgreSQL?

Developer 2: Yes, I used it at the last job for a reporting project, but I don't think many people have that experience. We should probably stick to using MySQL.

After interviewing all seven developers that were influential on the project, I found that the only person without hands-on experience with PostgreSQL was the project manager. Since the project manager didn't expect to have any technical involvement in the project, he approved the selection of PostgreSQL.

PostgreSQL is one of the dirty little secrets of web developers. They have about the same level of familiarity with it as they do with encryption and security. Because *only advanced users* will use it, they have a general geek requirement to look into it and presume that everyone else is too *inexperienced* to do the same. Everyone is trying to "dumb it down" for the other guy. They consider their own use of the tools at hand (MySQL) a sacrifice that they are willing to make in order to help the less experienced person down the hall. Comically, the person down the hall thinks that he's/she's making the same sacrifice for everyone else.

Lesson learned

Quit making choices for the *other guy*. He/she is just as experienced (and intelligent) as you are, or he/she might just want the opportunity to advance his/her skills.

Licensing

About 2 months after Oracle bought MySQL, they announced a plan that divided the development into two camps: a MySQL community edition and a professional version. The community edition would no longer gain any new features, and the professional version would become a commercial product.

There was a vast and thunderous sucking sound in the open source community, as they thrashed wildly about to find a new platform for Free and Open Source Software (FOSS) development.

Oracle immediately (in about 2 weeks) countermanded the order and declared that things will stay as they were for the indefinite future. Those with short memories, forgiving hearts, or who just weren't paying attention went on about their business. Many other open source projects either switched to PostgreSQL or suddenly grew PostgreSQL database support.

Today, we have MySQL and MySQL Enterprise Edition. If you want backup, high availability, enterprise scalability, and the MySQL Enterprise Monitor, you now have to pony up some dough. Capitalism is fine, and corporations have a right to charge money for their services and products in order to exist. But why should you, as a project manager or developer, have to pay for something that you can get for free?

Licensing is all about continued product availability and distribution. The PostgreSQL licensing model specifically states that you can have the source code, do anything with it, redistribute it however you jolly well please, and these rights extend indefinitely. Try to get this deal with a commercial vendor.

As a corporate developer, PostgreSQL wins the legal battle for risk management hands down. I have heard the argument "I want to go with a commercial vendor if I need someone to sue." I will encourage anyone who considers it a good argument to do a little research about how often these vendors have been sued, how often those suits were successful, and what the cost of court was for that success. I think you'll find that the only viable option is not to have the battle.

Predictability

This section could just as well have been titled *standards compliance*, but I decided against it because the benefits of standards compliance in corporate projects are not obvious. The limitations of the common databases are well-documented, and I will show you a few websites in a moment where you can make a comparison of who has the most *unintended behavior*. I will encourage you to read the following material while thinking about the question, "Which method of feature development is most likely to make my application break in the future?":

- http://www.sql-info.de/postgresql/postgres-gotchas.html
- http://www.sql-info.de/mysql/gotchas.html

Spoiler alert:

A stricter adherence to standards comes at the cost of not allowing ambiguous behavior. Not allowing ambiguous behavior makes the developer's life more difficult. Making the developer's life more difficult ensures that the interpretation of the commands that the developer gives will not change later, breaking the application.

Just how lazy can you afford to be? I'm not sure how to measure this. PostgreSQL is available for no-cost future predictability, so I don't have to answer the question.

Sure, PostgreSQL also has some bugs listed. However, changes to the database core have a tendency to make the engine work like the documentation says it does, not like the documentation should have said. PostgreSQL developers don't have to say, "Oops, I didn't think of that," very often. When they do, PostgreSQL just becomes more standards compliant.

Community

Oracle and SQL Server don't have a community. Please understand when I say that, I mean that the chance that you will get to talk to a developer of the core database is about the same as your chance of winning the lottery. By the time you do, it's probably because you found a bug so heinous that it couldn't be ignored and the only person who can understand your report is the guy who wrote the code in question. They have paid technical support and this support has proven in my experience to be generally competent, but not stellar. I have had to work around the problem that I originally requested help with about 40 percent of the time.

Compare this to MySQL and PostgreSQL, where just about anybody can speak to just about anybody else all day long. Many of the core developers of both the platforms can be found on IRC, met at conventions, contacted for contract development work, and for the most part, bribed remarkably easily with beer (hint, hint, wink, wink, nudge, nudge).

They are actively concerned about the health of the overall community and will answer just about any kind of question you ask, even if the question has a very tenuous relationship to database development. My personal experience, is that the PostgreSQL team has more core developers readily available than MySQL. They are also more personally available at conventions and meetings.

Did I mention they like beer?

Procedural languages

SQL Server allows you to create a **dynamic link library** (DLL) in any language that produces the **Common Language Runtime** (CLR). These DLLs must be loaded into the server at boot time. To create a procedure at runtime and have it immediately available, the only choice is the built-in SQL dialect, Transact SQL (TSQL).

MySQL has a feature called **plugins**. One of the legal plugin types is a procedural language. Several languages have been tooled to work with MySQL via the plugin system, including most of the popular ones such as PHP and Python. These functions cannot be used for stored procedures or triggers, but they can be invoked from the common SQL statements. For the rest, you are stuck with the built-in SQL.

PostgreSQL has full support for additional procedural languages, which can be used to create any legal entity in the database that can be created with PL/pgSQL. The language can be added (or removed) from a running version of PostgreSQL and any function defined using this language can also be created or dropped while PostgreSQL is running.

These languages have full access to PostgreSQL's internal functions and to all the data entities that the calling user has permission for. In addition to having access to internal PostgreSQL functions, entities, and data structures, some functions (in untrusted languages) can also access external services, create or delete files and directories, or send e-mails and invoke external processes. We will discuss trusted and untrusted languages in later chapters.

Many of these plugin language extensions are available for PostgreSQL. I have used the extensions for PHP, Python, Bash, and PL/pgSQL. Yes, this means that the standard language for PostgreSQL is also installed and managed using the same extension system as any other language.

This brings us to the point that we have more developers available for PostgreSQL than you might have originally thought. Software developers are not required to learn a new development language in order to write stored procedures. They can extend PostgreSQL with a language of their choice and continue to code in the manner and workflow that they choose.

Lesson learned
There are no second-class citizens in the PostgreSQL development community. Anyone can code in (almost) any language they choose.

Third-party tools

A frequent point of comparison among the database platforms is the number of third-party applications available. I'm not so sure that the total number matters, as much as the existence of the applications you actually need.

To this end, the following is a list of the products that I have used extensively with PostgreSQL:

- **Pentaho data integration (kettle)**: This is an outstanding **Extract, Transform and Load (ETL)** tool

- **Pentaho Report Server**: This is a great reporting engine

- **pgAdmin3**: This is an awesome database administration tool

- **php5-pgsql**: This is a package that allows native access to PostgreSQL from PHP

- **QCubed**: This is the PHP development framework with PostgreSQL support

- **Yii**: This is another great PHP development framework
- **Talend**: This is another ETL tool that works, but this is not my favorite
- **BIRT**: This is a great JAVA reporting tool with an easy report creation environment
- **psycopg2**: This is the Python bindings for PostgreSQL

These tools have made the PostgreSQL development experience a breeze, and this is no where near a complete list. We can fill this book with just a list of applications that support PostgreSQL, and thanks to its liberal license, PostgreSQL is embedded in many commercial applications that you never really know.

Lesson learned

Don't worry too much about how many tools are out there for the product. The ones that matter are available.

Platform compatibility

SQL Server is a Microsoft product. As such, it was, and will always be, a Microsoft platform tool. It is accessible to some limited degree via ODBC, but it is not a serious choice for cross-platform development.

MySQL and PostgreSQL support every operating system currently available today. This ability (or the lack of limitation) is a strong argument for long-term stability. If any particular operating system is no longer available, or no longer supports open source software, it is fairly simple to move the database server to another platform.

Lesson learned

In the commercial operating system wars, just say no.

Application design

"The thing that hath been, it is that which shall be; and that which is done is that which shall be done: and there is no new thing under the sun."

— *Ecclesiastes 1:9 (KJV)*

"... old things are passed away; behold, all things are become new."

— *2 Corinthians 5:16-18 (KJV)*

In software development, we are always running into the situation where what is old is new again, and developers who embrace a philosophy swear by it like a religion. We swing back and forth between thin servers and thin clients, flat and hierarchical storage, desktop applications and web applications and, most appropriately for this chapter, between client and server programming.

The reason for this swing between programming implementations has got nothing to do with the features that the client or the server offers. Developer experience is a much more likely influence, and this influence can go in either direction, depending on what the developer encountered first.

I encourage both the server-centric developer and the client-centric developer to lay down their pitchforks while reading the rest of this chapter.

We will discuss, in due time, most of the new features of *server programming*. If you're still not convinced, we will take a look at how you can harness the benefits of most of those features without leaving your application-centered point of view.

Databases are considered harmful

The simplest and least powerful way of looking at server programming, is to view the database as a data bucket. Using only the most basic SQL statements such as INSERT, SELECT, UPDATE, and DELETE, you can manipulate data, a single row at a time, and create application libraries for multiple databases easily.

This approach has some major drawbacks. Moving data back and forth to the database server one row at a time is extremely inefficient, and you will find that this method is simply not viable in a web-scale application.

This idea is usually associated with the concept of a **database abstraction layer**, a client library that allows the developer to switch the database out from under the application with little effort. This abstraction layer is very useful in the open source development community, which allows the use of many databases, but they have no financial incentive to get the best possible performance.

SQL, being based on relational algebra and tuple relational calculus, has the ability to quickly and efficiently perform set-based processing on large amounts of data; the application-side processing usually involves iterative looping, which is generally much slower.

In my 27-year career, I have never actually changed the database of an installed application without throwing away the application. One of the principles of agile software development is YAGNI (you ain't gonna need it). This is one of those cases.

Lesson learned

Data abstraction is valuable for projects that need to select a database platform at installation time. For anything else, just say no.

Encapsulation

Another technique used in more client-centric development philosophies, is to isolate the database-specific calls into a library of procedures. This design is usually aimed at leaving the application in control of all the business logic. The application is still the king, and the database is still just a necessary evil.

This view of database architecture sells the application developer short by ignoring a toolbox full of tools and choosing only the hammer. Everything in the application is then painted to look like a nail and is smacked with the hammer.

Lesson learned

Don't give up on the power of the database just because it is not familiar. Use procedural languages and check out extension toolkits. There are some awesome pieces of work in there.

What does PostgreSQL offer?

So far, we've mentioned procedural languages, functions, triggers, custom data types, and operators. These things can be created directly in the database via the CREATE commands or added as libraries using extensions.

Now, we will show you some things that you need to keep in mind when programming on the server in PostgreSQL.

Data locality

If possible, keep the data on the server. Believe me, it's happier there, and performance is much better when modifying data. If everything was done in the application layer, the data will need to be returned from the database with the modifications and then finally sent back to the database for a commit. If you are building a web-scalable application, this should be your last resort.

Let's walk through a small snippet that uses two methods in order to make an update to a single record:

```php
<?php
  $db = pg_connect("host port user password dbname schema");
  $sql = "SELECT * FROM customer WHERE id = 23";
  $row = pg_fetch_array($db,$sql);
  if ($row['account_balance'] > 6000) {
  $sql = "UPDATE customer SET valued_customer = true
    WHERE id = 23;";;";
  pg_query($db,$sql);
  }
  pg_close($db);
?>
```

This code snippet pulls a row of data from the database server to the client, makes an evaluation, and changes a customer account based on the evaluation. The result of the change is then sent back to the server for processing.

There are several things that are wrong with this scenario. First, the scalability is terrible. Imagine if this operation needed to be performed for thousands, or even millions of customers. This will be really slow because the code will process the records one by one, and each record will be sent over the network and then updated, which involves going over the network again for each record.

The second problem is transactional integrity. What happens if the user's account balance changes from some other transaction between the query and the update? Is the customer still valued? This will depend on the business reason for the evaluation.

Try out the following example:

```php
<?php
  $db = pg_connect('...');
  pg_query('UPDATE customer SET valued_customer = true
    WHERE balance > 6000;', $db);
  pg_close($db);
?>
```

This example is simple, has transactional integrity, and works for an incredibly large number of customers. Why point out such a simple and obvious example? The answer is because many development frameworks work incorrectly by default. The code generator will produce some equivalent form of this example in the interest of being cross-platform, predictable, and easy to integrate into a simple design model.

This method promotes terrible practices. For systems that have a very low number of concurrent transactions, you will probably see what you expect, but as concurrency increases, the number of unintended behaviors also increase.

The second example exposes a better philosophy: operate on columns (not on rows), leave the data on the server, and let the database do the transactional work for you. That's what the database is made for.

More basics

It helps to have some basic background information before you start programming for the server. In the next few sections, we will explore the general technical environment in which you will be working. We will cover a lot of information, but don't worry too much about remembering it all right now. Just try to pick up the general idea.

Transactions

The default transaction isolation level in PostgreSQL is called **Read Committed**. This means that if multiple transactions attempt to modify the same data, they must wait for each other to finish before acting on the resulting data. They wait in a first-come-first-serve order. The final result of the data is what most people will naturally expect: the last chronological change being reflected.

PostgreSQL does not provide any way to do a dirty read. A dirty read is the ability to view the data the way it appears in someone else's transaction and to use it as if it were committed. This ability is not available in PostgreSQL because of the way in which the multiversion concurrency control works.

There are other transaction isolation methods available; you can read about them in detail at `http://www.postgresql.org/docs/current/static/transaction-iso.html`.

It is important to note, that when no transaction blocks are specified (`BEGIN ..END`), PostgreSQL will treat each individual statement like a private transaction and commit immediately when the statement is finished. This gives other transactions a chance to settle between your statements. Some programming languages provide a transaction block around your statements, while some do not. Please check your language documentation to find out whether you are running in a transacted session.

When using the two main clients to interact with PostgreSQL, the transaction behavior is different. The `psql` command-line client does not provide transaction blocks. You are expected to know when to start/stop a transaction on your own. The **pgAdmin3** query window, on the other hand, wraps any statement that you submit into a transaction block for you. This way it provides a `cancel` option. If the transaction is interrupted, `ROLLBACK` will be performed and the database will go back to its former state.

Some operations are exempt from transactions. For example, a `sequence` object will continue to increment even if the transaction fails and is rolled back. `CREATE INDEX CONCURRENTLY` requires the management of its own transactions and should not be called from within a transaction block. The same is true for `VACUUM`, as well as `CLUSTER`.

General error reporting and error handling

If you want to provide a status to the user during execution, you should be familiar with the commands `RAISE`, `NOTICE`, and `NOTIFY`. From a transactional perspective, the difference is that `RAISE` and `NOTICE` will send the message immediately, even when wrapped in a transaction, while `NOTIFY` will wait for the transaction to settle before sending a message. `NOTIFY` will, therefore, actually not notify you of anything if the transaction fails and is rolled back.

User-defined functions

The ability to write user-defined functions is the powerhouse feature of PostgreSQL. Functions can be written in many different programming languages, can use any kind of control structures that the language provides, and in the case of "untrusted" languages, can perform any operation that is available in PostgreSQL.

Functions can provide features that are not even directly related to SQL. Some of the upcoming examples will show you how to get network address information, query the system, move files around, and do just about anything that your heart desires.

So, how do we access the sugary goodness of PostgreSQL? We start by declaring that we want a function:

```
CREATE OR REPLACE FUNCTION addition (integer, integer) RETURNS integer
AS $$
DECLARE retval integer;
BEGIN
```

```
      SELECT $1 + $2 INTO retval;
      RETURN retval;
   END;
   $$ LANGUAGE plpgsql;
```

What if we want to add three integers together? Using the following code we can add three integers together:

```
   CREATE OR REPLACE FUNCTION addition (integer, integer, integer)
   RETURNS integer
   AS $$
   DECLARE retval integer;
   BEGIN
      SELECT $1 + $2 +$3 INTO retval;
      RETURN retval;
   END;
   $$ LANGUAGE plpgsql;
```

We just invoked a concept called **function overloading**. This feature allows you to declare a function of the same name, but with different parameters that potentially behave differently. This difference can be just as subtle as changing the data type of one of the arguments to the function. The function that PostgreSQL invokes depends on the closest match to the function arguments and expected return type.

Suppose we want to add together any number of integers? Well, PostgreSQL has a way to do this also, as follows:

```
   CREATE OR REPLACE FUNCTION addition (VARIADIC arr integer[]) RETURNS
   integer
   AS $$
   DECLARE retval integer;
   BEGIN
      SELECT sum($1[i]) INTO retval FROM generate_subscripts($1, 1)
        g(i) ;
      RETURN retval;
   END;
   $$
   LANGUAGE plpgsql;
```

This will allow you to pass in any number of integers and get an appropriate response. These functions, of course, do not handle real or numeric data types. To handle other data types, simply declare the function again with those types and call them with the appropriate parameters.

For more information about variable parameters, check out http://www. postgresql.org/docs/9.3/static/xfunc-sql.html#XFUNC-SQL-VARIADIC-FUNCTIONS.

Other parameters

There is more than one way to get data into a function and out of it. We can also declare IN/OUT parameters, return a table, return a set of records, and use cursors for both the input and output.

This brings us to a pseudotype called ANY. It allows the parameter type to be undefined, and it allows any basic data type to be passed to the function. Then, it is up to the function to decide what to do with the data. There are several other pseudotypes available in PostgreSQL, also called the **polymorphic** types. These are anyelement, anyarray, anynonarray, anyenum, and anyrange. You can read more about these pseudotypes at http://www.postgresql.org/docs/9.3/static/datatype-pseudo.html.

Here is an example of the pseudotype anyarray. The following simple function takes an array of any type as an argument and returns an array by removing all the duplicates:

```
CREATE OR REPLACE FUNCTION remove_duplicates(anyarray)
RETURNS anyarray AS
$$
   SELECT ARRAY(SELECT DISTINCT unnest($1));
$$
LANGUAGE 'sql' ;


postgres=# SELECT remove_duplicates(ARRAY[1,1,2,2,3,3]);
 remove_duplicates
-------------------
 {1,2,3}
(1 row)


postgres=# SELECT remove_duplicates(ARRAY['a','a','b','c']);
 remove_duplicates
-------------------
 {b,a,c}
(1 row)
```

More control

Once you have your function written the way you need, PostgreSQL gives you additional control over how the function executes. You can control what data the function can access and how PostgreSQL will interpret the expense of running the function.

There are two statements that provide a security context for your functions. The first one is SECURITY INVOKER, which is the default security context. In the default context, the privileges of the calling user are respected by the function.

The other context is SECURITY DEFINER. In this context, the user privileges of the creator of the function are respected during the execution of the function. Generally, this is used to temporarily escalate user rights for a specific purpose.

This is very useful if you want to have a stricter control over your data. In an environment where security of the underlying data is important, and you don't want users to directly SELECT the data or change it using INSERT, UPDATE, or DELETE, you can create a set of functions with the security-definer attribute as APIs for the tables. This approach gives you complete control over your API behavior and how users can access the underlying objects.

Cost can also be defined for the function. This cost will help the query planner estimate how expensive it is to call the function. Higher orders of cost will cause the query planner to change the access path, so your function will be called as few times as possible. The PostgreSQL documentation shows these numbers to be a factor of cpu_operator_cost. That's more than a little misleading. These numbers have no direct correlation to CPU cycles. They are only relevant in comparison with one another. It's more like how some national money compares with the rest of the European Union. Some Euros are more equal than others.

To estimate your own function's complexity, start with the language you are implementing it in. For C, the default will be 1 * number of records returned, and it will be 100 for all other languages, according to the PostgreSQL documentation at http://www.postgresql.org/docs/current/static/sql-createfunction.html. For plsh, you may want to use 150 or more, depending on how many external tool calls are involved in getting an answer. The default is 100 and this seems to work reasonably well for PL/pgSQL.

Summary

Now you know a few things about the PostgreSQL environment, as well as some things that will help you in the unforeseeable future. PostgreSQL is built to handle your needs, but more importantly, it is built *not* to change underneath you in the future.

We touched upon the environment and called out some of the more important things to be kept in mind when programming on the server in PostgreSQL. Don't worry too much if you don't remember all of it. It is fine to go on to the next chapter, where we will actually start making some useful functions and learn about writing our first PL/pgSQL functions. You will also learn how to write conditional statements, loops, and different ways to return data. Then, come back and review this chapter when you have a clearer understanding of the features available to the function writer.

Your First PL/pgSQL Function

3

A function is the basic building block for extending PostgreSQL. A function accepts input in the form of parameters, and it can create output in the form of output parameters or return values. Many functions are provided by PostgreSQL itself, that is, common mathematical functions such as square roots and absolute values. For a comprehensive list of the functions that are already available, go to `http://www.postgresql.org/docs/current/static/functions.html`.

The functions that you create have the same privileges and ability that the built-in functions possess. The developers of PostgreSQL use the same libraries to extend the database that you use, as a developer, to write your business logic.

This means, that you have the tools available to be a first-class citizen of the PostgreSQL development community. In fact, there are no second-class seats on this bus.

A function accepts parameters that can be of any data type available in PostgreSQL, and it returns results to the caller using the same type. What you do within the function is entirely up to you. You have been empowered to do anything that PostgreSQL is capable of doing. You are herewith also warned that you are capable of doing anything that PostgreSQL is capable of doing. The training wheels are off.

In this chapter, you will learn the following topics:

- The basic building blocks of a PostgreSQL function
- Passing parameters into a function
- The basic control structures inside a function
- Returning results out of a function

Why PL/pgSQL?

PL/pgSQL is a powerful SQL scripting language, that is heavily influenced by PL/SQL, the stored procedure language distributed with Oracle. It is included in the vast majority of PostgreSQL installations as a standard part of the product, so it usually requires no setup at all to begin.

PL/pgSQL also has a dirty little secret. The PostgreSQL developers don't want you to know that it is a full-fledged SQL development language, capable of doing pretty much anything within the PostgreSQL database.

Why is this a secret? For years, PostgreSQL did not claim to have stored procedures. PL/pgSQL functions were originally designed to return scalar values and were intended for simple mathematical tasks and trivial string manipulations.

Over the years, PL/pgSQL developed a rich set of control structures and gained the ability to be used by triggers, operators, and indexes. In the end, developers were grudgingly forced to admit that they had a complete, stored procedure development system on their hands.

Along the way, the goal of PL/pgSQL changed from simple scalar functions, to providing access to all of the PostgreSQL system internals, with full control structure. The full list of what is available in the current version is provided at `http://www. postgresql.org/docs/current/static/plpgsql-overview.html`.

Today, the following are some of the benefits of using PL/pgSQL:

- It is easy to use
- It is available by default on most deployments of PostgreSQL
- It is optimized for the performance of data-intensive tasks

In addition to PL/pgSQL, PostgreSQL also allows many other languages such as PL/Perl, PL/Python, PL/Proxy, and PL/Tcl to be plugged in to the database, some of which will be covered in this book. You may also choose to write your functions in Perl, Python, PHP, bash, and a host of other languages, but they will likely need to be added to your instance of PostgreSQL.

The structure of a PL/pgSQL function

It doesn't take much to get a PL/pgSQL function working. Here's a basic example:

```
CREATE FUNCTION mid(varchar, integer, integer) RETURNS varchar
AS $$
BEGIN
  RETURN substring($1,$2,$3);
END;
$$
LANGUAGE plpgsql;
```

The preceding function shows the basic elements of a PL/pgSQL function. It creates an alias for the `substring` built-in function called `mid`. This is a handy alias to have around for developers that come from Microsoft SQL Server or MySQL and are wondering what happened to the `mid` function. It also illustrates the most basic parameter-passing strategy: parameters are not named and are accessed in the function by their relative location from left to right. The `$$` character in this example represents the start and end of the code block. This character sequence can be arbitrary and you can use something else of your choice, but this book uses `$$` in all the examples.

The basic elements of a PL/pgSQL function are name, parameters, return type, body, and language. It can be argued that parameters are not mandatory for a function and neither is the return value. This might be useful for a procedure that operates on data without providing a response, but it will be prudent to return the value TRUE to indicate that the procedure succeeded.

Accessing function arguments

Function arguments can also be passed and accessed by name, instead of just by the ordinal order. By accessing the parameters by name, it makes the resulting function code a little more readable. The following is an example of a function that uses named parameters:

```
CREATE FUNCTION mid(keyfield varchar, starting_point integer)
  RETURNS varchar
AS
$$
BEGIN
  RETURN substring(keyfield,starting_point);
END
$$
LANGUAGE plpgsql;
```

The preceding function also demonstrates the overloading of the mid function. Overloading is another feature of PostgreSQL functions, which allows multiple procedures to use the same name, but a different number or types of parameters. In this case, we first declared the mid function with three parameters. However, in this example, overloading is used to implement an alternative form of the mid function, where there are only two parameters. When the third parameter is omitted, the result will be a string starting from starting_point and continuing to the end of the input string, as shown here:

```
SELECT mid('Kirk L. Roybal',9);
```

The preceding line of code yields the following result:

```
   mid
 --------
  Roybal
 (1 row)
```

In order to access the function parameters by name, PostgreSQL makes a few educated guesses depending on the statement. Consider, for a moment, the following function:

```
CREATE OR REPLACE FUNCTION ambiguous(parameter varchar) RETURNS
    integer  AS $$
DECLARE retval integer;
BEGIN

INSERT INTO parameter (parameter) VALUES (parameter) RETURNING id
    INTO retval;
RETURN retval;

END;
$$
LANGUAGE plpgsql;

SELECT ambiguous ('parameter');
```

This is an example of positively atrocious programming since the argument, table, and its column are all called parameter. This should never occur outside an example of how *not* to write functions. However, PostgreSQL is intelligent enough to correctly deduce that the contents of the function parameter are only legal in the VALUES list. All other occurrences of parameter are actually physical PostgreSQL entities.

We also introduced an optional section to the function. We declare a variable before the BEGIN statement. Variables that appear in this section are valid during the execution of the function.

Also note, the `RETURNING id INTO retval` statement in this function. This feature allows the developer to specify the identity field of the record and returns the value of this field after the record has been inserted. Our function then returns this value to the caller as an indicator that the function succeeded, and as a way to find the record that has been inserted. This is a good way to return values inserted by default, such as the serial sequence numbers. You can use any expression with table column names, and the syntax will be similar to the column list in a `SELECT` statement.

Conditional expressions

Conditional expressions allow developers to control the action of the function, based on a defined criteria. PostgreSQL provides the `CASE` and `IF` statements to execute different commands based on conditions. The following is an example of the usage of a `CASE` statement to control how a string is treated based on its value. If the value is null or contains a zero-length string, it is treated the same as null:

```
CREATE OR REPLACE FUNCTION format_us_full_name(
                prefix text, firstname text,
                mi text, lastname text,
                suffix text)
    RETURNS text AS
$$
DECLARE
  fname_mi text;
  fmi_lname text;
  prefix_fmil text;
  pfmil_suffix text;
BEGIN
  fname_mi := CONCAT_WS(' ',
                CASE trim(firstname)
                WHEN ''
                THEN NULL
                ELSE firstname
                END,
                CASE trim(mi)
                WHEN ''
                THEN NULL
                ELSE mi
                END || '.');
  fmi_lname := CONCAT_WS(' ',
                CASE fname_mi
                WHEN ''
                THEN NULL
```

```
                        ELSE fname_mi
                        END,
                        CASE trim(lastname)
                        WHEN ''
                        THEN NULL
                        ELSE lastname
                        END);
        prefix_fmil := CONCAT_WS('. ',
                        CASE trim(prefix)
                        WHEN ''
                        THEN NULL
                        ELSE prefix
                        END,
                        CASE fmi_lname
                        WHEN ''
                        THEN NULL
                        ELSE fmi_lname
                        END);
        pfmil_suffix := CONCAT_WS(', ',
                        CASE prefix_fmil
                        WHEN ''
                        THEN NULL
                        ELSE prefix_fmil
                        END,
                        CASE trim(suffix)
                        WHEN ''
                        THEN NULL
                        ELSE suffix || '.'
                        END);
        RETURN pfmil_suffix;
    END;
    $$
    LANGUAGE plpgsql;
```

The idea here, is that when any element of a full name is missing, the surrounding punctuation and white spaces should also be missing. This function returns a well-formatted full name of a person in the USA, with as much of the name filled in as possible. When running this function, you will see the following:

```
postgres=# SELECT format_us_full_name('Mr', 'Martin', 'L', 'King',
            'Jr');

    format_us_full_name
------------------------
```

```
Mr. Martin L. King, Jr.
```

```
(1 row)
```

Now, let's try with a name missing:

```
postgres=# SELECT format_us_full_name('', 'Martin', 'L', 'King',
            'Jr');
```

```
 format_us_full_name
--------------------
 Martin L. King, Jr.
```

```
(1 row)
```

Another way to use conditional expressions, is using the IF/THEN/ELSE blocks. The following is the same function again, written using IF statements, rather than CASE statements:

```
CREATE OR REPLACE FUNCTION format_us_full_name(
                prefix text, firstname text,
                mi text, lastname text,
                suffix text)
RETURNS text AS
$$
DECLARE
  fname_mi text;
  fmi_lname text;
  prefix_fmil text;
  pfmil_suffix text;
BEGIN
  fname_mi := CONCAT_WS(' ',
                IF(trim(firstname)
                ='',NULL,firstname),
                IF(trim(mi) = '', NULL, mi ||
                '.')
                );
  fmi_lname := CONCAT_WS(' ',
                IF(fname_mi = '',NULL,
                fname_mi),
                IF(trim(lastname) =  '', NULL,
                lastname)
                );
  prefix_fmil := CONCAT_WS('. ',
```

```
                          IF(trim(prefix) = '', NULL,
                          prefix),
                          IF(fmi_lname = '', NULL,
                          fmi_lname)
                          );
     pfmil_suffix := CONCAT_WS(', ',
                          IF (prefix_fmil = '', NULL,
                          prefix_fmil),
                          IF (trim(suffix) = '',
                          NULL, suffix || '.')
                          );
     RETURN pfmil_suffix;
  END;
  $$
  LANGUAGE plpgsql;
```

PostgreSQL's PL/pgSQL provides several other syntactical variants of these conditional expressions. This introduction focuses on the most commonly used ones. For a more complete discussion of the topic, visit `http://www.postgresql.org/docs/current/static/functions-conditional.html`.

Loops with counters

The PL/pgSQL language provides a simple way to loop through some elements. The following is a function that returns the *n*th Fibonacci sequence number:

```
CREATE OR REPLACE FUNCTION fib(n integer)
RETURNS INTEGER AS $$

DECLARE
  counter integer := 0;
  a integer := 0;
  b integer := 1;
BEGIN
  IF (n < 1) THEN
    RETURN 0;
  END IF;
  LOOP
    EXIT WHEN counter = n;
    counter := counter + 1;
    SELECT  b,a+b INTO a,b;
     END LOOP;
  RETURN a;
END;
$$
```

```
LANGUAGE plpgsql;

SELECT fib(4);
```

The preceding code gives 3 as the output.

Just for the record, each element in the Fibonacci sequence is the sum of the previous two elements. Thus, the first few elements of the sequence should be 0, 1, 1, 2, 3, 5, 8, 13, 21, 34, and so on. There are a few PostgreSQL Fibonacci sequence functions out there on the interwebs, but they use the dreaded recursive method. In this case, recursion is a *bad thing*. Our example uses the iterative method that avoids the use of stacks for recursion, as this might result in the lack of stack space for large numbers.

In this function, we also introduced default values to the variables in the declarations section. When the function is invoked, the variables will be initially set to these values.

Also, take a quick gander at the statement SELECT b,a+b INTO a,b. This statement makes two variable assignments at the same time. It avoids the use of a third variable while acting on both a and b.

Another slight variation of the function using a FOR loop, is as follows:

```
CREATE OR REPLACE FUNCTION fib(n integer)
RETURNS INTEGER
AS $$
DECLARE
counter integer := 0;
  a integer := 0;
   b integer := 1;
BEGIN
  IF (n < 1) THEN
    RETURN 0;
  END IF;
  FOR counter IN 1..n
  LOOP
    SELECT  b,a+b INTO a,b;
  END LOOP;
  RETURN a;
END;
$$
  LANGUAGE plpgsql;
```

For some additional looping syntax, take a look at the PostgreSQL documentation page at http://www.postgresql.org/docs/current/static/plpgsql-control-structures.html.

Statement termination

In PL/pgSQL, all blocks and the statements within the blocks, must end with a semicolon. The exceptions are the statements that start a block with IF or BEGIN. Block-starting statements are not complete statements; therefore, the semicolon is always after the block-ending statement, such as END; or END IF;.

Looping through query results

Before we embark on this journey of query result loops, I think I should warn you, that if you are using this method, you are probably *doing it wrong*. This is one of the most processor- and memory-intensive operations that PostgreSQL offers. There are exceedingly few reasons to iterate through a result set on the database server that offset this cost. I would encourage you to think hard about how to implement the same idea using a VALUES list in a query, temporary table, and permanent table, or to precompute the values in any way possible, in order to avoid this operation. So, do you still think you have an overwhelming reason to use this technique? Okay, then read on. The following is the simple version:

```
    FOR row IN
EXECUTE 'SELECT * FROM job_queue q WHERE NOT processed LIMIT 100'
LOOP
    CASE row.process_type
      WHEN 'archive_point_of_sale'
        THEN  INSERT INTO hist_orders (...)
              SELECT ... FROM orders
                INNER JOIN order_detail ...
                INNER JOIN item ...;
      WHEN 'prune_archived_orders'
        THEN DELETE FROM order_detail
              WHERE order_id in (SELECT order_id FROM
                hist_orders);
            DELETE FROM orders
              WHERE order_id IN (SELECT order_id FROM
                hist_orders);
      ELSE
        RAISE NOTICE 'Unknown process_type: %', row.process_type;
    END;
    UPDATE job_queue SET processed = TRUE WHERE id = q.id;
END LOOP;
```

The preceding example shows a basic strategy pattern of processing messages in a job queue. Using this technique, the rows in a table contain a list of jobs that need to be processed.

We introduce the EXECUTE statement here as well. The SELECT statement is a string value. Using EXECUTE, we can dynamically build PL/pgSQL commands as strings and then invoke them as statements against the database. This technique comes in handy, when we want to change the table name or other SQL keywords that make up our statement. These parts of the SQL statement cannot be stored in variables and are not generally changeable. With EXECUTE, we can change any part of the statement we jolly well please. We must mention that EXECUTE has a cost associated with it: the queries are prepared each time before running.

The following is an example from the PostgreSQL documentation that shows dynamic commands running inside a loop:

```
CREATE FUNCTION cs_refresh_mviews() RETURNS integer AS $$
DECLARE
    mviews RECORD;
BEGIN
    PERFORM cs_log('Refreshing materialized views...');
    FOR mviews IN SELECT * FROM cs_materialized_views ORDER BY
      sort_key LOOP
        -- Now "mviews" has one record from cs_materialized_views
        PERFORM cs_log('Refreshing materialized view ' ||
          quote_ident(mviews.mv_name) || ' ...');
        EXECUTE 'TRUNCATE TABLE ' || quote_ident(mviews.mv_name);
        EXECUTE 'INSERT INTO ' || quote_ident(mviews.mv_name) || '
          ' || mviews.mv_query;
    END LOOP;
    PERFORM cs_log('Done refreshing materialized views.');
    RETURN 1;
END;
$$ LANGUAGE plpgsql;
```

The preceding looping example, shows a more complex function that refreshes the data in some staging tables. These staging tables are designated *materialized views* because the data is actually physically transferred to the staging tables. This method was a common way to reduce query execution overhead for many presentations of the same data, before materialized views were officially supported in PostgreSQL 9.3. In this case, the inefficiency of looping is trivial compared to the continued cost of repeated queries to the same data.

PERFORM versus SELECT

You may have noticed a statement in the previous example that we haven't covered yet. Use the PERFORM command when you want to just discard the results of a statement. Change the previous example to the following line:

```
SELECT cs_log("Done refreshing materialized views");
```

The query engine will return No destination for result data.

We can retrieve the results into variables, and then proceed to ignore the variables, but that's just a little too sloppy for my taste. By using the PERFORM statement, we have indicated that ignoring the results was not accidental. We were happy with the fact that the log was appended to blindly, and if it wasn't, oh well, we didn't fail to continue the execution because of a log entry issue.

Looping Through Arrays

There is a very convenient loop construct called FOREACH, which allows you to loop through the elements of an array. Let's dive into an example:

```
CREATE FUNCTION findmax(int[]) RETURNS int8 AS $$
DECLARE
  max int8 := 0;
  x int;
BEGIN
  FOREACH x IN ARRAY $1
  LOOP
    IF x > max THEN
      max := x;
    END IF;
  END LOOP;
  RETURN max;
END;
$$ LANGUAGE plpgsql;
```

This function is quite self-explanatory. It finds the maximum values from a given integer array. The point to be noted here is that unlike a normal FOR loop, a FOREACH loop can only use a counter variable that is already declared. You can see that we have declared x before we used it as a counter in the loop. You can run this function to see if it works:

```
postgres=# select findmax(ARRAY[1,2,3,4,5, -1]);
 findmax
---------
       5
(1 row)
```

Returning a record

So far, all of our function examples have featured a simple scalar value in the RETURN clause. In PL/pgSQL, you can also define **set-returning functions (SRF)**. These functions can return either a type defined by an existing table or a generic record type. Let's take a look at a simple example:

```
CREATE TABLE  names(id serial, name varchar);
INSERT  INTO names(name) VALUES('John');
INSERT  INTO names(name) VALUES('Martin');
INSERT  INTO names(name) VALUES('Peter');

CREATE OR REPLACE FUNCTION GetNames() RETURNS SETOF names AS
   'SELECT * FROM names;' LANGUAGE 'sql';
```

We just defined a very simple function, GetNames(), which will simply return all the rows from our newly defined names table.

If you run the GetNames() function now, you will get the following output:

```
postgres=# select GetNames();
  getnames
------------
 (1,John)
 (2,Martin)
 (3,Peter)
(3 rows)
```

You can use an SRF in place of a table or as a subquery in the FROM clause of a query. Here's an example:

```
postgres=# select * from GetNames() where id > 2;
 id | name
----+-------
  3 | Peter
(1 row)
```

In addition to the table types, we can also return generic types from an SRF. We can change our example a little to demonstrate this. Let's define a new return type and a new function:

```
CREATE TYPE nametype AS (id int, name varchar);

CREATE FUNCTION PlpgGetNames() RETURNS SETOF nametype AS
$$
DECLARE
r nametype%rowtype;
```

```
BEGIN
  FOR r IN SELECT id, name FROM names LOOP
    RETURN NEXT r;
  END LOOP;
  RETURN;
END ;
$$

LANGUAGE 'plpgsql';
```

The `PlpgGetNames()` function declares a variable `r` to be of `rowtype nametype`. This variable is used to store the rows queried in the loop. The function does a loop over the `names` table and sets `r` to each row in the result set. The `RETURN NEXT` command means that an output row is queued into the return set of the function. This does not cause the function to return. Finally, the `RETURN` statement after the loop returns all the rows, which were queued earlier using `RETURN NEXT`.

Let's run our new function, as shown here:

```
postgres=# SELECT PlpgGetNames();
 plpggetnames
--------------
 (1,John)
 (2,Martin)
 (3,Peter)
(3 rows)
```

For the sake of a second example, we will assume that you are in the middle of a big software development upgrade procedure that uses a name/value pair table structure to store settings. You have been asked to change the table structure from the key and value columns to a series of columns, where the column name is now the name of the key. This is similar to the pivot tables in Excel. By the way, you also need to preserve the settings for every version of the software you have ever deployed.

If you take a look at the existing CREATE TABLE statement for the table you have to work with, you will find the following:

```
CREATE TABLE application_settings_old (
version varchar(200),
key varchar(200),
value varchar(2000));
```

When you run a SELECT statement against the table, you will find out that there aren't many settings, but there have been quite a few versions of the settings. So, let's make a new table that is a little more explicit:

```
CREATE TABLE  application_settings_new (
version varchar(200),
full_name varchar(2000),
description varchar(2000),
print_certificate varchar(2000),
show_advertisements varchar(2000),
show_splash_screen varchar(2000));
```

Transforming the settings data into this new format can be accomplished with an INSERT statement and a function that conveniently returns our data in the new table format.

Let's add some test data, as follows:

```
INSERT INTO application_settings_old
  VALUES('3456','full_name','test_name');
INSERT INTO application_settings_old
  VALUES('3456','description','test_description');
INSERT INTO application_settings_old
  VALUES('3456','print_certificate','yes');
INSERT INTO application_settings_old
  VALUES('3456','show_advertisements','yes');
INSERT INTO application_settings_old
  VALUES('3456','show_splash_screen','no');
```

Let's go ahead and define the function:

```
CREATE OR REPLACE FUNCTION
flatten_application_settings(app_version varchar(200))
RETURNS setof application_settings_new
AS $$
   BEGIN
    -- Create a temporary table to hold a single row of data
    IF EXISTS (SELECT relname FROM pg_class WHERE
      relname='tmp_settings')
    THEN
      TRUNCATE TABLE tmp_settings;
    ELSE
      CREATE TEMP TABLE tmp_settings (LIKE
        application_settings_new);
    END IF;
```

```
            --the row will contain all of the data for this version
         INSERT INTO tmp_settings (version) VALUES (app_version);
      -- add the details to the record for this application version
      UPDATE tmp_settings
      SET full_name = (SELECT value
                         FROM application_settings_old
                       WHERE version = app_version
                         AND key='full_name'),
         description = (SELECT value
                          FROM application_settings_old
                        WHERE version = app_version
                          AND key='description'),
         print_certificate = (SELECT value
                                FROM application_settings_old
                              WHERE version = app_version
                                AND key='print_certificate'),
         show_advertisements = (SELECT value
                                  FROM application_settings_old
                                WHERE version = app_version
                                  AND key='show_advertisements'),
         show_splash_screen = (SELECT value
                                 FROM application_settings_old
                               WHERE version = app_version
                                 AND key='show_splash_screen');
   --hand back the results to the caller
      RETURN QUERY SELECT * FROM tmp_settings;
END;
$$ LANGUAGE plpgsql;
```

The preceding function returns a single row of data to the calling query. The row contains all the settings that were previously defined as key/value pairs, but are explicitly defined fields now. The function and the final table can also be enhanced to transform the data types of the settings to something more explicit. However, I'll leave that one up to you.

We then proceed to use the function in order to do the transformation:

```
INSERT INTO application_settings_new
SELECT ( flatten_application_settings(version)).*
FROM (
SELECT version
FROM application_settings_old
GROUP BY version)  AS ver;
```

Voilá! The data is now available in a tabular form in the new table structure.

Acting on the function's results

The previous example showed one way to retrieve, and further process, function results. The following are a few more useful ways to call a function:

```
SELECT fib(25);
SELECT (flatten_application_settings('9.08.97')).*;
SELECT * FROM flatten_application_settings('9.08.97');
```

Any of the preceding methods will create a legal field list in PostgreSQL, which, in turn, can be used in any way the fields in a simple SELECT statement on a table are used.

The example in the previous section used the results of the flatten_application_settings() function, a source of data for an INSERT statement. The following is an example of how to use the same function as a data source for UPDATE:

```
UPDATE application_settings_new
   SET full_name = flat.full_name,
       description  = flat.description,
       print_certificate = flat.print_certificate,
       show_advertisements = flat.show_advertisements,
       show_splash_screen = flat.show_splash_screen
  FROM flatten_application_settings('9.08.97') flat;
```

Using the application version as a key, we can update the records in the new table. Isn't this a really handy way to keep up with the changes to the application settings, while both the old and new applications are still active? I'll take any compliments in the form of cash (or beer), please.

Summary

Writing functions in PostgreSQL is an extremely powerful tool. PostgreSQL functions provide the ability to add functionality to the database core, in order to increase performance, security, and maintainability.

These functions can be written in just about any language that is available to the open source community and several that are proprietary. If the language that you want to write them in is not available, it can be made available quickly and easily through a very robust and complete compatibility layer. In this chapter, we only looked at PL/pgSQL functions.

In the next chapter, we will focus more on PL/pgSQL functions, and take a look at the different ways in which data can be returned using OUT parameters and return values.

4
Returning Structured Data

In the previous chapter, we saw functions that return single values. These functions return either a "scalar," simple type such as an integer, text, or data; or a more complex type, similar to a row in the database table. In this chapter, we will expand these concepts and show you how to return your data to the client in more powerful ways.

We will also examine the following topics:

- Differences between SETOF scalars, rows, and arrays
- Returning CURSORs, which are kind of "lazy" tables, that is, something that can be used to get a set of rows, but which may not have actually evaluated or fetched the rows yet, as the modern world is not about rigid table-structured data
- Ways to deal with more complex data structures, both predefined and dynamically created

Let's start with a simple example and then add more features and variants as we go.

Sets and arrays

Rowsets are similar to arrays in many ways, but they mainly differ in their usage. For most data manipulations, you will want to use rowsets, as the SQL language is designed to deal with them. Arrays, however, are most useful for static storage. They are more complicated for client applications to use than rowsets, with usability features missing, such as no simple and straightforward built-in ways to iterate over them.

Returning sets

When you write a set returning function, there are some differences from a normal scalar function. First, let's take a look at how to return a set of integers.

Returning a set of integers

We will revisit our Fibonacci number generating function; however, this time we will not just return the *n*th number, but the whole sequence of numbers up to the *n*th number, as shown here:

```
CREATE OR REPLACE FUNCTION fibonacci_seq(num integer)
  RETURNS SETOF integer AS $$
DECLARE
  a int := 0;
  b int := 1;
BEGIN
  IF (num <= 0)
    THEN RETURN;
  END IF;

  RETURN NEXT a;
  LOOP
    EXIT WHEN num <= 1;
    RETURN NEXT b;

    num = num - 1;
    SELECT b, a + b INTO a, b;
  END LOOP;
END;
$$ LANGUAGE plpgsql;
```

The first difference we see, is that instead of returning a single integer value, this function is defined to return a SETOF integer.

Then, if you examine the code carefully, you will see that there are two different types of RETURN statements. The first is the ordinary RETURN function in the following code snippet:

```
IF (num <= 0)
    THEN RETURN;
```

In this case, the IF function is used to terminate the fibonacci_seq function early, if the length of the desired sequence of Fibonacci numbers is zero or less.

The second kind of RETURN statement is used to return values and continue execution:

```
RETURN NEXT a;
```

RETURN NEXT appends rows to the result set of the function, and the execution continues until a normal RETURN statement is encountered or until the control reaches the end of the function. You may have noticed that there are a few other things we did differently in this Fibonacci example, than we did earlier. First, we declared and initialized the variables a and b inside the DECLARE section, instead of first declaring and then initializing them. We also used the argument as a down counter instead of using a separate variable to count from zero and then comparing it with the argument.

Let's test our function now. In the next section, we will discuss how to use the set returning functions in more detail:

```
postgres=# SELECT fibonacci_seq(5);
 fibonacci_seq
---------------
        0
        1
        1
        2
        3
(5 rows)
```

Both of these techniques save a few lines of code and can make the code more readable, depending on your preferences. However, the longer versions might be easier to follow and understand, so we don't particularly endorse either way.

Using a set returning function

A set returning function (also known as a table function) can be used in most places where a table, view, or subquery can be used. They are a powerful and flexible way to return data.

You can call the function in the SELECT clause, as you do with a scalar function:

```
postgres=# SELECT fibonacci_seq(3);
 fibonacci_seq
---------------
        0
        1
        1
(3 rows)
```

You can also call the function as part of the FROM clause:

```
postgres=# SELECT * FROM fibonacci_seq(3);
 fibonacci_seq
---------------
             0
             1
             1
(3 rows)
```

You can even call the function in the WHERE clause:

```
postgres=# SELECT * FROM fibonacci_seq(3) WHERE 1 = ANY
   (SELECT fibonacci_seq(3));
 fibonacci_seq
---------------
             0
             1
             1
(3 rows)
```

You can limit the result set, just as in the case of querying a table:

```
postgres=# SELECT * FROM fibonacci_seq(10) as fib WHERE fib > 3;
 fibonacci_seq
---------------
             5
             8
            13
            21
            34
(5 rows)
```

Using database-side functions for all the data access is a great way to secure your application; it also helps with performance and allows easy maintenance. Table functions allow you to use functions in all cases where you would have been forced to use more complex queries from the client if only scalar functions were available.

Returning rows from a function will often be helpful to return back to the client more information than just a set of integers. You may need all the columns from an existing table, and the simplest way to declare a return type for a function is to just use the table as part of the return definition, as shown here:

```
CREATE OR REPLACE FUNCTION installed_languages()
   RETURNS SETOF pg_language AS $$
BEGIN
```

```
        RETURN QUERY SELECT * FROM  pg_language;
END;
$$ LANGUAGE plpgsql;
```

Notice that you still need the SETOF part, but instead of defining it as a set of integers, we use pg_language, which is a table.

You can use TYPE, defined using the CREATE TYPE command or even VIEW:

```
hannu=# SELECT * FROM installed_languages();

-[ RECORD 1 ]-+----------
lanname       | internal
lanowner      | 10
lanispl       | f
lanpltrusted  | f
lanplcallfoid | 0
laninline     | 0
lanvalidator  | 2246
lanacl        |
-[ RECORD 2 ]-+----------
lanname       | c
lanowner      | 10
lanispl       | f
lanpltrusted  | f
lanplcallfoid | 0
laninline     | 0
lanvalidator  | 2247
lanacl        |
-[ RECORD 3 ]-+----------
lanname       | sql
lanowner      | 10
lanispl       | f
lanpltrusted  | t
lanplcallfoid | 0
laninline     | 0
lanvalidator  | 2248
lanacl        |
-[ RECORD 4 ]-+----------
lanname       | plpgsql
lanowner      | 10
lanispl       | t
lanpltrusted  | t
lanplcallfoid | 12596
laninline     | 12597
```

```
lanvalidator  |  12598
lanacl        |
-[ RECORD 5 ]-+----------
lanname       |  plpythonu
lanowner      |  10
lanispl       |  t
lanpltrusted  |  f
lanplcallfoid |  17563
laninline     |  17564
lanvalidator  |  17565
lanacl        |
```

Functions based on views

Creating a function based on a view definition is a very powerful and flexible way of providing information to users. As an example of this, I will tell you a story of how I started a simple utility view to answer the question, "What queries are running now, and which queries have been running for the longest time?" This evolved into a function based on this view, plus a few more views based on the function.

The way to get all the data to answer this question in PostgreSQL is by using the following query. Please note that the output is using an expanded mode of psql. You can turn it on using the \x meta-command:

```
hannu=# SELECT * FROM pg_stat_activity WHERE state='active';

-[ RECORD 1 ]----+--------------------------------
datid            |  17557
datname          |  hannu
pid              |  8933
usesysid         |  10
usename          |  postgres
application_name |  psql
client_addr      |
client_hostname  |
client_port      |  -1
backend_start    |  2013-03-19 13:47:45.920902-04
xact_start       |  2013-03-19 14:05:47.91225-04
query_start      |  2013-03-19 14:05:47.91225-04
state_change     |  2013-03-19 14:05:47.912253-04
waiting          |  f
state            |  active
query            |  select * from pg_stat_activity
                 |     where state='active';
```

The usual process is to use a variant of the following query, which is already wrapped into a view here:

```
CREATE VIEW running_queries AS
SELECT
    (CURRENT_TIMESTAMP - query_start) as runtime,
    pid,
    usename,
    waiting,
    query
FROM pg_stat_activity
WHERE state='active'
ORDER BY 1 DESC
LIMIT 10;
```

Soon, you will notice that putting this query into a view is not enough. Sometimes, you may want to vary the number of lowest queries, while sometimes you may not want to have the full query text, but just the beginning, and so on.

If you want to vary some parameters, the logical thing to do is to use a function instead of a view, as otherwise you will need to create different views of each new requirement:

```
CREATE OR REPLACE FUNCTION running_queries(rows int, qlen int)
    RETURNS SETOF running_queries AS
$$
BEGIN
    RETURN QUERY SELECT
        runtime,
        pid,
        usename,
        waiting,
        substring(query,1,qlen) as query
    FROM running_queries
    ORDER BY 1 DESC
    LIMIT rows;
END;
$$ LANGUAGE plpgsql;
```

As a security precaution, the default behavior of the pg_stat_activity view is that only superusers can see what other users are running. Sometimes, it may be necessary to allow the non-superusers to at least see the type of query (SELECT, INSERT, DELETE, or UPDATE) that other users are running, but hide the exact contents. To do this, you have to make two changes to the previous function.

First, replace the row to get `current_query` with the following code snippet:

```
(CASE WHEN ( usename = session_user )
        OR (SELECT usesuper
              FROM pg_user
              WHERE usename = session_user)
      THEN
        substring(query,1,qlen)
      ELSE
        substring(ltrim(query), 1, 6) || ' ***'
      END  ) as query
```

This code snippet checks each row to see whether the user running the function has permission to see the full query. If the user is a superuser, then he she has permission to see the full query. If the user is a regular user, he/she will only see the full query for his/her queries. All other rows will only show the first six characters followed by `***` to mark it as a shortened query string.

The other key point to allowing ordinary users to run the function, is to grant them the appropriate rights to do so. When a function is created, the default behavior is to run with the SECURITY INVOKER rights, which means that the function will be called with the rights of the user who called it. To easily grant the correct rights to call the function, the function needs to be created with the SECURITY DEFINER attribute. This causes the function to execute with the privileges of the user who created the function; therefore, creating the function as a superuser will allow it to execute as a superuser, regardless of the rights of the user who called it. This, however, should be done with caution because a superuser can be dangerous, and if you end up **executing** a string that is passed in, you will have all the issues of SQL injection attacks.

Now, you have a function, which you can use to get the start of the five longest-running queries using the following query:

```
SELECT * FROM running_queries(5,25);
```

In order to get a complete query, you can use the following:

```
SELECT * FROM running_queries(1000,1024);
```

You may want to define a few convenience views for the variants you use most, as follows:

```
CREATE OR REPLACE VIEW running_queries_tiny AS
SELECT * FROM running_queries(5,25);
CREATE VIEW running_queries_full AS
SELECT * FROM running_queries(1000,1024);
```

You can even redefine the original view to use the first version of the function:

```
CREATE OR REPLACE VIEW running_queries AS
SELECT * FROM running_queries(5,25);
```

This is usually not recommended, but it demonstrates the following three important things:

- Views and functions can have exactly the same name
- You can get a circular reference by basing a function on a view and then basing a view on that function
- If you get a circular reference in this way, you can't easily change either definition

To resolve this, simply avoid circular references.

Even without circular references, there is still a dependency on the view called from the function. If, for instance, you need to add a column to show the application name to the running_queries view, the function needs to change as well:

```
CREATE OR REPLACE VIEW running_queries AS
SELECT
    CURRENT_TIMESTAMP - query_start as runtime,
    pid,
    usename,
    waiting,
    query,
    application_name as appname
FROM pg_stat_activity
ORDER BY 1 DESC
LIMIT 10;
```

The view definition can be changed without an error, but the next time you try to run the running_queries(int, int) function, you will get an error:

```
hannu=# SELECT * FROM running_queries(5,25);
ERROR:  structure of query does not match function result type
DETAIL:  Number of returned columns (5) does not match expected
  column count (6).
CONTEXT:  PL/pgSQL function "running_queries" line 3 at RETURN
  QUERY
```

To fix this, you need to add an additional column to the function. This is one of the dangers of reusing types in this way: you might end up breaking functions unintentionally. PostgreSQL won't tell you, when you change a type in this way, whether any functions were using this type and will only fail when you try to run the query:

```
CREATE OR REPLACE FUNCTION running_queries(rows int, qlen int)
   RETURNS SETOF running_queries AS
$$
BEGIN
   RETURN QUERY SELECT
       runtime,
       pid,
       usename,
       waiting,
       (CASE WHEN ( usename= session_user )
          OR (select usesuper
                from pg_user
              where usename = session_user)
       THEN
          substring(query,1,qlen)
       ELSE
          substring(ltrim(query), 1, 6) || ' ***'
       END) as query,
       appname
    FROM running_queries
   ORDER BY 1 DESC
   LIMIT rows;
END;
$$
LANGUAGE plpgsql
SECURITY DEFINER;
```

OUT parameters and records

Using a pre-existing type, table, or view for compound return types is a simple mechanism for returning more complex structures. However, there is often a need to define the return type of the function with the function itself and not depend on other objects. This is especially true when managing changes to a running application; so, over a period of time, two better ways to handle this have been added to PostgreSQL.

OUT parameters

Until now, all the functions we created used parameters that are defined as IN parameters. The IN parameters are meant to just pass information into the function that can be used, but not returned. Parameters can also be defined as OUT or INOUT parameters if you want the function to return some information as well:

```
CREATE OR REPLACE FUNCTION positives(
                    INOUT a int,
                    INOUT b int,
                    INOUT c int)
AS $$
BEGIN
    IF a < 0 THEN a = null; END IF;
    IF b < 0 THEN b = null; END IF;
    IF c < 0 THEN c = null; END IF;
END;
$$ LANGUAGE plpgsql;
```

When we run the previous function, it only returns a single row of data with three columns, as shown here:

```
hannu=# SELECT * FROM positives(-1, 1, 2);
-[ RECORD 1 ]
a |
b | 1
c | 2
```

Returning records

If multiple rows of data need to be returned, a similar function that returns a set is achieved by adding RETURNS SETOF RECORD. This technique can only be used with functions using the INOUT or OUT arguments:

```
CREATE FUNCTION permutations(INOUT a int,
                            INOUT b int,
                            INOUT c int)
RETURNS SETOF RECORD
AS $$
BEGIN
    RETURN NEXT;
    SELECT b,c INTO c,b; RETURN NEXT;
    SELECT a,b INTO b,a; RETURN NEXT;
```

```
        SELECT b,c INTO c,b; RETURN NEXT;
        SELECT a,b INTO b,a; RETURN NEXT;
        SELECT b,c INTO c,b; RETURN NEXT;
    END;
    $$ LANGUAGE plpgsql;
```

Running the `permutations` function returns six rows, as expected:

```
    hannu=# SELECT * FROM permutations(1, 2, 3);
    -[ RECORD 1 ]
    a | 1
    b | 2
    c | 3
    -[ RECORD 2 ]
    a | 1
    b | 3
    c | 2
    -[ RECORD 3 ]
    a | 3
    b | 1
    c | 2
    -[ RECORD 4 ]
    a | 3
    b | 2
    c | 1
    -[ RECORD 5 ]
    a | 2
    b | 3
    c | 1
    -[ RECORD 6 ]
    a | 2
    b | 1
    c | 3
```

This works well, but it seems a bit verbose for what is a pretty simple operation. This is because we cannot directly call RETURN NEXT a,b,c, but we need to first assign values to variables declared by the INOUT incantations. We also want to avoid the even clumsier syntax of tmp = a; a = b; b = tmp;.

Due to design decisions in the PL/pgSQL language, there is currently no good way to construct the return structure at runtime, that is, no RETURN a,b,c.

However, let's try to do it anyway and see what happens.

Using RETURNS TABLE

You may think that if there are no visible OUT parameters in a function declared as RETURNS TABLE (...), the following code might work:

```
CREATE FUNCTION permutations2(a int, b int, c int)
  RETURNS TABLE(a int, b int, c int)
AS $$
BEGIN
    RETURN NEXT a,b,c;
END;
$$ LANGUAGE plpgsql;
```

However, when we try to do it this way, we get an error:

```
ERROR:  parameter name "a" used more than once
CONTEXT:  compilation of PL/pgSQL function "permutations2" near
    line 1
```

This error hints that the fields in the return table definition are also actually just OUT parameters and the whole RETURNS TABLE syntax is just another way to spell CREATE FUNCTION f(OUT ..., OUT...) RETURNS RECORD ....

This can be verified further by changing the input parameters, so that the definition can be fed into PostgreSQL:

```
CREATE FUNCTION permutations2(ia int, ib int, ic int)
  RETURNS TABLE(a int, b int, c int)
AS $$
BEGIN
    RETURN NEXT a,b,c;
END;
$$ LANGUAGE plpgsql;
```

When we try to create the function, we get the following output:

```
ERROR:  RETURN NEXT cannot have a parameter in function with OUT
    parameters
LINE 5:     RETURN NEXT a,b,c;
                    ^
```

So yes, the fields of the table in the RETURNS definition are actually just OUT parameters.

Returning with no predefined structure

Sometimes, you really need to write a function where the return structure is unknown. One good thing about PostgreSQL function declarations, is that you can use the return type RECORD, which can be left undefined until the function is called:

```
CREATE OR REPLACE FUNCTION run_a_query(query TEXT)
  RETURNS SETOF RECORD
AS $$
DECLARE
    retval RECORD;
BEGIN
    FOR retval IN EXECUTE query LOOP
        RETURN NEXT retval;
    END LOOP ;
END;
$$ LANGUAGE plpgsql;
```

This is a function that lets a user execute a query; it is quite useless as such, but it can be used as the basis for more useful functions that, for example, let users run queries only at a certain time, or can be used to perform some checks on queries before running them.

Simply run the following query:

```
SELECT * FROM run_a_query('SELECT usename, usesysid FROM
  pg_user');
```

You will get the following error:

```
ERROR:  a column definition list is required for functions
  returning "record"
LINE 1: select * from run_a_query('select usename, usesysid from
  pg_...
```

To use this kind of a function, you need to tell PostgreSQL what the return values will be, by adding a column definition list at the time of calling a function in the following way:

```
SELECT * FROM run_a_query('SELECT usename,usesysid FROM pg_user')
  AS ("user" text, uid int);
```

So, will this work? No, you will get the following error:

```
ERROR:  wrong record type supplied in RETURN NEXT
DETAIL:  Returned type name does not match expected type text in
  column 1.
CONTEXT:  PL/pgSQL function run_a_query(text) line 6 at RETURN
  NEXT
```

By changing things slightly, we finally arrive at something that works, as follows:

```
hannu=# SELECT * FROM run_a_query('SELECT usename::text,usesysid::int
FROM pg_user') AS
  ("user" text, uid int);
-[ RECORD 1 ]--
user | postgres
uid  | 10
-[ RECORD 2 ]--
user | hannu
uid  | 17573
```

What do we learn from this? PostgreSQL will let you return an arbitrary record from a function, but it is very particular in how it does this. When you call the function, you will need to be very deliberate about things, especially data types. PostgreSQL will use default casts to convert data to different data types if it has enough information. However, in a function such as this, much of that information is not known.

Returning SETOF ANY

There is another way to define functions that can operate on, and return, incomplete type definitions: using the ANY* pseudotypes.

Let's define a function, which turns a simple one-dimensional PostgreSQL array of any type into a set of rows with one element of the same type:

```
CREATE OR REPLACE FUNCTION array_to_rows( array_in ANYARRAY )
  RETURNS TABLE(row_out ANYELEMENT)
AS $$
BEGIN
    FOR i IN 1.. array_upper(array_in,1) LOOP
        row_out =  array_in[i];
        RETURN NEXT ;
    END LOOP;
END;
$$ LANGUAGE plpgsql;
```

This works well on an array of integers:

```
hannu=# SELECT array_to_rows('{1,2,3}'::int[]);
-[ RECORD 1 ]-+--
array_to_rows | 1
-[ RECORD 2 ]-+--
array_to_rows | 2
-[ RECORD 3 ]-+--
array_to_rows | 3
```

It also works well on an array of dates, as shown here:

```
hannu=# SELECT array_to_rows('{"1970-1-1","2012-12-12"}'::date[]);
-[ RECORD 1 ]-+-----------
array_to_rows | 1970-01-01
-[ RECORD 2 ]-+-----------
array_to_rows | 2012-12-12
```

The function even works on arrays of records from user-defined tables:

```
hannu=# CREATE TABLE mydata(id serial primary key, data text);
CREATE TABLE

hannu=# INSERT INTO mydata VALUES(1, 'one'), (2,'two');
INSERT 0 2
hannu=# SELECT array_to_rows(array(SELECT m FROM mydata m));
-[ RECORD 1 ]-+--------
array_to_rows | (1,one)
-[ RECORD 2 ]-+--------
array_to_rows | (2,two)

hannu=# SELECT * FROM array_to_rows
   (array(SELECT m FROM mydata m));
-[ RECORD 1 ]
id   | 1
data | one
-[ RECORD 2 ]
id   | 2
data | two
```

The last two SELECT statements return a one-column table of the type mydata and a two-column table of the same type expanded into its component columns. This single function is flexible enough to handle several different types of data without any changes.

There is a more potent version of `array_to_rows` built into PostgreSQL called `unnest()`. The built-in function is faster than our sample function and can also deal with arrays with more than one dimension:

```
hannu=# SELECT unnest('{{1,2,3}, {4,5,6}}'::int[]);
-[ RECORD 1 ]
unnest | 1
-[ RECORD 2 ]
unnest | 2
-[ RECORD 3 ]
unnest | 3
-[ RECORD 4 ]
unnest | 4
-[ RECORD 5 ]
unnest | 5
-[ RECORD 6 ]
unnest | 6
```

PostgreSQL has a weird array type, which can hold the arrays of any number of dimensions. It is even weirder than this, as the array slices in any dimension can also start with any positive index (and they are, by default, 1-based). For example, an array with indices ranging from -2 to 2 is produced by the following incantation:

```
hannu=# SELECT '[-2:2]={1,2,3,4,5}'::int[];
-[ RECORD 1 ]------------
int4 | [-2:2]={1,2,3,4,5}
```

To check whether this really is the case, use the following code snippet:

```
hannu=# SELECT array_dims('[-2:2]={1,2,3,4,5}'::int[]);
-[ RECORD 1 ]------
array_dims | [-2:2]
```

The third element of the array is 3, and this is the middle element.

Variadic argument lists

PostgreSQL allows you to write a function with a variable number of arguments. This is accomplished using `VARIADIC`. Let's take a look at a practical example. Suppose you want to limit the results of a query in your function, based on the `VARIADIC` list of arguments; here's one way to do this:

```
CREATE OR REPLACE FUNCTION get_nspc_tbls(VARIADIC arr name[])
RETURNS TABLE(table_name name,id oid,nspname name)
```

```
AS $$
BEGIN
RETURN QUERY SELECT c.relname , c.oid , n.nspname from pg_class c,
  pg_namespace n where c.relnamespace = n.oid and n.nspname =
  any(arr);
END;
$$ LANGUAGE plpgsql;
```

The preceding function lets you list the tables, which are in specified namespaces. The variable list allows you to provide one or more namespace names. This trick can be quite handy in various situations. Notice the use of the `any` function; you can't substitute it with an `IN` clause, as this will try to compare a `name` type with `name[]`:

```
postgres=# SELECT * FROM get_nspc_tbls('public','pg_temp');
-[ RECORD 1 ]-----------------------
table_name | a
id         | 16434
nspname    | public
-[ RECORD 2 ]-----------------------
table_name | parameter
id         | 24682
nspname    | public
-[ RECORD 3 ]-----------------------
table_name | application_settings_old
id         | 24690
nspname    | public
-[ RECORD 4 ]-----------------------
table_name | foo
id         | 16455
nspname    | pg_temp
```

A summary of the RETURN SETOF variants

You learned that you can return table-like datasets from a function using one of the following:

RETURNS	RECORD structure	INSIDE function
SETOF <type>	This is obtained from the type definition	DECLARE row variable of the ROW or RECORD type ASSIGN to row variable RETURN NEXT var;
SETOF <table/view>	This is the same as the table or view structure	

RETURNS	RECORD structure	INSIDE function
SETOF RECORD	Dynamic using **AS (name type, ...)** at call site	
SETOF RECORD	This uses the OUT and INOUT function arguments. Assigned to the OUT variables	RETURN NEXT;
TABLE (...)	This is declared inline, in parentheses, after the TABLE keyword and is converted to the OUT variable for use in functions. It is assigned to the OUT variables from the TABLE (...) part of the declaration.	RETURN NEXT;

Returning cursors

Another method that can be used to get tabular data out of a function, is using CURSOR.

CURSOR, or a portal, as it is sometimes referred to in PostgreSQL documentation, is an internal structure that contains a prepared query plan, ready to return rows from the query. Sometimes, the cursor needs to retrieve all the data for the query at once, but for many queries it does lazy fetching. For example, queries that need to scan all of the data in a table, such as SELECT * FROM xtable, only read the amount of data that is needed for each FETCH from the cursor.

In plain SQL, CURSOR is defined as follows:

```
DECLARE mycursor CURSOR  FOR <query >;
```

Later, the rows are fetched using the following statement:

```
FETCH NEXT FROM  mycursor;
```

While you can use a cursor to handle the data from a set returning function the usual way, by simply declaring the cursor as DECLARE mycursor CURSOR FOR SELECT * FROM mysetfunc();, many times it is more beneficial to have the function itself just return a cursor.

You will want to do this if you need different cursors based on argument values, or if you need to return dynamically structured data out of a function, without defining the structure when calling the function.

The cursor in PL/pgSQL is represented by a variable of the type `refcursor` and must be declared in one of the following three ways:

```
DECLARE
    curs1 refcursor;
    curs2 CURSOR FOR SELECT * FROM tenk1;
    curs3 CURSOR (key integer) IS SELECT * FROM tenk1 WHERE
      unique1 = key;
```

The first variant declares an unbound cursor that needs to be bound to a query at OPEN time. The two remaining variants declare a cursor bound to a query.

 You can read a good technical overview on how to use cursors in PL/pgSQL functions from the official PostgreSQL documentation at `http://www.postgresql.org/docs/current/static/plpgsql-cursors.html`.

One thing to note about the documentation is that you don't really need to "return" the cursor, at least not now because cursors can also be passed back to the caller in OUT parameters.

The PostgreSQL documentation states:

"The following example shows one way to return multiple cursors from a single function:

CREATE FUNCTION myfunc(refcursor, refcursor) RETURNS SETOF
  refcursor AS $$

BEGIN

  *OPEN $1 FOR SELECT * FROM table_1;*

  RETURN NEXT $1;

  *OPEN $2 FOR SELECT * FROM table_2;*

  RETURN NEXT $2;

END;

$$ LANGUAGE plpgsql;

-- need to be in a transaction to use cursors.

BEGIN;

*SELECT * FROM myfunc('a', 'b');*

FETCH ALL FROM a;

FETCH ALL FROM b;

COMMIT;"

You can also write the `myfunc` function using the `OUT` parameters:

```
CREATE FUNCTION myfunc2(cur1 refcursor, cur2 refcursor)
RETURNS VOID AS $$
BEGIN
    OPEN cur1 FOR SELECT * FROM table_1;
    OPEN cur2 FOR SELECT * FROM table_2;
END;
$$ LANGUAGE plpgsql;
```

You will still run the function in exactly the same way as the function returning the cursor variable.

Iterating over cursors returned from another function

To wrap up our cursors' discussion, let's go through an example of returning a cursor and then iterating over the returned cursor in another PL/pgSQL function:

1. First, let's create a five-row table and fill it with data:

    ```
    CREATE TABLE fiverows(id serial PRIMARY KEY, data text);
    INSERT INTO fiverows(data) VALUES ('one'), ('two'),
                        ('three'), ('four'), ('five');
    ```

2. Next, let's define our cursor returning function. This function will open a cursor for a query, based on its argument and then return that cursor:

    ```
    CREATE FUNCTION curtest1(cur refcursor, tag text)
      RETURNS refcursor
    AS $$
    BEGIN
        OPEN cur FOR SELECT id, data || '+' || tag FROM
          fiverows;
        RETURN cur;
    END;
    $$ LANGUAGE plpgsql;
    ```

3. Next, we define a function, which uses the function we just created to open two additional cursors, and then process the query results. To show that we are not cheating and that the function really creates the cursors, we use the function twice and iterate over the results in parallel:

    ```
    CREATE FUNCTION curtest2(tag1 text, tag2 text)
      RETURNS SETOF fiverows
    AS $$
    ```

```
DECLARE
    cur1 refcursor;
    cur2 refcursor;
    row record;
BEGIN
    cur1 = curtest1(NULL, tag1);
    cur2 = curtest1(NULL, tag2);
    LOOP
        FETCH cur1 INTO row;
        EXIT WHEN NOT FOUND ;
        RETURN NEXT row;
        FETCH cur2 INTO row;
        EXIT WHEN NOT FOUND ;
        RETURN NEXT row;
    END LOOP;
END;
$$ LANGUAGE plpgsql;
```

Please note, that once a `record` variable inside a `plpgsql` function is **defined** by being used, it can't be changed from `record` type for the duration of that session because PL/pgSQL stores and reuses the plan built with the record type.

By passing in `NULL` to the first parameters of `curtest1`, PostgreSQL automatically generates the cursor names so that multiple invocations of this function will not get name conflicts with any other functions, which also create cursors.

Wrapping up of functions returning cursors

The pros of using cursors are as follows:

- Cursors are a useful tool if you don't want to always execute the query and wait for the full result set before returning from a function

- Currently, they are also the only way to return multiple result sets out of a user-defined function

The cons of using cursors are as follows:

- They mainly work to pass data between functions on the server, and you are still limited to one record set per call returned to the database client

- They are sometimes confusing to use, and bound and unbound cursors are not always interchangeable

You can read more about cursors at `http://www.postgresql.org/docs/current/static/plpgsql-cursors.html`.

Other ways to work with structured data

We now have covered the traditional ways of returning sets of structured data from functions. We will now start with the more interesting part. Other methods to pass around complex data structures have evolved in the world.

Complex data types for the modern world – XML and JSON

In the real world, most of the data is not in a single table and the database is not the main thing that most programmers focus on. Often, they don't even think about it at all, or at least they would rather not think about it.

If you are a database developer who works on the database side of things, it is often desirable to talk to the clients (be it web or application developers as your client, or programs as database clients) in the language they speak. Currently, the two most widely spoken data languages by the web applications and their developers are XML and JSON.

Both XML and JSON are text-based data formats, and as such, they can be easily saved into fields of the type `text`. PostgreSQL, being a DBMS, built for being user-extendable, also has extensive support for both these formats.

XML data type and returning data as XML from functions

One of the extensions added to PostgreSQL, in order to support XML data, is a native XML data type. While the XML data type is largely just a text field, it differs from text in the following ways:

- The XML stored in an XML field is checked on inserts and updates to be well-formed
- There are support functions to produce and work with known well-formed XML

An XML value can be produced in a couple of ways, including the standard SQL method:

```
XMLPARSE ( { DOCUMENT | CONTENT } value)
```

PostgreSQL also has a specific syntax that will produce an XML value:

```
xml '<foo>bar</foo>'
'<foo>bar</foo>'::xml
```

An XML value can be easily converted to a text representation using the XMLSERIALIZE function, as follows:

```
XMLSERIALIZE ( { DOCUMENT | CONTENT } value AS type )
```

Additionally, PostgreSQL allows you to simply cast the XML value as text.

 The full description of the XML data type and its associated functions is available at http://www.postgresql.org/docs/current/static/datatype-xml.html. As each version of PostgreSQL has improved, the support for XML has also improved.

There are several *_to_xml functions in PostgreSQL, which take either a SQL query, or a table, or view as input and return its corresponding XML representation.

Let's take a look at this using the fiverows table we defined previously in the *Returning cursors* section.

First, let's get the table data as an XML:

```
hannu=# SELECT table_to_xml('fiverows',true, false, '') AS s;
-[ RECORD 1 ]------------------------------------------------------
s | <fiverows xmlns:xsi="http://www.w3.org/2001/XMLSchema-instance">
  |
  | <row>
  |   <id>1</id>
  |   <data>one</data>
  | </row>
  |
  | <row>
  |   <id>2</id>
  |   <data>two</data>
  | </row>
  |
```

```
|   <row>
|     <id>3</id>
|     <data>three</data>
|   </row>
|
|   <row>
|     <id>4</id>
|     <data>four</data>
|   </row>
|
|   <row>
|     <id>5</id>
|     <data>five</data>
|   </row>
|
| </fiverows>
|
```

If you have a client that can handle XML, then the `*_to_xml` functions can be the best way to return complex data.

Another good thing about the `*_to_xml` functions is that you can create a function which returns several different XML documents in one go and, thus, returns data rows with different structures. A good example, will be a payment order and rows, where the first record returned by the function is the XML for the order header followed by one or more records of XML for the order rows, all returned by the same function in one call.

There are, at the time of writing this book, five variants of the `*_to_xml` functions:

```
cursor_to_xml(cursor refcursor, count integer,
              nulls bool, tableforest bool, targetns text)
query_to_xml(query text,
             nulls bool, tableforest bool, targetns text)
table_to_xml(tbl regclass,
             nulls boolean, tableforest boolean, targetns text)
schema_to_xml(schema name,
              nulls boolean, tableforest boolean, targetns text)
database_to_xml(nulls boolean, tableforest bool, targetns text)
```

The `cursor_to_xml(...)` function, which iterates over an open cursor, is recommended for large data sets, as it can convert the data into chunks of rows without first accumulating all the data in memory.

The next three functions return a string that represents a SQL query, a table name, or a schema name, and return all the data from the named object. The `table_to_xml()` function also works on views. Then, there is the `database_to_xml(...)` function, which converts the current database to an XML document. However, a common result of running it on a production database is an out-of-memory error if the output is too big:

```
hannu=# SELECT database_to_xml(true, true, 'n');
ERROR:  out of memory
DETAIL:  Failed on request of size 1024.
```

Returning data in the JSON format

In PostgreSQL 9.2, there is a new native data type for JSON values. This new support for JSON followed the same growth pattern as XML. It initially started with two functions to convert arrays and records to the JSON format, but in PostgreSQL 9.3, there are many new functions introduced. The following is a summary of improvements in the PostgreSQL 9.3 JSON support:

- There are dedicated JSON operators such as `->`, `->>`, and `#>`
- There are ten new JSON functions

The JSON parser is exposed as an API. The API provides hooks for the significant parser event, such as the beginning and end of objects and arrays, and providing functions to handle these hooks allows a wide variety of JSON processing functions to be created.

The `hstore` extension has two new JSON-related functions, `hstore_to_json(hstore)` and `hstore_to_json_loose(hstore)`.

> You can read about the new JSON operators and the functions in the official documentation at `http://www.postgresql.org/docs/current/static/functions-json.html`.

The `row_to_json(record, bool)` function is used to convert any record to JSON, and `array_to_json(anyarray, bool)` is used to convert any array to JSON.

The following are some simple examples of the usage of these functions:

```
hannu=# SELECT array_to_json(array[1,2,3]);
-[ RECORD 1 ]-+--------
array_to_json | [1,2,3]

hannu=# SELECT * FROM test;
```

```
-[ RECORD 1 ]--------------------
id      | 1
data    | 0.26281
tstampt | 2012-04-05 13:21:03.235
-[ RECORD 2 ]--------------------
id      | 2
data    | 0.1574
tstampt | 2012-04-05 13:21:05.201

hannu=# SELECT row_to_json(t) FROM test t;
-[ RECORD 1 ]-----------------------------------------------
row_to_json | {"id":1,"data":0.26281,"tstampt":"2012-04-05
  13:21:03.235"}
-[ RECORD 2 ]-----------------------------------------------
row_to_json | {"id":2,"data":0.1574,"tstampt":"2012-04-05
  13:21:05.201"}
```

These functions are very useful as they enable us to write functions returning much more complex data than was possible using the standard RETURNS TABLE syntax, but the real power of these functions comes from being able to convert arbitrarily complex rows.

Let's first create a simple table with some data:

```
CREATE TABLE test(
    id serial PRIMARY KEY,
    data text,
    tstamp timestamp DEFAULT current_timestamp
);
INSERT INTO test(data) VALUES(random()), (random());
```

Now, let's create another table, which has one column with the data type of the previous table, and insert rows from this table in the new table:

```
hannu=# CREATE TABLE test2(
hannu(#     id serial PRIMARY KEY,
hannu(#     data2 test,
hannu(#     tstamp timestamp DEFAULT current_timestamp
hannu(# );
hannu=# INSERT INTO test2(data2) SELECT test FROM test;
INSERT 0 2

hannu=# SELECT * FROM test2;
```

```
-[ RECORD 1 ]-----------------------------------
id     | 5
data2  | (1,0.26281,"2012-04-05 13:21:03.235204")
tstamp | 2012-04-30 15:42:11.757535
-[ RECORD 2 ]-----------------------------------
id     | 6
data2  | (2,0.15740,"2012-04-05 13:21:05.2033")
tstamp | 2012-04-30 15:42:11.757535
```

Now, let's see how `row_to_json()` handles this table:

```
hannu=# SELECT row_to_json(t2, true) FROM test2 t2;
                          row_to_json
-------------------------------------------------------------
 {"id":5,
  "data2":{"id":1,"data":"0.26281",
          "tstamp":"2012-04-05 13:21:03.235204"},
  "tstamp":"2012-04-30 15:42:11.757535"}
 {"id":6,
  "data2":{"id":2,"data":"0.15740",
          "tstamp":"2012-04-05 13:21:05.2033"},
  "tstamp":"2012-04-30 15:42:11.757535"}
(2 rows)
```

The result was converted to JSON without any problems.

Just to be sure, let's push the complexity up a bit more and create a `test3` table, which has an array of the `table2` rows as its data value:

```
CREATE TABLE test3(
    id serial PRIMARY KEY,
    data3 test2[],
    tstamp timestamp DEFAULT current_timestamp
);
INSERT INTO test3(data3)
SELECT array(SELECT test2 FROM test2);
```

Let's see whether `row_to_json` still works, as shown here:

```
SELECT row_to_json(t3, true) FROM test3 t3;
-------------------------------------------
{"id":1,
 "data3":[ {"id":1,
           "data2":{"id":1,
                   "data":"0.262814193032682",
```

```
                         "tstamp":"2012-04-05 13:21:03.235204"},
               "tstamp":"2012-04-05 13:25:03.644497"
               },
               {"id":2,
                "data2":{"id":2,
                         "data":"0.157406373415142",
                         "tstamp":"2012-04-05 13:21:05.2033"},
                "tstamp":"2012-04-05 13:25:03.644497"
               }
             ],
   "tstamp":"2012-04-16 14:40:15.795947"}
 (1 row)
```

Yes, it does!

Well, actually I had to manually format it a little, as the `prettyprint` flag to `row_to_json()` only forks for the top level, and the second row of the result (the one that follows `"data3"`) was all in one line. However, JSON itself was completely functional!

Summary

The main points you learned in this chapter are that you can return multiple rows and return data using OUT parameters, as well as return multiple rows of complex data, similar to a SELECT query. You also learned that several sets of tables can be returned, and you can possibly have them evaluated in a lazy manner using refcursors. Moreover, you can return data as complex as you want using either XML or JSON.

So, there really are very few reasons for not using database functions as your main interaction mechanism with the database. In the next chapter, we will learn how to call functions when different types of events occur in the database.

5
PL/pgSQL Trigger Functions

While it is generally a good practice to keep related code together and avoid *hidden* actions as part of the main application code workflows, there are valid cases where it is a good practice to add some kind of general or cross-application functionality to the database using automated actions, which happen each and every time a table is modified. That is, actions are part of your data model and not your application code and you want to be sure that it is not possible to forget or bypass them, which is similar to how constraints make it impossible to insert invalid data.

The method used to add automated function calls to a table modifying event is called a **trigger**. Triggers are especially useful for the cases where there are multiple different client applications — possibly from different sources and using different programming styles — accessing the same data using multiple different functions or simple SQL.

From a standard's perspective, triggers are standardized in SQL3 (SQL1999). Triggers are generally defined using an **event-condition-action** (**ECA**) model. Events occur in the database, which trigger the invocation of a certain function if the conditions are satisfied. All data actions performed by the trigger execute within the same transaction in which the trigger is executing. Triggers cannot contain transaction control statements such as COMMIT and ROLLBACK. Triggers can be statement level or row level (more on this later in the chapter).

In PostgreSQL, a trigger is defined in two steps:

1. Define a trigger function using CREATE FUNCTION.
2. Bind this trigger function to a table using CREATE TRIGGER.

In this chapter, we will cover the following topics:

- Creating a trigger and a trigger function
- Taking a look at some of the use cases of triggers, such as an audit trigger, and disallowing certain operations using triggers

- Discussing conditional triggers and triggers on specific field changes
- Describing the list of variables passed on to a trigger in brief, which can be used in the trigger function for conditional lookups

Creating the trigger function

The trigger function's definition looks mostly like an ordinary function definition, except that it has a return value type, `trigger`, and it does not take any arguments:

```
CREATE FUNCTION mytriggerfunc() RETURNS trigger AS $$ …
```

Trigger functions are passed information about their calling environment through a special `TriggerData` structure, which in the case of PL/pgSQL is accessible through a set of local variables. The local variables, `OLD` and `NEW`, represent the row in which the trigger is in before and after triggering the event. Additionally, there are several other local variables that start with the prefix `TG_`, such as `TG_WHEN` or `TG_TABLE_NAME` for general context. Once your trigger function is defined, you can bind it to a specific set of actions on a table.

Creating the trigger

The simplified syntax to create a user-defined `TRIGGER` statement is given as follows:

```
CREATE TRIGGER name
    { BEFORE | AFTER | INSTEAD OF } { event [ OR ... ] }
    ON table_name
    [ FOR [ EACH ] { ROW | STATEMENT } ]
    EXECUTE PROCEDURE function_name ( arguments )
```

In the preceding code, the event is either `INSERT`, `UPDATE`, `DELETE`, or `TRUNCATE`. There are a few more options which we will come back to in a later section.

The `arguments` variable seemingly passed to the trigger function in the trigger definition are not used as arguments when calling the trigger. Instead, they are available to the trigger function as a text array (`text []`) in the `TG_ARGV` variable (the length of this array is in `TG_NARGS`). Let's slowly start investigating how triggers and trigger functions work.

Starting from PostgreSQL 9.3, there is support for DDL triggers. We will learn more about DDL triggers, also called *event triggers*, in the next chapter.

First, we will use a simple trigger example and move on to more complex examples step by step.

Working on a simple "Hey, I'm called" trigger

The first trigger we will work on simply sends a notice back to the database client each time the trigger is fired and provides some feedback on its firing conditions:

```
CREATE OR REPLACE FUNCTION notify_trigger()
  RETURNS TRIGGER AS $$
BEGIN
    RAISE NOTICE 'Hi, I got % invoked FOR % % % on %',
                           TG_NAME,
                           TG_LEVEL,
                           TG_WHEN,
                           TG_OP,
                           TG_TABLE_NAME;
END;
$$ LANGUAGE plpgsql;
```

Next, we need a table to bind this function to the following line of code:

```
CREATE TABLE notify_test(i int);
```

Now we are ready to define the trigger. As this is a simple example, we define a trigger which is invoked on INSERT and calls the function once on each row:

```
CREATE TRIGGER notify_insert_trigger
  AFTER INSERT ON notify_test
  FOR EACH ROW
EXECUTE PROCEDURE notify_trigger();
```

Let's test this out:

```
postgres=# INSERT INTO notify_test VALUES(1),(2);

NOTICE:  Hi, I got notify_insert_trigger invoked FOR ROW AFTER INSERT
on notify_test
ERROR:  control reached end of trigger procedure without RETURN
CONTEXT:  PL/pgSQL function notify_trigger()
```

Hmm, it seems we need to return something from the function even though it is not needed for our purposes. The function definition says CREATE FUNCTION ... RETURNS but we definitely cannot return a trigger from a function.

Let's get back to the documentation. OK, here it is. The trigger needs to return a value of the ROW or RECORD type and it is ignored in the AFTER triggers.

For now, let's just return NEW as this is the right type and is always present even though it will be NULL in the DELETE trigger:

```
CREATE OR REPLACE FUNCTION notify_trigger()
RETURNS TRIGGER AS $$
BEGIN
    RAISE NOTICE 'Hi, I got % invoked FOR % % % on %',
                 TG_NAME,
                 TG_LEVEL, TG_WHEN, TG_OP, TG_TABLE_NAME;
    RETURN NEW;
END;
$$ LANGUAGE plpgsql;
```

We can use RETURN NULL as well here, as the return value of the AFTER trigger is ignored anyway:

```
postgres=# INSERT INTO notify_test VALUES(1),(2);
NOTICE:  Hi, I got notify_insert_trigger invoked FOR ROW AFTER INSERT
on notify_test
NOTICE:  Hi, I got notify_insert_trigger invoked FOR ROW AFTER INSERT
on notify_test
INSERT 0 2
```

As you saw, the trigger function is indeed called once for each row that is inserted, so let's use the same function to also report the UPDATE and DELETE functions:

```
CREATE TRIGGER notify_update_trigger
  AFTER UPDATE ON notify_test
  FOR EACH ROW
EXECUTE PROCEDURE notify_trigger();

CREATE TRIGGER notify_delete_trigger
  AFTER DELETE ON notify_test
  FOR EACH ROW
EXECUTE PROCEDURE notify_trigger();
```

Check whether the preceding code works.

First, let's test the UPDATE trigger:

```
postgres=# update notify_test set i = i * 10;
NOTICE:  Hi, I got notify_update_trigger invoked FOR ROW AFTER UPDATE
on notify_test
NOTICE:  Hi, I got notify_update_trigger invoked FOR ROW AFTER UPDATE
on notify_test
UPDATE 2
```

This works fine—we get a notice for two invocations of our trigger function.

Now, let's test the DELETE trigger:

```
postgres=# delete from notify_test;
NOTICE:  Hi, I got notify_delete_trigger invoked FOR ROW AFTER DELETE
on notify_test
NOTICE:  Hi, I got notify_delete_trigger invoked FOR ROW AFTER DELETE
on notify_test
DELETE 2
```

If you only want to be notified each time an operation is performed on the table, the preceding code is enough. One small improvement can be made in how we define triggers. Instead of creating one trigger for each of the INSERT, UPDATE, or DELETE functions, we can create a single trigger to be called for any of them. So, let's replace the previous three triggers with just the following:

```
CREATE TRIGGER notify_trigger
  AFTER INSERT OR UPDATE OR DELETE
  ON notify_test
  FOR EACH ROW
EXECUTE PROCEDURE notify_trigger();
```

The ability to put more than one of the INSERT, UPDATE, or DELETE functions in the same trigger definition is a PostgreSQL extension to the SQL standard. Since the action part of the trigger definition is nonstandard anyway, especially when using a PL/pgSQL trigger function, this should not be a problem.

Let's now drop the individual triggers, truncate the table, and test again:

```
postgres=# DROP TRIGGER notify_insert_trigger ON notify_test;
DROP TRIGGER
postgres=# DROP TRIGGER notify_update_trigger ON notify_test;
DROP TRIGGER
postgres=# DROP TRIGGER notify_delete_trigger ON notify_test;
DROP TRIGGER
postgres=# TRUNCATE notify_test;
TRUNCATE TABLE
postgres=# INSERT INTO notify_test VALUES(1);
NOTICE:  Hi, I got notify_trigger invoked FOR ROW AFTER INSERT on
notify_test
INSERT 0 1
```

This works fine but it reveals one weakness: we did not get any notification on TRUNCATE.

Unfortunately, we cannot simply add OR TRUNCATE in the preceding trigger definition. The TRUNCATE command does not act on single rows, so the FOR EACH ROW triggers make no sense for truncating and are not supported.

You need to have a separate trigger definition for TRUNCATE. Fortunately, we can still use the same function, at least for this simple "Hey, I'm called" trigger:

```
CREATE TRIGGER notify_truncate_trigger
  AFTER TRUNCATE ON notify_test
  FOR EACH STATEMENT
EXECUTE PROCEDURE notify_trigger();
```

Now we get a notification on TRUNCATE as well, as shown here:

```
postgres=# TRUNCATE notify_test;
NOTICE:  Hi, I got notify_truncate_trigger invoked FOR STATEMENT AFTER
TRUNCATE on notify_test
TRUNCATE TABLE
```

While it may seem cool to get these messages in each **Data Manipulation Language (DML)** operation, it has little production value.

So, let's develop this a bit further and log the event in an audit log table instead of sending something back to the user.

The audit trigger

One of the most common uses of triggers is to log data changes to tables in a consistent and transparent manner. When creating an audit trigger, we first must decide what we want to log.

A logical set of things that can be logged are who changed the data, when the data was changed, and which operation changed the data. This information can be saved in the following table:

```
CREATE TABLE audit_log (
    username text, -- who did the change
    event_time_utc timestamp, -- when the event was recorded
    table_name text, -- contains schema-qualified table name
    operation text, -- INSERT, UPDATE, DELETE or TRUNCATE
    before_value json, -- the OLD tuple value
    after_value json -- the NEW tuple value
);
```

Here's some additional information on what we will log:

- The username will get the SESSION_USER variable, so we know who was logged in and not which role he had potentially assumed using SET ROLE

- event_time_utc will contain the event time converted to **Coordinated Universal Time (UTC)** so that all complex date arithmetic calculations around daylight saving change times can be avoided

- table_name will be in the schema.table format

- The operation will be directly from TG_OP, although it could be just the first character (I/U/D/T), without the loss of any information

- Finally, the before and after images of rows are stored as rows converted to json, which is available as its own data type starting in PostgreSQL Version 9.2 for easy human-readable representation of the row values

Next, the trigger function:

```
CREATE OR REPLACE FUNCTION audit_trigger()
  RETURNS trigger AS $$
DECLARE
    old_row json := NULL;
    new_row json := NULL;
BEGIN
    IF TG_OP IN ('UPDATE','DELETE') THEN
        old_row = row_to_json(OLD);
    END IF;
    IF TG_OP IN ('INSERT','UPDATE') THEN
        new_row = row_to_json(NEW);
    END IF;
    INSERT INTO  audit_log(
        username,
        event_time_utc,
        table_name,
        operation,
        before_value,
        after_value
    ) VALUES (
        session_user,
        current_timestamp AT TIME ZONE 'UTC',
        TG_TABLE_SCHEMA ||  '.' || TG_TABLE_NAME,
        TG_OP,
        old_row,
        new_row
    );
```

```
    RETURN NEW;
END;
$$ LANGUAGE plpgsql;
```

> The conditional expressions that check the operations at the beginning of the function are needed to overcome the fact that NEW and OLD are not NULL for the DELETE and INSERT triggers correspondingly. Rather, they are unassigned. Using an unassigned variable in any way except assigning to it in PL/pgSQL results in an error. Any error in the trigger will usually abort the trigger and the current transaction.

We are now ready to define our new logging trigger, as shown here:

```
CREATE TRIGGER audit_log
  AFTER INSERT OR UPDATE OR DELETE
  ON notify_test
  FOR EACH ROW
EXECUTE PROCEDURE audit_trigger();
```

Let's run a small test: we remove our original notify triggers from the `notify_test` table and perform a few simple operations:

```
postgres=# DROP TRIGGER notify_trigger ON notify_test;
DROP TRIGGER
postgres=# DROP TRIGGER notify_truncate_trigger ON notify_test;
DROP TRIGGER
postgres=# TRUNCATE notify_test;
TRUNCATE TABLE
postgres=# INSERT INTO notify_test VALUES (1);
INSERT 0 1
postgres=# UPDATE notify_test SET i = 2;
UPDATE 1
postgres=# DELETE FROM notify_test;
DELETE 1
postgres=# SELECT * FROM audit_log;
-[ RECORD 1 ]--+---------------------------
username       | postgres
event_time_utc | 2013-04-14 13:14:18.501529
table_name     | public.notify_test
operation      | INSERT
before_value   |
after_value    | {"i":1}
-[ RECORD 2 ]--+---------------------------
username       | postgres
event_time_utc | 2013-04-14 13:14:18.51216
```

```
table_name     | public.notify_test
operation      | UPDATE
before_value   | {"i":1}
after_value    | {"i":2}
-[ RECORD 3 ]--+---------------------------
username       | postgres
event_time_utc | 2013-04-14 13:14:18.52331
table_name     | public.notify_test
operation      | DELETE
before_value   | {"i":2}
after_value    |
```

This works well. Depending on your needs, this function will likely need some tweaking. Enough of just watching and recording DML, it is time to start influencing what goes in there.

 Triggers are called in alphabetical order, and the latter triggers can change what gets inserted, so caution needs to be applied when naming triggers, particularly when auditing.

Disallowing DELETE

What if our business requirements are such that the data can only be added and modified in some tables, but not deleted?

One way to handle this will be to just revoke the DELETE rights on these tables from all the users (remember to also revoke DELETE from PUBLIC), but this can also be achieved using triggers because of reasons such as auditing or returning custom exception messages.

A generic cancel trigger can be written as follows:

```
CREATE OR REPLACE FUNCTION cancel_op()
  RETURNS TRIGGER AS $$
BEGIN
    IF TG_WHEN = 'AFTER' THEN
        RAISE EXCEPTION 'YOU ARE NOT ALLOWED TO % ROWS IN %.%',
          TG_OP, TG_TABLE_SCHEMA, TG_TABLE_NAMENAME;
    END IF;
    RAISE NOTICE '% ON ROWS IN %.% WON'T HAPPEN',
          TG_OP, TG_TABLE_SCHEMA, TG_TABLE_NAMENAME;
    RETURN NULL;
END;
$$ LANGUAGE plpgsql;
```

The same trigger function can be used for both the BEFORE and AFTER triggers. If you use it as a BEFORE trigger, the operation is skipped with a message. However, if you use it as an AFTER trigger, an ERROR trigger is raised and the current (sub)transaction is rolled back.

It will also be easy to add a log of the deleted attempts into a table in this same trigger function in order to help enforce the company policy—just add INSERT to a log table that is similar to the table in the previous example.

Of course, you can make one or both the messages more menacing if you want, by adding something such as "Authorities will be notified!" or "You will be terminated!".

Let's take a look at how this works in the following code:

```
postgres=# CREATE TABLE delete_test1(i int);
CREATE TABLE
postgres=# INSERT INTO delete_test1 VALUES(1);
INSERT 0 1
postgres=# CREATE TRIGGER disallow_delete AFTER DELETE ON delete_test1
FOR EACH ROW  EXECUTE PROCEDURE cancel_op();
CREATE TRIGGER

postgres=# DELETE FROM delete_test1 WHERE i = 1;
ERROR:  YOU ARE NOT ALLOWED TO DELETE ROWS IN public.delete_test1
```

Notice that the AFTER trigger raised an error:

```
postgres=# CREATE TRIGGER skip_delete BEFORE DELETE ON delete_test1
FOR EACH ROW  EXECUTE PROCEDURE cancel_op();
CREATE TRIGGER

postgres=# DELETE FROM delete_test1 WHERE i = 1;
NOTICE:  DELETE ON ROWS IN public.delete_test1 WON'T HAPPEN
DELETE 0
```

This time, the BEFORE trigger canceled the delete and the AFTER trigger, although still there, was not reached.

The same trigger can also be used to enforce a no-update policy or even disallow inserts to a table that needs to have immutable contents.

Disallowing TRUNCATE

You may have noticed that the preceding trigger can easily be bypassed for DELETE if you delete everything using TRUNCATE.

While you cannot simply skip TRUNCATE by returning NULL as opposed to the row-level BEFORE triggers, you can still make it impossible by raising an error if TRUNCATE is attempted. Create an AFTER trigger using the same function as the one used previously for DELETE:

```
CREATE TRIGGER disallow_truncate
  AFTER TRUNCATE ON delete_test1
  FOR EACH STATEMENT
EXECUTE PROCEDURE cancel_op();
```

Here you are, without TRUNCATE:

```
postgres=# TRUNCATE delete_test1;
ERROR:  YOU ARE NOT ALLOWED TO TRUNCATE ROWS IN public.delete_test1
```

Of course, you can also raise the error in a BEFORE trigger, but in that case you will need to write your own unconditional raise-error trigger function instead of cancel_op().

Modifying the NEW record

Another form of auditing that is frequently used is to log information in fields in the same row as the data. As an example, let's define a trigger that logs the time and the active user in the last_changed_at and last_changed_by fields at each INSERT and UPDATE trigger. In the row-level BEFORE triggers, you can modify what actually gets written by changing the NEW record. You can either assign values to some fields or even return a different record with the same structure. For example, if you return OLD from the UPDATE trigger, you effectively make sure that the row can't be updated.

The timestamping trigger

To form the basis of our audit logging in the table, we start by creating a trigger that sets the user who made the last change and when the change occurred:

```
CREATE OR REPLACE FUNCTION changestamp()
  RETURNS TRIGGER AS $$
BEGIN
    NEW.last_changed_by = SESSION_USER;
    NEW.last_changed_at = CURRENT_TIMESTAMP;
```

```
        RETURN NEW;
END;
$$ LANGUAGE plpgsql;
```

Of course, this works only in a table that has the correct fields:

```
CREATE TABLE modify_test(
     id serial PRIMARY KEY,
     data text,
     created_by text default SESSION_USER,
     created_at timestamptz default CURRENT_TIMESTAMP,
     last_changed_by text default SESSION_USER,
     last_changed_at timestamptz default CURRENT_TIMESTAMP
);

CREATE TRIGGER changestamp
  BEFORE UPDATE ON modify_test
  FOR EACH ROW
EXECUTE PROCEDURE changestamp();
```

Now, let's take a look at our newly created trigger:

```
postgres=# INSERT INTO modify_test(data) VALUES('something');
INSERT 0 1
postgres=# UPDATE modify_test SET data = 'something else' WHERE id =
1;
UPDATE 1
postgres=# SELECT * FROM modify_test;
-[RECORD 1]---+--------------------------
id              | 1
data            | something else
created_by      | postgres
created_at      | 2013-04-15 09:28:23.966179
last_changed_by | postgres
last_changed_at | 2013-04-15 09:28:31.937196
```

The immutable fields trigger

When you are depending on the fields in the rows as part of your audit record, you need to ensure that the values reflect reality. We were able to make sure that the last_ changed_* fields always contain the correct value, but what about the created_by and created_at values? These can be easily changed in later updates, but they should never change. Even initially, they can be set to false values, since the default values can be easily overridden by giving any other value in the INSERT statement.

So, let's modify our `changestamp()` trigger function into a `usagestamp()` function, which makes sure that the initial values are what they should be and that they stay like that:

```
CREATE OR REPLACE FUNCTION usagestamp()
  RETURNS TRIGGER AS $$
BEGIN
    IF TG_OP = 'INSERT' THEN
        NEW.created_by = SESSION_USER;
        NEW.created_at = CURRENT_TIMESTAMP;
    ELSE
        NEW.created_by = OLD.created_by;
        NEW.created_at = OLD.created_at;
    END IF;

    NEW.last_changed_by = SESSION_USER;
    NEW.last_changed_at = CURRENT_TIMESTAMP;
    RETURN NEW;
END;
$$ LANGUAGE plpgsql;
```

In case of `INSERT`, we set the `created_*` fields to the required values, regardless of what the `INSERT` query tries to set them to. In case of `UPDATE`, we just carry over the old values, again overriding any attempted changes.

This function then needs to be used in order to create a `BEFORE INSERT OR UPDATE` trigger:

```
CREATE TRIGGER usagestamp
  BEFORE INSERT OR UPDATE ON modify_test
  FOR EACH ROW
EXECUTE PROCEDURE usagestamp();
```

Now, let's try to update the created audit log information. First, we will need to drop the original trigger so that we don't have two triggers firing on the same table. Then, we will try to change the values of `created_by` and `created_at`:

```
postgres=# DROP TRIGGER changestamp ON modify_test;
DROP TRIGGER
postgres=# UPDATE modify_test SET created_by = 'notpostgres',
created_at = '2000-01-01';
UPDATE 1
postgres=# select * from modify_test;
-[ RECORD 1 ]---+--------------------------
id              | 1
data            | something else
```

```
created_by      | postgres
created_at      | 2013-04-15 09:28:23.966179
last_changed_by | postgres
last_changed_at | 2013-04-15 09:33:25.386006
```

From the results, you can see that the created information is still the same, but the last changed information has been updated.

Controlling when a trigger is called

While it is relatively easy to perform trigger actions conditionally inside the PL/pgSQL trigger function, it is often more efficient to skip invoking the trigger altogether. The performance effects of firing a trigger are not generally noticed when only a few events are fired. However, if you are bulk loading data or updating large portions of your table, the cumulative effects can certainly be felt. To avoid the overhead, it's best to call the trigger function only when it is actually needed.

There are two ways to narrow down when a trigger will be called in the CREATE TRIGGER command itself.

So, use the same syntax once more but with all the options this time:

```
CREATE TRIGGER name
    { BEFORE | AFTER | INSTEAD OF } { event [ OR event ... ] }
    [ OF column_name  [ OR column_name ... ] ] ON table_name
    [ FOR [ EACH ] { ROW | STATEMENT } ]
    [ WHEN ( condition ) ]
    EXECUTE PROCEDURE function_name ( arguments )
```

You can use the WHEN clause to only fire a trigger based on a condition (such as a certain time of the day) or only when certain fields are updated. We will now take a look at a couple of examples.

Conditional triggers

A flexible way to control triggers is to use a generic WHEN clause that is similar to WHERE in SQL queries. With a WHEN clause, you can write any expression, except a subquery, that is tested before the trigger function is called. The expression must result in a Boolean value, and if the value is FALSE (or NULL, which is automatically converted to FALSE), the trigger function is not called.

For example, you can use this to enforce a "No updates on Friday afternoon" policy:

```
CREATE OR REPLACE FUNCTION cancel_with_message()
  RETURNS TRIGGER AS $$
BEGIN
    RAISE EXCEPTION '%', TG_ARGV[0];
    RETURN NULL;
END;
$$ LANGUAGE plpgsql;
```

This code just raises an exception with the string passed as an argument in the CREATE TRIGGER statement. Notice that we cannot use TG_ARGV[0] directly as the message because the PL/pgSQL syntax requires a string constant as the third element of RAISE.

Using the previous trigger function, you can set up triggers in order to enforce various constraints by specifying both the condition (in the WHEN(...) clause) and the message to be raised if this condition is met as the argument to the trigger function:

```
CREATE TABLE new_tasks(id SERIAL PRIMARY KEY, sample TEXT);

CREATE TRIGGER no_updates_on_friday_afternoon
  BEFORE INSERT OR UPDATE OR DELETE OR TRUNCATE ON new_tasks
  FOR EACH STATEMENT
  WHEN (CURRENT_TIME > '12:00' AND extract(DOW from CURRENT_TIMESTAMP)
= 5)
EXECUTE PROCEDURE cancel_with_message('Sorry, we have a "No task
change on Friday afternoon" policy!');
```

Now, if anybody tries to modify the new_tasks table on a Friday afternoon, they get a message about this policy, as shown here:

```
postgres=# insert into new_tasks(sample) values("test");
ERROR:  Sorry, we have a "No task change on Friday afternoon" policy!
```

One thing to note about trigger arguments is that the argument list is always an array of text (text []).

All of the arguments given in the CREATE TRIGGER statement are converted to strings, and this includes any NULL values.

This means that putting NULL in the argument list results in the text NULL in the corresponding slot in TG_ARGV.

Triggers on specific field changes

Another way to control when a trigger is fired is using a list of columns. In the UPDATE triggers, you can specify one or more comma-separated columns to tell PostgreSQL that the trigger function should only be executed if any of the listed columns change.

It is possible to construct the same conditional expression with a WHEN clause, but the list of columns has cleaner syntax:

```
WHEN(
    NEW.column1 IS DISTINCT FROM OLD.column1
    OR
    NEW.column2 IS DISTINCT FROM OLD.column2)
```

A common example of how this conditional expression is used is raising an error each time someone tries to change a primary key column. The IS DISTINCT FROM function makes sure that the trigger is only executed when the new value of column1 is different from the old value. This can be easily done by declaring an AFTER trigger using the cancel_op() trigger function (defined previously in this chapter), as follows:

```
CREATE TRIGGER disallow_pk_change
  AFTER UPDATE OF id ON table_with_pk_id
  FOR EACH ROW
EXECUTE PROCEDURE cancel_op();

postgres=# INSERT INTO new_tasks DEFAULT VALUES;
INSERT 0 1
packt=# SELECT * FROM new_tasks ;
 id | sample
----+--------
  1 |
(1 row)


packt=# UPDATE new_tasks SET id=0 where id=1;
ERROR:  YOU ARE NOT ALLOWED TO UPDATE ROWS IN public.new_tasks
```

Visibility

Sometimes, your trigger functions might run into the **Multiversion Concurrency Control (MVCC)** visibility rules of how PostgreSQL's system interacts with changes to data.

A function declared as STABLE or IMMUTABLE will never see changes applied to the underlying table by the previous triggers.

A VOLATILE function follows more complex rules which are, in a nutshell, as follows:

- The statement-level BEFORE triggers detects whether no changes are made by the current statement, and the statement-level AFTER triggers detects all of the changes made by the statement.

- Data changes by the operation to the row causing the trigger to fire are, of course, not visible to the BEFORE triggers, as the operation has not occurred yet. Changes made by other triggers to other rows in the same statement are visible, and as the order of the rows processed is undefined, you need to be cautious. Starting from PostgreSQL 9.3, an error is thrown if a tuple to be updated or deleted has already been updated or deleted by a BEFORE trigger.

- The same is true for the INSTEAD OF triggers. The changes made by the triggers fired in the same command in the previous rows are visible to the current invocation of the trigger function. Row-level AFTER triggers are fired when all of the changes to all the rows of the outer command are complete and visible to the trigger function.

All these rules apply to functions that query data in the database; the OLD and NEW rows are, of course, visible as described previously.

 The same information in, perhaps, different words is available at http://www.postgresql.org/docs/current/static/spi-visibility.html.

Most importantly – use triggers cautiously!

Triggers are an appropriate tool for use in database-side actions, such as auditing, logging, enforcing complex constraints, and even replication (several logical replication systems such as Slony are based on triggers used in production). However, for most application logic, it is much better to avoid triggers as they can lead to really weird and hard-to-debug problems. As a good practice, follow the rules provided in the following table:

Rule	Description
Rule 1	Do not change data in the primary key, foreign key, or unique key columns of any table
Rule 2	Do not update records in the table that you read during the same transaction
Rule 3	Do not aggregate over the table you are updating
Rule 4	Do not read data from a table that is updated during the same transaction

Variables passed to the PL/pgSQL TRIGGER function

The following is a complete list of the variables available to a trigger function written in PL/pgSQL:

OLD, NEW	RECORD	This records the before and after images of the row on which the trigger is called. OLD is unassigned for INSERT and NEW is unassigned for DELETE. Both are UNASSIGNED in statement-level triggers.
TG_NAME	name	This denotes the name of the trigger (this and following from the trigger definition).
TG_WHEN	text	BEFORE, AFTER, or INSTEAD OF are the possible values of the variable.
TG_LEVEL	text	ROW or STATEMENT are the possible values of the variable.
TG_OP	text	INSERT, UPDATE, DELETE, or TRUNCATE are the possible values of the variable..
TG_RELID	oid	This denotes the OID of the table on which the trigger is created.
TG_TABLE_NAME	name	This denotes the name of the table (the old spelling TG_RELNAME is deprecated but still available).
TG_TABLE_SCHEMA	name	This denotes the schema name of the table.
TG_NARGS, TG_ARGV[]	Int, text[]	This denotes the number of arguments and the array of the arguments from the trigger definition.
TG_TAG	text	This is used in DDL or event triggers. This variable contains the name of the command that resulted in the trigger invocation. More information on this in the next chapter.

You can read more about the variables at http://www.postgresql.org/docs/current/static/plpgsql-trigger.html.

Summary

A trigger is a binding of a set of actions to certain operations performed on a table or view. This set of actions is defined in a special trigger function which is distinguished by specifying the type of the returned value to be of a special pseudotype trigger. So, each time an operation (INSERT, UPDATE, DELETE, or TRUNCATE) is performed on the table, this trigger function is called by the system.

It can be executed either *for each row* or *for each statement*. If executed for each row (row-level trigger), the function is passed special variables such as OLD and NEW.

This will contain the row's contents, as it is currently in the database (OLD) and as it is the moment the trigger function is called (NEW). Where the OLD or NEW value is missing, it is passed as undefined. If executed once per statement (the statement-level trigger), both OLD and NEW are unassigned for all the operations.

The trigger function for row-level triggers on INSERT, UPDATE, and DELETE can be set to execute either BEFORE or AFTER the operation on a table and can be set to execute the INSTEAD OF operation on view.

The trigger function for statement-level triggers on INSERT, UPDATE, and DELETE can be set to execute either BEFORE or AFTER the operation on both tables and views.

While TRUNCATE is logically a special, non-MVCC form of a "delete all" statement, no ON DELETE triggers will fire in the case of TRUNCATE. Instead, you can use a special ON TRUNCATE trigger on the same table. Only statement-level on TRUNCATE triggers are possible. While you cannot skip statement triggers by returning NULL, you can *raise an exception* and abort the transaction.

It is also not possible to define any ON TRUNCATE triggers on views.

In the next chapter, we will take a look at the new PostgreSQL event trigger feature. Event triggers allow you to execute triggers when a **Data Definition Language (DDL)** statement is executed on a table.

6
PostgreSQL Event Triggers

PostgreSQL 9.3 introduced a special type of triggers to complement the trigger mechanism we discussed in the preceding chapter. These triggers, are database-specific and are not attached to a specific table. Unlike regular triggers, event triggers capture DDL events. Event triggers can be the BEFORE and AFTER triggers, and the trigger function can be written in any language except SQL. Other popular database vendors such as Oracle and SQL Server also provide a similar functionality.

One can think of several use cases for DDL triggers. The most popular one among the DBAs normally is to do an audit trail. You, as a DBA, might want to audit the users and the DDL commands. Schema changes, in a production environment, should be done very carefully; hence, the need for an audit trail is apparent. Event triggers are disabled in the single user mode and can only be created by a superuser.

In this chapter, we will cover the following topics:

- Use cases for event triggers
- A full audit trail example using PL/pgsql
- Preventing schema changes using event triggers

Use cases for creating event triggers

In addition to an audit trail, the following can be valid use cases for an event trigger:

- Replicating DDL changes to a remote location
- Cascading a DDL
- Preventing changes to tables, except during a predefined window
- Providing limited DDL capability to developers / support staff using security definer functions

- Disabling certain DDL commands based on a criteria
- Performance analysis to see how long a command takes between `ddl_command_start` and `ddl_command_end`

Note that the event trigger support for PL/pgsql is not yet complete in 9.3. There are several features that are being worked upon and will be available in future PostgreSQL versions, hopefully. These are a few of the most notable features that are missing so far:

- There's no information about the object that a DDL targets
- There's no access to the command string
- There's no support for the generated commands

A command such as `CREATE TABLE foo (id serial PRIMARY KEY)` will also result in the `CREATE SEQUENCE` and `CREATE INDEX` commands to be executed internally. However, the current DDL triggers will not be able to log these generated commands.

Creating event triggers

Event triggers are created using the `CREATE EVENT TRIGGER` command. Before you can create an event trigger, you need a function that the trigger will execute. This function must return a special type called `EVENT_TRIGGER`. If you happen to define multiple event triggers, they are executed in the alphabetical order of their names.

Currently, event triggers are supported on three events, as follows:

- `ddl_command_start`: This event occurs just before a `CREATE`, `ALTER`, or `DROP` DDL command is executed
- `ddl_command_end`: This event occurs just after a `CREATE`, `ALTER`, or `DROP` command has finished executing
- `sql_drop`: This event occurs just before the `ddl_command_end` event for the commands that drop database objects

You can specify a `WHEN` clause with the `CREATE EVENT TRIGGER` command, so that the event is fired only for the specified commands.

The event trigger PL/pgSQL functions have access to the following new variables introduced in 9.3:

- `TG_TAG`: This variable contains the "tag" or the command for which the trigger is executed. This variable does not contain the full command string, but just a tag such as `CREATE TABLE`, `DROP TABLE`, `ALTER TABLE`, and so on.

- TG_EVENT: This variable contains the event name, which can be ddl_command_start, ddl_comman_end, and sql_drop.

 A complete matrix of the event trigger firing mechanism can be found in the PostgreSQL documentation at http://www.postgresql.org/docs/current/static/event-trigger-matrix.html.

Creating an audit trail

Let's now take a look at the complete example of an event trigger that creates an audit trail of some DDL commands in the database:

```
CREATE TABLE track_ddl
(
  event text,
  command text,
  ddl_time timestamptz,
  usr text
);

CREATE OR REPLACE FUNCTION track_ddl_function()
RETURNS event_trigger
AS
$$
BEGIN
  INSERT INTO track_ddl values(tg_tag, tg_event, now(), session_user);
  RAISE NOTICE 'DDL logged';
END
$$ LANGUAGE plpgsql SECURITY DEFINER;

CREATE EVENT TRIGGER track_ddl_event ON ddl_command_start
WHEN TAG IN ('CREATE TABLE', 'DROP TABLE', 'ALTER TABLE')
EXECUTE PROCEDURE track_ddl_function();

CREATE TABLE event_check(i int);

SELECT * FROM track_ddl;

-[ RECORD 1 ]--------------------
event     | CREATE TABLE
```

```
command  | ddl_command_start
ddl_time | 2014-04-13 16:58:40.331385
usr      | testusr
```

The example is actually quite simple. Here's what we have done in the example:

1. First, we created a table where we store the audit log. The table is quite simple at the moment, due to a limited amount of information that is currently available to a PL/pgSQL function. We store the tag, the event, the timestamp when this trigger is executed, and the user who executed the command.

2. We then create a function that is executed by the trigger whenever it is fired. The function is simple enough for now. It must return the type EVENT_TRIGGER. It logs the DDL information in the audit trail table. The function created is SECURITY DEFINER. The reason why this is done is because other users in the database don't have any privileges on the audit trail table and we don't actually want them to know it is there. This function is executed as the definer (which is a superuser), and the use of session_user ensures that we log the user who logged in to the database, and not the one whose privileges are used to execute the function.

3. We then create an event trigger that only executes when certain commands such as CREATE, DROP, or ALTER TABLE are executed by a user.

We then create an example table and note that the command is indeed logged in the audit trail table.

Preventing schema changes

Another common use case for event triggers is to prevent the execution of certain commands based on a specific condition. If you only want to stop users from executing some commands, you can always revoke the privileges using more conventional means. The triggers may come in handy if you want to do this based on a certain condition, let's say, time of the day:

```
CREATE OR REPLACE FUNCTION abort_create_table_func()
RETURNS event_trigger
AS
$$
DECLARE
    current_hour int := extract(hour from now());
BEGIN
    if current_hour BETWEEN 9 AND 16
    then
```

```
        RAISE EXCEPTION 'Not a suitable time to create tables';
    end if;
END;
$$ LANGUAGE plpgsql SECURITY DEFINER;

CREATE EVENT TRIGGER abort_create_table ON ddl_command_start
WHEN TAG IN ('CREATE TABLE')
EXECUTE PROCEDURE abort_create_table_func();
```

The preceding code is, again, quite simple:

1. First, we create a trigger function that prevents a change if the current hour of the day is between 9 to 16.

2. We create a trigger that executes this function only when a CREATE TABLE command is executed.

You can extend this example to include more complex conditions and also base the decision on the current state of the database. This kind of flexibility is not available when you use simple privilege management based on GRANT and REVOKE.

A roadmap of event triggers

As you can see, the current implementation of event triggers in PL/pgsql and PostgreSQL 9.4 is rather limited. However, there are more changes and features planned for the upcoming releases that will expand the scope, in which event triggers will become more useful. Here are the highlights of what we can look forward to in the future:

- **Access to more information**: More TG_* variables are going to be available, in order to provide more information about the command that is running and on which object it is running. We can look forward to the following variables in future PostgreSQL versions:

  - TG_OBJECTID
  - TG_OBJECTNAME
  - TG_SCHEMANAME
  - TG_OPERATION
  - TG_OBTYPENAME
  - TG_CONTEXT

- **Accessors**: These are just functions which give you some information. In this case the pg_get_event_command_string function will give the full command string of the DDL command that caused the event trigger to fire.

  ° pg_get_event_command_string()

- **Support of DROP CASCADE**: Here, event triggers will be fired for each object effected in a DROP CASCADE call.

- **INSTEAD OF**: The idea here, is for an event trigger to take control of a command, analogous to the INSTEAD OF DML triggers.

- **CREATE TABLE on INSERT**: The idea here, is to just create a new table whenever we receive an insert for the first time and the table doesn't exist.

> If you want to learn more about the features in progress and the patches, which are being discussed related to event trigger support in PostgreSQL, please follow the wiki page at https://wiki.postgresql.org/wiki/Event_Triggers.

Summary

Event triggers are new in PostgreSQL 9.3, and the community is still working on various features in order to make them more useful. You can use these triggers for various purposes, including auditing DDL commands and making local customized policies regarding the execution of DDL commands in the database. Event triggers are disabled in single user mode.

Event triggers are created using the CREATE EVENT TRIGGER command, and they execute a function that returns a special type called EVENT_TRIGGER. There are three types of events that are currently supported: ddl_command_start, ddl_command_end, and sql_drop. You can limit a trigger execution by a tag using a WHEN clause, if you want to fire it for specific commands only.

Currently, there are two new variables available in the event trigger function called TG_TAG and TG_EVENT that provide information about the tag and the event of the trigger. Future releases of PostgreSQL will expose more variables that make it possible to audit complete information about firing DDL, including objects and the command string.

In the next chapter, we will discuss the differences between restricted and unrestricted languages and we will take a look at the practical examples of both.

7
Debugging PL/pgSQL

This chapter is entirely optional. Since you have only produced the highest quality bug-free code using the best possible algorithms, this text is probably a waste of your time. Of course, your functions parse perfectly on the first try. Your views show exactly what they should — according to the enviously complete business and technical documentation that you wrote last month. There is no need for version control on your procedures, as there has only ever been a Version 1.

Since you are still reading this, I'm sure that you're a whole lot more like me. I spend about 10 percent of my time writing new code and about 90 percent of it editing the mistakes and oversights that I (and others) made in the first 10 percent. In fact, it can be argued that no new code is ever written at all. Actually, a more accurate description of the process is that a dumb assertion is made and then it is edited until the customer can no longer stand the Quality Assurance (QA) process. We then ship the result in the hopes of being useful to the end user. Was that too much of reality for you? Sorry.

The objective of this chapter is to make you faster at making mistakes. As a by-product, you will also learn how to diagnose and fix them at an alarming rate. The net effect of this, we are hoping, is that your boss will assume you wrote it correctly the first time. This is, of course, a lie but a very useful one.

This concept is critical to agile software development. In this philosophy, it is called "prototyping." The idea is to create a feature quickly and demonstrate it as a conversation point, rather than trying to produce an entire system (presumably perfectly) from conceptual documentation. Other authors refer to it as "failing quickly." It recognizes the fact that the first three or four development iterations will probably not be acceptable to the customer and shouldn't be advertised as final until some discussion has taken place.

This process effectively requires the developer to "live" in the debugger. The developer continually changes the outputs and routines until the desired effect is achieved. PostgreSQL has a wonderful set of debugging tools available to help you fix your mess. Let me show you how they work.

Manual debugging with RAISE NOTICE

Here's the first promised example:

```
CREATE OR REPLACE FUNCTION format_us_full_name_debug(
  prefix text,
    firstname text,
    mi text,
    lastname text,
    suffix text)
  RETURNS text AS
$BODY$
DECLARE
  fname_mi text;
  fmi_lname text;
  prefix_fmil text;
  pfmil_suffix text;
BEGIN
  fname_mi := CONCAT_WS(' ', CASE trim(firstname) WHEN ''
    THEN NULL ELSE firstname END, CASE trim(mi) WHEN ''
    THEN NULL ELSE mi END || '.');
  RAISE NOTICE 'firstname mi.: %', fname_mi;
  fmi_lname := CONCAT_WS(' ', CASE fname_mi WHEN ''
    THEN NULL ELSE fname_mi END,CASE trim(lastname) WHEN ''
    THEN NULL ELSE lastname END);
  RAISE NOTICE 'firstname mi. lastname: %', fmi_lname;
  prefix_fmil := CONCAT_WS('. ', CASE trim(prefix) WHEN ''
    THEN NULL ELSE prefix END, CASE fmi_lname WHEN ''
    THEN NULL ELSE fmi_lname END);
  RAISE NOTICE 'prefix. firstname mi lastname: %', prefix_fmil;
  pfmil_suffix := CONCAT_WS(', ', CASE prefix_fmil WHEN ''
    THEN NULL ELSE prefix_fmil END, CASE trim(suffix) WHEN ''
    THEN NULL ELSE suffix || '.' END);
  RAISE NOTICE 'prefix. firstname mi lastname, suffix.: %',
    pfmil_suffix;

  RETURN pfmil_suffix;
END;
$BODY$
  LANGUAGE plpgsql VOLATILE;
```

In this example, we format a person's full name using the magic of the
NULL propagation.

The NULL propagation is what occurs when any or all of the members of an expression are null. In the myvar := null || 'something' expression, myvar will evaluate to null. PostgreSQL 9.1 introduced a handy new function named CONCAT_WS (concatenate with a separator) to take advantage of this effect.

Take an example of the following line of code:

```
lastfirst := CONCAT_WS(', ', lastname, firstname);
```

The preceding code will not print the comma and whitespace between lastname and firstname if either firstname or lastname is not present. This effect is used in the format_us_address() function with many levels of nesting in order to provide an address that is visually appealing as well as postal-processing friendly.

There are several statements in the code example that show you how to use RAISE NOTICE along with some text and a variable to provide debugging information as the function is being called. For example, running our function in pgAdmin3 will produce some notification messages, as shown here:

```
NOTICE:   firstname mi.: Kirk L.
NOTICE:   firstname mi. lastname: Kirk L. Roybal
NOTICE:   prefix. firstname mi lastname: Mr. Kirk L. Roybal
NOTICE:   prefix. firstname mi lastname, suffix.: Mr. Kirk L. Roybal,
Author.
```

You can see these messages in pgAdmin3 under the **Messages** tab, as shown in the following screenshot:

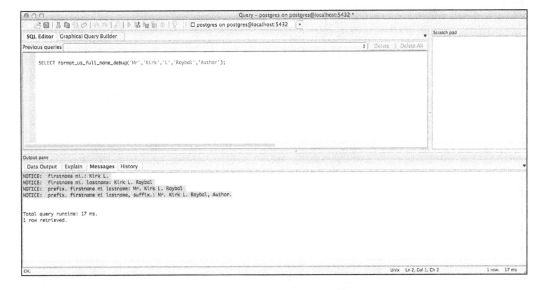

The output of the same query in the command-line psql client is shown in the following code:

```
kroybal=# SELECT format_us_full_name_debug('Mr','Kirk','L',
   'Roybal','Author');
NOTICE:  firstname mi.: Kirk L.
NOTICE:  firstname mi. lastname: Kirk L. Roybal
NOTICE:  prefix. firstname mi lastname: Mr. Kirk L. Roybal
NOTICE:  prefix. firstname mi lastname, suffix.: Mr. Kirk L. Roybal,
Author.
   format_us_full_name_debug
-----------------------------
 Mr. Kirk L. Roybal, Author.
(1 row)
```

If you don't see the RAISE NOTICE messages on your screen, you should check client_min_messages in your session, as shown in the following code. It should be NOTICE or higher to see the messages:

```
kroybal=# SHOW client_min_messages;
 client_min_messages
---------------------
 notice
(1 row)
```

Throwing exceptions

The RAISE command takes several operators except NOTICE. The command will also throw exceptions that are intended for the calling code to catch. The following is an example of how to create an exception:

```
CREATE OR REPLACE FUNCTION validate_us_zip(zipcode TEXT)
   RETURNS boolean
AS $$
DECLARE
   digits text;
BEGIN
   -- remove anything that is not a digit (POSIX compliantly,
     please)
   digits := (SELECT regexp_replace
     (zipcode,'[^[:digit:]]','','g'));

   IF digits = '' THEN
     RAISE EXCEPTION 'Zipcode does not contain any digits
       --> %', digits USING HINT = 'Is this a US zip code?',
       ERRCODE = 'P9999';
```

```
      ELSIF length(digits) < 5 THEN
        RAISE EXCEPTION 'Zipcode does not contain enough digits
          --> %', digits USING HINT = 'Zip code has less than 5
          digits.', ERRCODE = 'P9998';
      ELSIF length(digits) > 9 THEN
        RAISE EXCEPTION 'Unnecessary digits in zip code --> %'
          , digits USING HINT = 'Zip code is more than 9 digits
          .', ERRCODE = 'P9997';
      ELSIF length(digits) > 5 AND length(digits) < 9 THEN
        RAISE EXCEPTION 'Zip code cannot be processed
          --> %', digits USING HINT = 'Zip code abnormal length
          .', ERRCODE = 'P9996';
      ELSE
        RETURN true;
      END IF;
  END;
  $$ LANGUAGE plpgsql;
```

The developer defines the ERRCODE values. In this example, I used the general PL/pgSQL error code value (P0001 or plpgsql_error), started at the top of the range (P9999) of errors, and decremented for each type of error that I wished to expose. This is a very simplistic technique designed to prevent overlap in the future from error codes used by PL/pgSQL. You are free to invent any error codes you want, but you would be well advised to avoid those already listed in the documentation at http://www.postgresql.org/docs/current/static/errcodes-appendix.html.

The following code is used to capture any errors thrown in the previous example:

```
CREATE OR REPLACE FUNCTION get_us_zip_validation_status(zipcode text)
returns text
AS
$$
BEGIN
  SELECT validate_us_zip(zipcode);
  RETURN 'Passed Validation';
EXCEPTION
  WHEN SQLSTATE 'P9999' THEN RETURN 'Non-US Zip Code';
  WHEN SQLSTATE 'P9998' THEN RETURN 'Not enough digits.';
  WHEN SQLSTATE 'P9997' THEN RETURN 'Too many digits.';
  WHEN SQLSTATE 'P9996' THEN RETURN 'Between 6 and 8 digits.';
  RAISE;   -- Some other SQL error.
END;
$$
LANGUAGE 'plpgsql';
```

This code can be called as follows:

```
SELECT get_us_zip_validation_status('34955');
 get_us_zip_validation_status
------------------------------
 Passed Validation
(1 row)

root=# SELECT get_us_zip_validation_status('349587');
 get_us_zip_validation_status
------------------------------
 Between 6 and 8 digits.
(1 row)

root=# SELECT get_us_zip_validation_status('3495878977');
 get_us_zip_validation_status
------------------------------
 Too many digits.
(1 row)

root=# SELECT get_us_zip_validation_status('BNHCGR');
 get_us_zip_validation_status
------------------------------
 Non-US Zip Code
(1 row)

root=# SELECT get_us_zip_validation_status('3467');
 get_us_zip_validation_status
------------------------------
 Not enough digits.
(1 row)
```

Logging to a file

The RAISE statement expression can be sent to a log file using `log_min_messages`. This parameter is set in `postgresql.conf`. The valid values are `debug5`, `debug4`, `debug3`, `debug2`, `debug1`, `info`, `notice`, `warning`, `error`, `log`, `fatal`, and `panic`.

The default logging level is dependent on the packaging system. On Ubuntu, the default logging level is `info`. The logging levels correspond to the same expressions for the RAISE statement. As a developer, you can raise any of the messages that are available and have them recorded in the log file for analysis later.

The simplest way to post a message to the PostgreSQL daemon log file is using RAISE LOG:

```
RAISE LOG 'Why am I doing this?';
```

This log file is usually located in the `<data_directory>/pg_log` folder.

The advantages of RAISE NOTICE

Using the RAISE NOTICE form of debugging has several advantages. It can be used easily and repeatedly with scripts for regression testing. This is very easily accomplished with the command-line client. Consider the following statement:

```
psql -qtc "SELECT format_us_full_name_debug
   ('Mr','Kirk','L.','Roybal','Author');"
```

The preceding statement produces the following output to stdout:

```
NOTICE:  firstname mi.: Kirk L..
NOTICE:  firstname mi. lastname: Kirk L.. Roybal
NOTICE:  prefix. firstname mi lastname: Mr. Kirk L.. Roybal
NOTICE:  prefix. firstname mi lastname, suffix.: Mr. Kirk L.. Roybal,
Author.
 Mr. Kirk L.. Roybal, Author.
```

Because a constant set of input parameters should always produce a known output, it is very easy to use command-line tools in order to test for expected outputs. When you are ready to deploy your newly modified code to the production system, run your command-line tests to verify that all of your functions still work as expected.

RAISE NOTICE is included with the product and requires no installation. Its advantage will become clearer later in the chapter where the rather painful installation procedure for the PL/pgSQL debugger is explained.

The RAISE statement is easy to understand. The syntax is straightforward, and it is well documented at `http://www.postgresql.org/docs/current/static/plpgsql-errors-and-messages.html`.

RAISE works in any development environment and has been around for a very long time, in almost every version of PostgreSQL on every operating system. I have used it with pgAdmin3, phpPgAdmin, as well as the command-line tool psql.

These attributes, taken together, make RAISE a very attractive tool for small -scale debugging.

The disadvantages of RAISE NOTICE

Unfortunately, there are some disadvantages to using this method of debugging. The primary disadvantage is that you need to remove the RAISE statements when they are no longer necessary. The messages tend to clutter up the psql command-line client and are generally annoying to other developers. The log may fill up quickly with useless messages from previous debugging sessions. The RAISE statements need to be written, commented out, and restored when needed. They may not cover the actual bug being sought. They also slow down the execution of the routine.

You will also find *Chapter 13, Publishing Your Code as PostgreSQL*, quite informative. This chapter includes some examples (and an extremely handy way to install them) that will be useful here in this part of the book. The examples will be shown in the text of this chapter as well, but they will be quite a bit easier for you to install as an extension.

Visual debugging

The PL/pgSQL debugger is a project hosted on PostgreSQL Git that provides a debugging interface into PostgreSQL Version 8.2 or higher. The project is hosted at `http://git.postgresql.org/gitweb/?p=pldebugger.git;a=summary`.

The PL/pgSQL debugger lets you step through the PL/pgSQL code, set and clear breakpoints, view and modify variables, and walk through the call stack.

As you can see from the description, the PL/pgSQL debugger can be quite a handy little tool to have in your arsenal.

Installing the debugger

OK, now we will move past the glamour and actually get the debugger running on our system. If you install PostgreSQL with one of the packages that contains the debugger, the installation is pretty simple. Otherwise, you will need to build it from the source.

A detailed discussion of how to install the PL/pgSQL debugger from the source is beyond the scope of this book, but I will just list the set of steps to install the debugger quickly. The best way to build the source will be to pull the latest version from the Git repository and follow the README file in the directory. If you want to get started with it quickly and you have a Windows machine available, the simplest way to use the debugger is using the PostgreSQL Windows installer from `http://www.postgresql.org/download/windows/`.

Installing the debugger from the source

Here is a set of simple steps that should get you up and running if you want to install from the source:

1. Clone the Git repository as shown. You can view the repository at
    `http://git.postgresql.org/gitweb/?p=pldebugger.git;a=summary`:

    `git clone http://git.postgresql.org/git/pldebugger.git`

2. Copy this `pldebugger/` directory to `contrib/` in your PostgreSQL source tree.

3. Run `make && make install` in the `pldebugger` folder.

4. Modify the `shared_preload_libraries` configuration option in
    `postgresql.conf` as follows:

    `shared_preload_libraries = '$libdir/plugin_debugger'`

5. Restart PostgreSQL.

6. Create the debugger extension:

    `CREATE EXTENSION pldbgapi;`

This should install the PL debugger and you should be able to use it with pgAdmin3.

 You can also install PostgreSQL using EnterpriseDB's one-click installers for most platforms, which also includes the PL debugger at `http://www.enterprisedb.com/products-services-training/pgdownload`.

Installing pgAdmin3

The PL/pgSQL debugger module works with pgAdmin3. You don't need to perform special steps with the installation of pgAdmin3 for the debugger to function. Install it as usual from your package manager on the platform that you are using. For Ubuntu 10.04 LTS, the command is as follows:

```
sudo apt-get install pgadmin3
```

Using the debugger

When the debugger is available for a particular database, it can be seen in the context menu when you right-click on a PL/pgSQL function. We have already created some of the debuggers in the earlier part of this chapter. Using `format_us_full_name` as an example, right-click on it and navigate to **Debugging | Debug**:

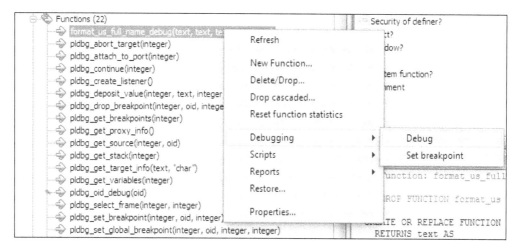

As a result, you will see the following dialog:

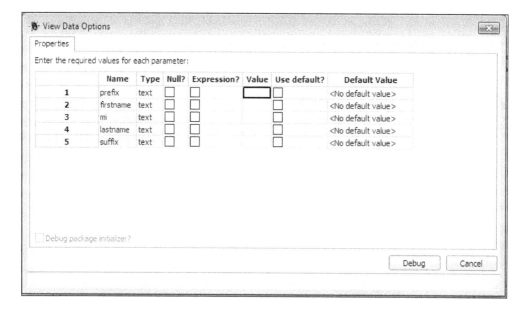

Enter some values into the columns, as seen in the preceding screenshot, and click on the **Debug** button. You will be deposited into the debugger:

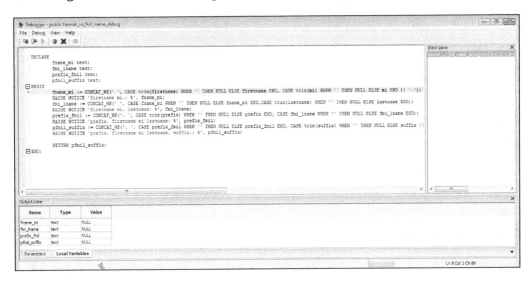

This will allow you to step through the code and see the values of any variables as they are being changed. Click on the **step-into** button a few times to see how the values are modified as the function is performed.

The advantages of the debugger

The PL/pgSQL debugger does not require any resources on the server when not actually in use. Because it is invoked manually from within pgAdmin3, it is not resident in memory until it is actually called upon. This architecture does not require any background processes or additional daemons for the sake of debugging.

Also, the PL/pgSQL debugger does not require any special "calling" functions to be written in order to invoke the debugging process. There are no errors to trap and no tables of error codes to interpret. Everything necessary to the debugging process is available in a simple window.

If you connect to your database as a superuser, you also have the ability to set a global break point. This break point can be set on any function or trigger and it will stop the next time any code path calls the function. This is particularly useful if you want to debug your functions or triggers in the context of your entire running application.

The greatest advantage of the PL/pgSQL debugger is that it does not require any special rigging in the functions that are being debugged.

There is no code to be inserted or removed, and good coding practices don't need to be modified with respect to debugging. There is no possibility to "forget" the debugging code when moving to production. All of your PL/pgSQL functions are now instantly ready to debug without any special action.

The disadvantages of the debugger

As you have become painfully aware, the installation of the debugger leaves a lot to be desired. This debugger has not become very popular in the PostgreSQL community at large because of the rather large learning curve involved, and that's just to get it installed.

This form of debugging is meant for personal productivity while actively developing functions. It does not work well as an automation tool.

Summary

The debugging methods that we have seen in this chapter are designed to be used in conjunction with one another. They complement each other at different points in the development process. Where debugging using the PL/pgSQL debugger is highly effective while editing an existing (hopefully well-written) function, other forms of debugging may be better suited to the quality assurance or automated data processing applications.

Because the PL/pgSQL debugger is meant to be a visual tool to work within pgAdmin3, it is possible that the developer may want to forego the visual debugger in the interest of some other feature.

In the next chapter, we will take a look at how to write some advanced functions in C.

8
Using Unrestricted Languages

You may have noticed, that some of the PLs in PostgreSQL can be declared as untrusted. They all end in the letter u to remind you that they are untrusted each time you use them to create a function. Unrestricted languages allow you to do things that restricted or trusted languages are not allowed to do; for example, interacting with the environment and creating files and opening sockets. In this chapter, we will look at some examples in detail.

This untrustedness brings up many questions:

- Does being untrusted mean that such languages are somehow inferior to trusted ones?
- Can I still write an important function in an untrusted language?
- Will they silently eat my data and corrupt the database?

The answers are no, yes, and maybe respectively. Let's now discuss these questions in order.

Are untrusted languages inferior to trusted ones?

No, on the contrary, these languages are untrusted in the same way that a sharp knife is untrusted and should be kept out of the reach of very small children, unless there is adult supervision. They have extra powers that ordinary SQL, or even the trusted languages (such as PL/pgSQL) and trusted variants of the same language (PL/Perl versus PL/PerlU) don't have.

You can use the untrusted languages to directly read and write on the server's disks, and you can use it to open sockets and make Internet queries to the outside world. You can even send arbitrary signals to any process running on the database host. Generally, you can do anything the native language of the PL can do.

However, you probably should not trust arbitrary database users to have the right to define functions in these languages. Always think twice before giving *all privileges* on an untrusted language to a user or group, by using the *u languages for important functions.

Can you use untrusted languages for important functions?

Absolutely! Sometimes, it may be the only way to accomplish some tasks from inside the server. Performing simple queries and computations should do nothing harmful to your database, and neither should connecting to the external world for sending e-mails, fetching web pages, or performing SOAP requests. However, be careful about performing operations that may cause delays and even queries that get stuck, but these can usually be dealt with by setting an upper limit as to how long a query can run, by using an appropriate statement time-out value. Setting a reasonable statement time-out value by default is a good practice anyway.

So, if you don't deliberately do risky things, the probability of harming the database is no bigger than using a "trusted" (also known as restricted) variant of the language. However, if you give the language to someone who starts changing bytes on the production database "to see what happens", you will get what you asked for.

Will untrusted languages corrupt the database?

The power to corrupt the database is definitely there, since the functions run as the system user of the database server with full access to the filesystem. So, if you blindly start writing into the data files and deleting important logs, it is possible that your database will be corrupted.

Additional types of denial-of-service attacks are also possible, such as using up all memory or opening all IP ports. But, there are ways to overload the database using plain SQL as well, so that part is not much different from the trusted database access with the ability to just run arbitrary queries.

So yes, you can corrupt the database, but please don't do it on a production server. If you do, you will be sorry.

Why untrusted?

PostgreSQL's ability to use an untrusted language is a powerful way to perform some non-traditional things from database functions. Creating these functions in a PL is a task of smaller magnitude than writing an extension function in C. For example, a function to look up a hostname for an IP address is only a few lines in PL/PythonU:

```
CREATE LANGUAGE plpythonu;
CREATE FUNCTION gethostbyname(hostname text)
  RETURNS inet
AS $$
  import socket
  return socket.gethostbyname(hostname)
$$ LANGUAGE plpythonu SECURITY DEFINER;
```

You can test it immediately after creating the function by using `psql`:

```
hannu=# SELECT gethostbyname('www.postgresql.org');
 gethostbyname
----------------
 98.129.198.126
(1 row)
```

Creating the same function in the most untrusted language, C, involves writing tens of lines of boilerplate code, worrying about memory leaks, and all the other problems coming from writing code in a low-level language. While we will look at extending PostgreSQL in C in the next chapter, I recommend prototyping in a PL language if possible, and in an untrusted language if the function needs something that the restricted languages do not offer.

Why PL/Python?

All of these tasks could be done equally well using PL/PerlU or PL/TclU. I chose PL/PythonU mainly because Python is the language I am most comfortable with. This also translates to having written some PL/Python code, which I plan to discuss and share with you in this chapter.

Quick introduction to PL/Python

In the previous chapters, we discussed PL/pgSQL which is one of the standard procedural languages distributed with PostgreSQL. PL/pgSQL is a language unique to PostgreSQL and was designed to add blocks of computation and SQL inside the database. While it has grown in its breadth of functionality, it still lacks the completeness of syntax of a full programming language. PL/Python allows your database functions to be written in Python with all the depth and maturity of writing a Python code outside the database.

A minimal PL/Python function

Let's start from the very beginning, yet again:

```
CREATE FUNCTION hello(name text)
  RETURNS text
AS $$
    return 'hello %s !' %  name
$$ LANGUAGE plpythonu;
```

Here, we see that creating a function starts by defining it as any other PostgreSQL function with a RETURNS definition of a text field:

```
CREATE FUNCTION hello(name text)
  RETURNS text
```

The difference from what we have seen before, is that the language part is specifying plpythonu (the language ID for the PL/PythonU language):

```
$$ LANGUAGE plpythonu;
```

Inside the function body, it is very much a normal Python function returning a value obtained by the name passed as an argument formatted into a string `'hello %s !'`, using the standard Python formatting operator %:

```
    return 'hello %s !' %  name
```

Finally, let's test how this works:

```
hannu=# SELECT hello('world');
    hello
---------------
 hello world !
(1 row)
```

And yes, it returns exactly what is expected!

Data type conversions

The first and last things happening when a PL function is called by PostgreSQL, are converting argument values between the PostgreSQL and PL types. The PostgreSQL types need to be converted to the PL types on entering the function, and then the return value needs to be converted back into the PostgreSQL types.

Except for PL/pgSQL, which uses PostgreSQL's own native types in computations, the PLs are based on existing languages with their own understanding of what types (integer, string, date, and so on) are, how they should behave, and how they are represented internally. They are mostly similar to PostgreSQL's understanding but quite often are not exactly the same. PL/Python converts data from PostgreSQL types to Python types, as shown in the following table:

PostgreSQL	Python 2	Python 3	Comments
`int2, int4`	`int`	`int`	
`int8`	`long`	`int`	
`real, double, numeric`	`float`	`float`	This may lose precision for numeric values.
`bytea`	`str`	`bytes`	No encoding conversion is done, nor should any encoding be assumed.
`text, char()`, `varchar()`, and other text types	`str`	`str`	On Python 2, the string will be in server encoding. On Python 3, it is a unicode string.
All other types	`str`	`str`	PostgreSQL's `type` output function is used to convert to this string.

Inside the function, all computation is done using Python types and the return value is converted back to PostgreSQL using the following rules (these rules are the direct quotes from official PL/Python documentation at `http://www.postgresql.org/docs/current/static/plpython-data.html`):

- When the PostgreSQL return type is Boolean, the return value will be evaluated for truth, according to the Python rules. That is, `0` and empty strings are `false`, but notably `f` is `true`.

- When the PostgreSQL return type is `bytea`, the return value will be converted to a string (Python 2) or bytes (Python 3) using the respective Python built-ins, with the result being converted `bytea`.

- For all other PostgreSQL return types, the returned Python value is converted to a string using Python's built-in `str`, and the result is passed to the input function of the PostgreSQL data type.

Strings in Python 2 are required to be in the PostgreSQL server encoding when they are passed to PostgreSQL. Strings that are not valid in the current server encoding will raise an error. But not all encoding mismatches can be detected, so garbage data can still result when this is not done correctly. Unicode strings are converted to the correct encoding automatically, so it can be safer and more convenient to use those. In Python 3, all strings are Unicode strings.

In other words, anything but 0, False, and an empty sequence, including empty strings ' ', or a dictionary becomes PostgreSQL false.

One notable exception to this, is that the check for None is done before any other conversions. Even for Booleans, None is always converted to NULL and not to the Boolean value false.

For the bytea type, the PostgreSQL byte array, the conversion from Python's string representation, is an exact copy with no encoding or other conversions applied.

Writing simple functions in PL/Python

Writing functions in PL/Python is not much different in principle from writing functions in PL/pgSQL. You still have the exact same syntax around the function body in $$, and the argument name, types, and returns all mean the same thing, regardless of the exact PL/language used.

A simple function

So, a simple add_one() function in PL/Python looks like this:

```
CREATE FUNCTION add_one(i int)
  RETURNS int AS $$
return i + 1;
$$ LANGUAGE plpythonu;

usm=# SELECT add_one(2);
 add_one
---------
       3
(1 row)
```

It can't get any simpler than that, can it?

What you see here is that the PL/Python arguments are passed to the Python code after converting them to appropriate types, and the result is passed back and converted to the appropriate PostgreSQL type for the return value.

Functions returning a record

To return a record from a Python function, you can use:

- A sequence or list of values in the same order as the fields in the return record
- A dictionary with keys matching the fields in the return record
- A class or type instance with attributes matching the fields in the return record

Here are samples of the three ways to return a record:

First, using an instance:

```
CREATE OR REPLACE FUNCTION userinfo(
                    INOUT username name,
                    OUT user_id oid,
                    OUT is_superuser boolean)
AS $$
    class PGUser:
        def __init__(self,username,user_id,is_superuser):
            self.username = username
            self.user_id = user_id
            self.is_superuser = is_superuser
    u = plpy.execute("""\
            select usename,usesysid,usesuper
              from pg_user
            where usename = '%s'""" % username)[0]
    user = PGUser(u['usename'], u['usesysid'], u['usesuper'])
    return user
$$ LANGUAGE plpythonu;
```

Then, a little simpler one using a dictionary:

```
CREATE OR REPLACE FUNCTION userinfo(
                    INOUT username name,
                    OUT user_id oid,
                    OUT is_superuser boolean)
AS $$
    u = plpy.execute("""\
            select usename,usesysid,usesuper
              from pg_user
            where usename = '%s'""" % username)[0]
    return {'username':u['usename'], 'user_id':u['usesysid'], 'is_
superuser':u['usesuper']}
$$ LANGUAGE plpythonu;
```

Finally, using a tuple:

```
CREATE OR REPLACE FUNCTION userinfo(
                    INOUT username name,
                    OUT user_id oid,
                    OUT is_superuser boolean)
AS $$
    u = plpy.execute("""\
            select usename,usesysid,usesuper
              from pg_user
             where usename = '%s'""" % username)[0]
    return (u['usename'], u['usesysid'], u['usesuper'])
$$ LANGUAGE plpythonu;
```

Notice `[0]` at the end of `u = plpy.execute(...)[0]` in all the examples. It is there to extract the first row of the result, as even for one-row results `plpy.execute` still returns a list of results.

Danger of SQL injection!

As we have neither executed a `prepare()` method and executed a `execute()` method with arguments after it, nor have we used the `plpy.quote_literal()` method (both techniques are discussed later) to safely quote the username before merging it into the query, we are open to a security flaw known as **SQL injection**. So, make sure that you only let trusted users call this function or supply the username argument.

Calling the function defined via any of these three CREATE commands will look exactly the same:

```
hannu=# SELECT * FROM userinfo('postgres');
 username | user_id | is_superuser
----------+---------+--------------
 postgres |      10 | t
(1 row)
```

It usually does not make sense to declare a class inside a function just to return a record value. This possibility is included mostly for cases where you already have a suitable class with a set of attributes matching the ones the function returns.

Table functions

When returning a set from PL/Python functions, you have three options:

- Return a list or any other sequence of return type
- Return an iterator or generator
- The `yield` keyword in python just returns a generator

Here, we have three ways to generate all even numbers up to the argument value using these different styles:

First, returning a list of integers:

```
CREATE FUNCTION even_numbers_from_list(up_to int)
  RETURNS SETOF int
AS $$
    return range(0,up_to,2)
$$ LANGUAGE plpythonu;

libro=# SELECT * FROM even_numbers_from_list(10);
 even_numbers_from_list
------------------------
            0
            2
            4
            6
            8
(5 rows)
```

The list here, is returned by a built-in Python function called `range`, which returns a result of all even numbers below the argument. This gets returned as a table of integers, one integer per row from the PostgreSQL function. If the RETURNS clause of the function definition would say int [] instead of SETOF int, the same function would return a single number of even integers as a PostgreSQL array.

The next function returns a similar result using a generator and returning both the even number and the odd one following it. Also, notice the different PostgreSQL syntax RETURNS TABLE (...) used this time for defining the return set:

```
CREATE FUNCTION even_numbers_from_generator(up_to int)
  RETURNS TABLE (even int, odd int)
```

```
AS $$
    return ((i,i+1) for i in xrange(0,up_to,2))
$$ LANGUAGE plpythonu;

libro=# SELECT * FROM even_numbers_from_generator(10);
 even | odd
------+-----
    0 |   1
    2 |   3
    4 |   5
    6 |   7
    8 |   9
(5 rows)
```

The generator is constructed using a generator expression (x for x in <seq>). Finally, the function is defined using a generator using an explicit yield syntax, and yet another PostgreSQL syntax is used for returning SETOF RECORD with the record structure defined this time by OUT parameters:

```
CREATE FUNCTION even_numbers_with_yield(up_to int,
                                        OUT even int,
                                        OUT odd int)
  RETURNS SETOF RECORD
AS $$
    for i in xrange(0,up_to,2):
        yield i, i+1
$$ LANGUAGE plpythonu;
```

The important part here, is that you can use any of the preceding ways to define a PL/Python set returning function and they all work the same. Also, you are free to return a mixture of different types for each row of the set:

```
CREATE FUNCTION birthdates(OUT name text, OUT birthdate date)
  RETURNS SETOF RECORD
AS $$
    return (
        {'name': 'bob', 'birthdate': '1980-10-10'},
        {'name': 'mary', 'birthdate': '1983-02-17'},
        ['jill', '2010-01-15'],
    )
$$ LANGUAGE plpythonu;
```

This yields the result, as follows:

```
hannu=# SELECT * FROM birthdates();
 name | birthdate
------+------------
 bob  | 1980-10-10
 mary | 1983-02-17
 jill | 2010-01-15
(3 rows)
```

As you can see, the data returning a part of PL/PythonU is much more flexible than returning data from a function written in PL/pgSQL.

Running queries in the database

If you have ever accessed a database in Python, you know that most database adapters conform to a somewhat loose standard called **Python Database API Specification v2.0** or **DB API 2** for short. You can find the reference online at `http://legacy.python.org/dev/peps/pep-0249/`

The first thing you need to know about database access in PL/Python is that in-database queries *do not* follow this API.

Running simple queries

Instead of using the standard API, there are just three functions for doing all database access. There are two variants: `plpy.execute` for running a query, and `plpy.prepare()` for turning a query text into a query plan or a prepared query.

The simplest way to do a query is with:

```
res = plpy.execute(<query text>, [<row count>])
```

This takes a textual query and an optional row count, and returns a result object, which emulates a list of dictionaries, one dictionary per row.

As an example, if you want to access a field `'name'` of the third row of the result, you use:

```
res[2]['name']
```

The index is 2 and not 3 because Python lists are indexed starting from 0, so the first row is `res[0]`, the second row `res[1]`, and so on.

Using prepared queries

In an ideal world, this would be all that is needed, but `plpy.execute(query, cnt)` has two shortcomings:

- It does not support parameters
- The plan for the query is not saved, requiring the query text to be parsed and run through the optimizer at each invocation

We will show a way to properly construct a query string later, but for most uses simple parameter passing is enough. So, the `execute(query, [maxrows])` call becomes a set of two statements:

```
plan = plpy.prepare(<query text>, <list of argument types>)
res = plpy.execute(plan, <list of values>, [<row count>])
```

For example, to query if a user 'postgres' is a superuser, use the following:

```
plan = plpy.prepare("select usesuper from pg_user where  usename =
$1", ["text"])
res = plpy.execute(plan, ["postgres"])
print res[0]["usesuper"]
```

The first statement prepares the query, which parses the query string into a query tree, optimizes this tree to produce the best query plan available, and returns the `prepared_query` object. The second row uses the prepared plan to query for a specific user's `superuser` status.

The prepared plan can be used multiple times, so that you could continue to see if user bob is `superuser`.

```
res = plpy.execute(plan, ["bob"])
print res[0]["usesuper"]
```

Caching prepared queries

Preparing the query can be quite an expensive step, especially for more complex queries where the optimizer has to choose from a rather large set of possible plans. So, it makes sense to re-use results of this step, if possible.

The current implementation of PL/Python does not automatically cache query plans (prepared queries), but you can do it yourself easily.

```
try:
    plan = SD['is_super_qplan']
except:
    SD['is_super_qplan'] = plpy.prepare("....
    plan = SD['is_super_qplan']
<the rest of the function>
```

The global dictionary SD is available to store data between function calls. This variable is private static data. The global dictionary GD is public data, available to all Python functions within a session. Use with care. The values in SD[] and GD[] only live inside a single database session, so it only makes sense to do the caching in case you have long-lived connections.

Writing trigger functions in PL/Python

As with other PLs, PL/PythonU can be used to write trigger functions. The declaration of a trigger function is different from an ordinary function by the return type RETURNS TRIGGER. So, a simple trigger function that just notifies the caller that it is indeed called, looks like this:

```
CREATE OR REPLACE FUNCTION notify_on_call()
  RETURNS TRIGGER
AS $$
plpy.notice('I was called!')
$$ LANGUAGE plpythonu;
```

After creating this function, the trigger can be tested on a table using a trigger function:

```
hannu=# CREATE TABLE ttable(id int);
CREATE TABLE
hannu=# CREATE TRIGGER ttable_notify BEFORE INSERT ON ttable EXECUTE
PROCEDURE notify_on_call();
CREATE TRIGGER
hannu=# INSERT INTO ttable VALUES(1);
NOTICE:  I was called!
CONTEXT:  PL/Python function "notify_on_call"
INSERT 0 1
```

Of course, the preceding trigger function is quite useless, as will be any trigger without knowing when and on what data change, the trigger was called. All the data needed by a trigger, when it is called, is passed in via the **trigger dictionary** called **TD**. In TD, you have the following values:

Key	Value
TD["event"]	The event the trigger function is called for; one of the following strings is contained as the event: INSERT, UPDATE, DELETE, or TRUNCATE
TD["when"]	One of BEFORE, AFTER, or INSTEAD OF
TD["level"]	ROW or STATEMENT
TD["old"]	This is the before-command image of the row. For low-level UPDATE and DELETE triggers, this contains a dictionary for the values of the triggering row, before the changes have been made by the command. It is None for other cases.
TD["new"]	This is the after-command image of the row. For low-level INSERT and UPDATE triggers, this contains a dictionary for the values of the triggering row, after the changes have been made by the command. It is None for other cases. If you are in a BEFORE or INSTEAD OF trigger, you can make changes to this dictionary and then signal PostgreSQL to use the changed tuple by returning the string MODIFY from the trigger function.
TD["name"]	The trigger name from the CREATE TRIGGER command.
TD["table_name"]	The name of the table on which the trigger occurred.
TD["table_schema"]	The schema of the table on which the trigger occurred.
TD["relid"]	The **object identifier** (**OID**) of the table on which the trigger occurred.
TD["args"]	If the CREATE TRIGGER command included arguments, they are available from TD["args"][0] to TD["args"][n-1].

In addition to doing anything you can do in ordinary PL/Python functions, such as modifying data in tables, writing to files and sockets, and sending e-mails, you can also affect the behavior of the triggering command.

If TD["when"] is ("BEFORE", "INSTEAD OF") and TD["level"] == "ROW", you can return SKIP to abort the event. Returning None or OK indicates that the row is unmodified and it is OK to continue. Returning None is also the default behavior for Python if the function does a simple return or runs to the end without a return statement, in which case, you don't need to do anything.

In case you have modified values in the TD["new"] and you want PostgreSQL to continue with the new values, you can return MODIFY to indicate to PL/Python that you've modified the new row. This can only be done if TD["event"] is INSERT or UPDATE, otherwise the return value is ignored.

Exploring the inputs of a trigger

The following trigger function is useful when developing triggers, so that you can easily see what the trigger function is really getting when called:

```
CREATE OR REPLACE FUNCTION explore_trigger()
  RETURNS TRIGGER
AS $$
import pprint
nice_data = pprint.pformat(
  (
    ('TD["table_schema"]' , TD["table_schema"] ),
    ('TD["event"]'        , TD["event"] ),
    ('TD["when"]'         , TD["when"] ),
    ('TD["level"]'        , TD["level"] ),
    ('TD["old"]'          , TD["old"] ),
    ('TD["new"]'          , TD["new"] ),
    ('TD["name"]'         , TD["name"] ),
    ('TD["table_name"]'   , TD["table_name"] ),
    ('TD["relid"]'        , TD["relid"] ),
    ('TD["args"]'         , TD["args"] ),
  )
)
plpy.notice('explore_trigger:\n' + nice_data)
$$ LANGUAGE plpythonu;
```

This function formats all the data passed to the trigger in TD using pprint.pformat, and then sends it to the client as a standard Python info message using plpy.notice. For testing this out, we create a simple table and then put an AFTER ... FOR EACH ROW ... trigger using this function on that table:

```
CREATE TABLE test(
    id serial PRIMARY KEY,
    data text,
    ts timestamp DEFAULT clock_timestamp()
);

CREATE TRIGGER test_explore_trigger
```

```
    AFTER INSERT OR UPDATE OR DELETE ON test
      FOR EACH ROW
    EXECUTE PROCEDURE explore_trigger('one', 2, null);
```

Now, we can explore what the trigger function actually gets:

```
hannu=# INSERT INTO test(id,data) VALUES(1, 'firstrowdata');
NOTICE:  explore_trigger:
(('TD["table_schema"]', 'public'),
 ('TD["event"]', 'INSERT'),
 ('TD["when"]', 'AFTER'),
 ('TD["level"]', 'ROW'),
 ('TD["old"]', None),
 ('TD["new"]',
  {'data': 'firstrowdata', 'id': 1, 'ts': '2013-05-13
12:04:03.676314'}),
 ('TD["name"]', 'test_explore_trigger'),
 ('TD["table_name"]', 'test'),
 ('TD["relid"]', '35163'),
 ('TD["args"]', ['one', '2', 'null']))
CONTEXT:  PL/Python function "explore_trigger"
INSERT 0 1
```

Most of this is expected and corresponds well to the table of the TD dictionary values given in the previous table. What may be a little unexpected, is the fact that the arguments given in the CREATE TRIGGER statement are all converted to strings, even the NULL. When developing your own triggers, either in PL/Python or any other language, it may be useful to put this trigger on the table as well, to check that the inputs to the trigger are as expected. For example, it is easy to see that if you omit the FOR EACH ROW part, the TD['old'] and TD['new'] will both be empty, as the trigger definition defaults to FOR EACH STATEMENT.

A log trigger

Now, we can put this knowledge to work and write a trigger that logs changes to the table to either a file or to a special log-collector process over the network. Logging to a file is the simplest way to permanently log the changes in transactions which were rolled back. If these were logged to a log table, the ROLLBACK command would also remove the log records. This may be a crucial audit requirement for your business.

Of course, this also has a downside. You will be logging the changes that may not be permanent due to the transaction being rolled back. Unfortunately, this is the price you have to pay for not losing the log records.

```
CREATE OR REPLACE FUNCTION log_trigger()
```

```
RETURNS TRIGGER AS $$
    args = tuple(TD["args"])
    if not SD.has_key(args):
        protocol = args[0]
        if protocol == 'udp':
            import socket
            sock = socket.socket( socket.AF_INET,
                                  socket.SOCK_DGRAM )
            def logfunc(msg, addr=args[1],
                        port=int(args[2]), sock=sock):
                sock.sendto(msg, (addr, port))
        elif protocol == 'file':
            f = open(args[1], 'a+')
            def logfunc(msg,f=f):
                f.write(msg+'\n')
                f.flush()
        else:
            raise ValueError, 'bad logdest in CREATE TRIGGER'
        SD[args] = logfunc
        SD['env_plan'] = plpy.prepare("""
            select clock_timestamp(),
                   txid_current(),
                   current_user,
                   current_database()""", [])
    logfunc = SD[args]
    env_info_row = plpy.execute(SD['env_plan'])[0]
    import json
    log_msg = json.dumps(
        {'txid' : env_info_row['txid_current'],
         'time' : env_info_row['clock_timestamp'],
         'user' : env_info_row['current_user'],
         'db'   : env_info_row['current_database'],
         'table' : '%s.%s' % (TD['table_name'],
                              TD['table_schema']),
         'event' : TD['event'],
         'old' : TD['old'],
         'new' : TD['new'],
        }
    )
    logfunc(log_msg)
$$ LANGUAGE plpythonu;
```

First, this trigger checks if it already has a logger function defined and cached in the function's local dictionary SD[]. As the same trigger may be used with many different log destinations, the log function is stored under the key constructed as a Python tuple from the trigger function arguments in the CREATE TRIGGER statement. We cannot use the TD["args"] list directly as a key, as Python dictionary keys have to be immutable, which a list is not, but a tuple is.

If the key is not present, meaning this is the first call to this particular trigger, we have to create an appropriate log function and store it. To do this, we examine the first argument for the log destination type.

For the udp log type, we create a UDP socket for writing. Then, we define a function passing in this socket and also the other two trigger arguments as default arguments for the function. This is the most convenient way to create a closure and to bundle a function with some data values in Python.

For the file type, we just open this file in the append mode (a+) and also create a log function. The log function writes a message to this file and flushes the write, so the data is written to the file immediately and not some time later when the write buffer fills up (this is not preferable for performance critical systems). The log function created in either of these cases is stored in SD[tuple(TD["args"])].

At this point, we also prepare and save a query plan for getting other data we want to log and save this in SD['env_plan']. Now that we are done with the one-time preparations, we can proceed with the actual logging part, which is really very simple.

Next, we retrieve the logging function (logfunc = SD[args]) and get the row of the other logged data:

```
env_info_row = plpy.execute(SD['env_plan'])[0]
```

Finally, we convert all the logged data into one JSON object (log_msg = json.dumps({...})) and then use the logging function to send it to the log, logfunc(log_msg).

And that's it.

Next, let's test it out to see how it works by adding another trigger to our test table we created earlier:

```
CREATE TRIGGER test_audit_trigger
 AFTER INSERT OR UPDATE OR DELETE ON test
   FOR EACH ROW
 EXECUTE PROCEDURE log_trigger('file', '/tmp/test.json.log');
```

Any changes to the table done via INSERT, UPDATE, or DELETE are logged into /tmp/
test.json.log. This file is initially owned by the same user running the server,
usually postgres. So, to look at it you need to either be that user or root user, or you
have to change the permissions on the file created to allow reading.

If you want to test the UDP logging part, you just have to define another trigger
with different arguments:

```
CREATE TRIGGER test_audit_trigger_udp
    AFTER INSERT OR UPDATE OR DELETE ON test
    FOR EACH ROW
    EXECUTE PROCEDURE log_trigger('udp', 'localhost', 9999);
```

Of course, you need something to listen at the UDP port there. A minimalist UDP
listener is provided for testing in the log_udp_listener.py file under chapter07/
logtrigger/. Just run it, and it prints any UDP packets received to stdout.

Constructing queries

PL/Python does a good job of managing values passed to prepared query plans, but
a standard PostgreSQL query plan can take an argument in a very limited number of
places. Sometimes, you may want to construct whole queries, not just pass values to
predefined queries. For example, you can't have an argument for a table name, or a
field name.

So, how would you proceed if you want to construct a query from the function's
arguments and be sure that everything is quoted properly and no SQL injection
would be possible? PL/Python provides three functions to help you with proper
quoting of identifiers and data, just for this purpose.

The function plpy.quote_ident(name is meant for quoting identifiers, that is,
anything that names a database object or its attribute like a table, a view, a field
name, or function name. It surrounds the name with double quotes and takes care
of properly escaping anything inside the string which would break the quoting:

```
hannu=# DO LANGUAGE plpythonu $$ plpy.notice(plpy.quote_ident
        (r'5"\"'))
$$;
NOTICE:  "5"" \"""
CONTEXT:  PL/Python anonymous code block
DO
```

And yes, 5" \" is a legal table or field name in PostgreSQL; you just have to always
quote it if you use it in any statement.

The DO syntax creates an anonymous block inside your database session. It is a very handy way to run some procedural language code without needing to create a function.

The other two functions are for quoting literal values. The function, `plpy.quote_literal(litvalue)`, is for quoting strings and `plpy.quote_nullable(value_or_none)` is for quoting a value, which may be `None`. Both of these functions quote strings in a similar way, by enclosing them in single quotes (`str` becomes `'str'`) and doubling any single quotes or backslashes:

```
hannu=# DO LANGUAGE plpythonu $$ plpy.notice(plpy.quote_literal(r"
        \' "))
$$;
NOTICE:  E' \\'' '
CONTEXT:  PL/Python anonymous code block
DO
```

The only difference between these two, is that `plpy.quote_nullable()` can also take a value `None`, which will be rendered as a string `NULL` without any surrounding quotes. The argument to both of these has to be a string or a unicode string. If you want it to work with a value of any Python type, wrapping the value in `str(value)` usually works well.

Handling exceptions

With any bit of code, you need to make sure you handle when errors occur and your PL/Python functions are not an exception.

Before Version 9.1 of PostgreSQL, any error in an SQL query caused the surrounding transaction to be rolled back:

```
DO LANGUAGE plpythonu $$
plpy.execute('insert into ttable values(1)')
plpy.execute('fail!')
$$;
ERROR:  spiexceptions.SyntaxError: syntax error at or near "fail"
LINE 1: fail!
        ^
QUERY:  fail!
CONTEXT:  Traceback (most recent call last):
  PL/Python anonymous code block, line 3, in <module>
    plpy.execute('fail!')
PL/Python anonymous code block
```

You can manually use the SAVEPOINT attributes to control the boundaries of the rolled-back block, at least as far back as Version 8.4 of PostgreSQL. This will reduce the amount of the transaction that is rolled back:

```
CREATE OR REPLACE FUNCTION syntax_error_rollback_test()
  RETURNS void
AS $$
plpy.execute('insert into ttable values(1)')
try:
    plpy.execute('SAVEPOINT foo;')
    plpy.execute('insert into ttable values(2)')
    plpy.execute('fail!')
except:
    pass
plpy.execute('insert into ttable values(3)')
$$ LANGUAGE plpythonu;

hannu=# SELECT syntax_error_rollback_test();
 syntax_error_rollback_test
----------------------------

(1 row)
```

When the SAVEPOINT foo; command is executed in PL/Python, an SQL error will not cause full ROLLBACK; but an equivalent of ROLLBACK TO SAVEPOINT foo;, so, only the effects of commands between SAVEPOINT and the error are rolled back:

```
hannu=# SELECT * FROM ttable ;
 id
----
  1
  3
(2 rows)
```

Starting in Version 9.1, there are two important changes in how PostgreSQL exceptions are handled. If no SAVEPOINT or subtransaction is used, each invocation of plpy.prepare() and plpy.execute() is run in its own subtransaction, so that an error will only rollback this subtransaction and not all of the current transaction. Since using a separate subtransaction for each database interaction involves extra costs, and you may want to control the subtransaction boundaries anyway, a new Python context manager, plpy.subtransaction() , is provided.

For an explanation of Python's context managers, refer to http://docs.python. org/library/stdtypes.html#context-manager-types, so that you can use the with statement in Python 2.6, or newer, to wrap a group of database interactions in one subtransaction in a more Pythonic way:

```
hannu=# CREATE TABLE test_ex(i int);
CREATE TABLE
DO LANGUAGE plpythonu $$
plpy.execute('insert into test_ex values(1)')
try:
  with plpy.subtransaction():
    plpy.execute('insert into test_ex values(2)')
    plpy.execute('fail!')
  except plpy.spiexceptions.SyntaxError:
    pass # silently ignore, avoid doing this in prod. code
    plpy.execute('insert into test_ex values(3)')
$$;
DO
hannu=# SELECT * FROM test_ex;
 i
---
 1
 3
(2 rows)
```

Atomicity in Python

While the subtransactions manage data changes in the PostgreSQL database, the variables on the Python side of the fence live their separate lives. Python does not provide even a single-statement level atomicity, as demonstrated by the following:

```
>>> a = 1
>>> a[1] = a = 2
Traceback (most recent call last):
  File "<stdin>", line 1, in <module>
TypeError: 'int' object does not support item assignment
>>> a
1
>>> a = a[1] = 2
Traceback (most recent call last):
  File "<stdin>", line 1, in <module>
TypeError: 'int' object does not support item assignment
>>> a
2
```

As you can see, it is possible that even a single multi-assignment statement can be executed only halfway through. This means that you have to be prepared to fully manage your Python data yourself. The function, `plpy.subtransaction()`, won't help you in any way with managing Python variables.

Debugging PL/Python

First, let's start by stating that there is no debugger support when running functions in PL/Python; so, it is a good idea to develop and debug a PL/Python function as a pure Python function as much as possible and only do the final integration in PL/Python. To help with this, you can have a similar environment in your Python development environment using the `plpy` module.

Just put the module in your path and do import `plpy` before you try running your prospective PL/PythonU functions in an ordinary interpreter. If you use any of the `plpy.execute(...)` or `plpy.prepare()` functions , you also need to set up a database connection before using these by calling `plpy.connect(<connectstring>)`.

Using plpy.notice() to track the function's progress

The debugging technology I use most often in any language, is printing out intermediate values as the function progresses. If the printout rolls past too fast, you can slow it down by sleeping a second or two after each print.

In standard Python, it would look like this:

```
def fact(x):
    f = 1
    while (x > 0):
        f = f * x
        x = x - 1
        print 'f:%d, x:%d' % (f, x)
    return f
```

It will print out all intermediate values for f and x as it runs:

```
>>> fact(3)
f:3, x:2
f:6, x:1
f:6, x:0
6
```

If you try to use print in a PL/Python function, you will discover that nothing is printed. In fact, there is no single logical place to print to when running a pluggable language inside a PostgreSQL server.

The closest thing to print in PL/Python is the function `plpy.notice()`, which sends a PostgreSQL NOTICE to the client and also to the server log if `log_min_messages` is set to the value `notice` or smaller.

```
CREATE FUNCTION fact(x int) RETURNS int
AS $$
    global x
    f = 1
    while (x > 0):
        f = f * x
        x = x - 1
        plpy.notice('f:%d, x:%d' % (f, x))
    return f
$$ LANGUAGE plpythonu;
```

Running this is much more verbose than the version with print, because each NOTICE also includes information about the CONTEXT from where the NOTICE comes:

```
hannu=# SELECT fact(3);
NOTICE:   f:3, x:2
CONTEXT:   PL/Python function "fact"
NOTICE:   f:6, x:1
CONTEXT:   PL/Python function "fact"
NOTICE:   f:6, x:0
CONTEXT:   PL/Python function "fact"
 fact
------
    6
(1 row)
```

PL/PythonU function arguments are passed in as globals

If you compared the `fact(x)` function in Python and PL/Python, you noticed an extra line at the beginning of the PL/Python function:

```
    global x
```

This is needed to overcome an implementation detail that often surprises PL/PythonU developers; the function arguments are not the function arguments in the Python sense and neither are they locals. They are passed in as variables in the function's global scope.

Using assert

Similar to ordinary Python programming, you can also use Python's `assert` statement to catch conditions which should not happen:

```
CREATE OR REPLACE FUNCTION fact(x int)
  RETURNS int
AS $$
    global x
    assert x>=0, "argument must be a positive integer"
    f = 1
    while (x > 0):
        f = f * x
        x = x - 1
    return f
$$ LANGUAGE plpythonu;
```

To test this, call `fact()` with a negative number:

```
hannu=# SELECT fact(-1);
ERROR:  AssertionError: argument must be a positive integer
CONTEXT:  Traceback (most recent call last):
  PL/Python function "fact", line 3, in <module>
    assert x>=0, "argument must be a positive integer"
PL/Python function "fact"
```

You will get a message about `AssertionError`, together with the location of the failing line number.

Redirecting sys.stdout and sys.stderr

If all the code you need to debug is your own, the preceding two techniques will cover most of your needs. However, what do you do in cases where you use some third party libraries which print out debug information to `sys.stdout` and/or `sys.stderr`?

Well, in those cases you can replace Python's `sys.stdout` and `sys.stdin` with your own pseudo file object that stores everything written there for later retrieval. Here is a pair of functions, the first of which does the capturing of `sys.stdout` or uncapturing if it is called with the argument, `do_capture` set to `false`, and the second one returns everything captured:

```
CREATE OR REPLACE FUNCTION capture_stdout(do_capture bool)
  RETURNS text
AS $$
    import sys
```

```
        if do_capture:
            try:
                sys.stdout = GD['stdout_to_notice']
            except KeyError:
                class WriteAsNotice:
                    def __init__(self, old_stdout):
                        self.old_stdout = old_stdout
                        self.printed = []
                    def write(self, s):
                        self.printed.append(s)
                    def read(self):
                        text = ''.join(self.printed)
                        self.printed = []
                        return text
                GD['stdout_to_notice'] = WriteAsNotice(sys.stdout)
                sys.stdout = GD['stdout_to_notice']
            return "sys.stdout captured"
        else:
            sys.stdout = GD['stdout_to_notice'].old_stdout
            return "restored original sys.stdout"
$$ LANGUAGE plpythonu;

CREATE OR REPLACE FUNCTION read_stdout()
  RETURNS text
AS $$
    return GD['stdout_to_notice'].read()
$$ LANGUAGE plpythonu;
```

Here is a sample session using the preceding functions:

```
hannu=# SELECT capture_stdout(true);
    capture_stdout
---------------------
 sys.stdout captured
(1 row)

DO LANGUAGE plpythonu $$
print 'TESTING sys.stdout CAPTURING'
import pprint
pprint.pprint( {'a':[1,2,3], 'b':[4,5,6]} )
$$;
DO
hannu=# SELECT read_stdout();
```

```
          read_stdout
---------------------------------
 TESTING sys.stdout CAPTURING    +
 {'a': [1, 2, 3], 'b': [4, 5, 6]}+


(1 row)
```

Thinking out of the "SQL database server" box

We'll wrap up the chapter on PL/Python with a couple of sample PL/PythonU functions for doing some things you would not usually consider doing inside the database function or trigger.

Generating thumbnails when saving images

Our first example, uses Python's powerful **Python Imaging Library** (PIL) module to generate thumbnails of uploaded photos. For ease of interfacing with various client libraries, this program takes the incoming image data as a Base64 encoded string:

```
CREATE FUNCTION save_image_with_thumbnail(image64 text)
  RETURNS int
AS $$
import Image, cStringIO
size = (64,64) # thumbnail size

# convert base64 encoded text to binary image data
raw_image_data = image64.decode('base64')

# create a pseudo-file to read image from
infile = cStringIO.StringIO(raw_image_data)
pil_img = Image.open(infile)
pil_img.thumbnail(size, Image.ANTIALIAS)

# create a stream to write the thumbnail to
outfile = cStringIO.StringIO()
pil_img.save(outfile, 'JPEG')
raw_thumbnail = outfile.getvalue()

# store result into database and return row id
q = plpy.prepare('''
```

```
        INSERT INTO photos(image, thumbnail)
        VALUES ($1,$2)
        RETURNING id''', ('bytea', 'bytea'))
    res = plpy.execute(q, (raw_image_data,raw_thumbnail))

    # return column id of first row
    return res[0]['id']
$$ LANGUAGE plpythonu;
```

The Python code is more or less a straight rewrite from the PIL tutorial, except that the files to read the image from, and write the thumbnail image to, are replaced with Python's standard file-like `StringIO` objects. For all this to work, you need to have PIL installed on your database server host.

In Debian/Ubuntu, this can be done by running `sudo apt-get install python-imaging`. On most modern Linux distributions, an alternative is to use Python's own package distribution system by running `sudo easy_install PIL`.

Sending an e-mail

The next sample is a function for sending e-mails from inside a database function:

```
CREATE OR REPLACE FUNCTION send_email(
    sender text,        -- sender e-mail
    recipients text,    -- comma-separated list of recipient addresses
    subject text,       -- email subject
    message text,       -- text of the message
    smtp_server text    -- SMTP server to use for sending
) RETURNS void
AS $$
    import smtplib;
    msg = "From: %s\r\nTo: %s\r\nSubject: %s\r\n\r\n%s" % \
        (sender, recipients, subject, message)
    recipients_list = [r.strip() for r
                                  in recipients.split(',')]
    server = smtplib.SMTP(smtp_server)
    server.sendmail(sender, recipients_list, msg)
    server.quit()
$$ LANGUAGE plpythonu;

test=# SELECT send_email('dummy@gmail.com', 'abv@postgresql.org',
        'test subject', 'message', 'localhost');
```

This function formats a message (msg = ""), converts a comma-separated **To:** address into a list of e-mail addresses (recipients_list = [r.strip()...]), connects to a SMTP server, and then passes the message to the SMTP server for delivery.

To use this function in a production system, it would probably require a bit more checking on the formats and some extra error handling, in case something goes wrong. You can read more about Python's smtplib at http://docs.python.org/library/smtplib.html.

Listing directory contents

Here is another interesting use case for an untrusted language. The function below can list the contents of a directory in your system:

```
CREATE OR REPLACE FUNCTION list_folder(
directory VARCHAR -- directory that will be walked
) RETURNS  SETOF VARCHAR
AS $$
import os;
file_paths = [];

# Walk the tree.
for root, directories, files in os.walk(directory):
    for filename in files:
        # Join the two strings in order to form the full filepath.
        filepath = os.path.join(root, filename)
        file_paths.append(filepath)  # Add it to the list.

return file_paths
$$ LANGUAGE plpythonu;
```

Let us now try and run the function:

```
test_db=# SELECT list_folder('/usr/local/pgsql/bin');
            list_folder
------------------------------------
 /usr/local/pgsql/bin/clusterdb
 /usr/local/pgsql/bin/createdb
 /usr/local/pgsql/bin/createlang
 /usr/local/pgsql/bin/createuser
 /usr/local/pgsql/bin/dropdb
 /usr/local/pgsql/bin/droplang
 /usr/local/pgsql/bin/dropuser
```

```
/usr/local/pgsql/bin/ecpg
/usr/local/pgsql/bin/initdb
/usr/local/pgsql/bin/pg_basebackup
/usr/local/pgsql/bin/pg_config
/usr/local/pgsql/bin/pg_controldata
/usr/local/pgsql/bin/pg_ctl
/usr/local/pgsql/bin/pg_dump
/usr/local/pgsql/bin/pg_dumpall
/usr/local/pgsql/bin/pg_isready
/usr/local/pgsql/bin/pg_receivexlog
/usr/local/pgsql/bin/pg_resetxlog
/usr/local/pgsql/bin/pg_restore
/usr/local/pgsql/bin/postgres
/usr/local/pgsql/bin/postmaster
/usr/local/pgsql/bin/psql
/usr/local/pgsql/bin/reindexdb
/usr/local/pgsql/bin/vacuumdb
(24 rows)
```

The function above uses the Python `os` module and walks the directory tree, top-down. This function will not walk down into symbolic links that resolve to directories. The errors are ignored by default. You can learn more about how Python's `os.walk()` behaves in Python 2's (since that is what the example uses) documentation here `https://docs.python.org/2/library/os.html`.

Summary

In this chapter, we saw that it is relatively easy to do things way beyond what a simple SQL database server normally supports; thanks to its pluggable language's support.

In fact, you can do almost anything in the PostgreSQL server that you could do in any other application server. Hopefully, this chapter just scratched the surface of what can be done inside a PostgreSQL server.

In the next chapter, we will learn about writing PostgreSQL's more advanced functions in C. This will give you deeper access to PostgreSQL, allowing you to use a PostgreSQL server for much more powerful things.

Writing Advanced Functions
in C

In the previous chapter, we introduced you to the possibilities of *untrusted* pluggable languages being available to a PostgreSQL developer to achieve things impossible in most other relational databases.

While using a pluggable scripting language is enough for a large class of problems, there are two main categories, where they may fall short: *performance* and *depth* of functionality.

Most scripting languages are quite a bit slower than optimized C code when executing the same algorithms. For a single function, this may not be the case because common things such as dictionary lookups or string matching have been optimized so well over the years. But in general, C code will be faster than scripted code. Also, in cases where the function is called millions of times per query, the overhead of actually calling the function and converting the arguments and return values to and from the scripting language counterparts can be a significant portion of the run time.

The second potential problem with pluggable languages is that most of them just do not support the full range of possibilities that are provided by PostgreSQL. There are a few things that simply cannot be coded in anything else but C. For example, when you define a completely new type for PostgreSQL, the type input and output functions, which convert the type's text representation to internal representation and back, need to handle PostgreSQL's pseudotype `cstring`. This is basically the C string or a zero-terminated string. Returning `cstring` is simply not supported by any of the PL languages included in the core distribution, at least not as of PostgreSQL Version 9.3. The PL languages also do not support pseudotypes ANYELEMENT, ANYARRAY and especially "any" VARIADIC.

In the following sections, we will go step-by-step through writing some PostgreSQL extension functions in increasing complexity in C.

We will start from the simplest **add 2 arguments** function which is quite similar to the one in PostgreSQL manual, but we will present the material in a different order. So, setting up the build environment comes early enough so that you can follow us hands-on from the very beginning.

After that, we will describe some important things to be aware of when designing and writing code that runs inside the server, such as memory management, executing queries, and retrieving results.

As the topic of writing C-language PostgreSQL functions can be quite large and our space for this topic is limited, we will occasionally skip some of the details and refer you to the PostgreSQL manual for extra information and specifications. We are also limiting this section to reference PostgreSQL 9.3. While most things will work perfectly fine across versions, there are references to paths that will be specific to a version.

The simplest C function – return (a + b)

Let's start with a simple function, which takes two integer arguments and returns the sum of these. We first present the source code and then will move on to show you how to compile it, load it into PostgreSQL, and then use it as any native function.

add_func.c

A C source file implementing add(int, int) returns int function looks like the following code snippet:

```
#include "postgres.h"
#include "fmgr.h"

PG_MODULE_MAGIC;

PG_FUNCTION_INFO_V1(add_ab);

Datum
add_ab(PG_FUNCTION_ARGS)
{
    int32    arg_a = PG_GETARG_INT32(0);
    int32    arg_b = PG_GETARG_INT32(1);

    PG_RETURN_INT32(arg_a + arg_b);
}
```

Let's go over the code explaining the use of each segment:

- `#include "postgres.h"`: This includes most of the basic definitions and declarations needed for writing any C code for running in PostgreSQL.

- `#include "fmgr.h"`: This includes the definitions for `PG_*` macros used in this code.

- `PG_MODULE_MAGIC;`: This is a "magic block" defined in `fmgr.h`. This block is used by the server to ensure that it does not load code compiled by a different version of PostgreSQL, potentially crashing the server. It was introduced in Version 8.2 of PostgreSQL. If you really need to write code which can also be compiled for PostgreSQL versions before 8.2 you need to put this between `#ifdef PG_MODULE_MAGIC` / `#endif`. You see this a lot in samples available on the Internet, but you probably will not need to do the `ifdef` for any new code. The latest pre-8.2 Version became officially obsolete (that is unsupported) in November 2010, and even 8.2 community support ended in December 2011.

- `PG_FUNCTION_INFO_V1(add_ab);`: This introduces the function to PostgreSQL as Version 1 calling a convention function. Without this line, it will be treated as an old-style Version 0 function. (See the information box following the Version 0 reference.)

- `Datum`: This is the return type of a C-language PostgreSQL function.

- `add_ab(PG_FUNCTION_ARGS)`: The function name is `add_ab` and the rest are its arguments. The `PG_FUNCTION_ARGS` definition can represent any number of arguments and has to be present, even for a function taking no arguments.

- `int32   arg_a = PG_GETARG_INT32(0);`: You need to use the `PG_GETARG_INT32(<argnr>)` macro (or corresponding `PG_GETARG_xxx(<argnr>)` for other argument types) to get the argument value. The arguments are numbered starting from `0`.

- `int32   arg_b = PG_GETARG_INT32(1);`: Similar to the previous description.

- `PG_RETURN_INT32(arg_a + arg_b);`: Finally, you use the `PG_RETURN_<rettype>(<retvalue>)` macro to build and return a suitable return value.

You could also have written the whole function body as the following code:

```
PG_RETURN_INT32(PG_GETARG_INT32(0) + PG_GETARG_INT32(1));
```

But, it is much more readable as written, and most likely a good optimizing C compiler will compile both into an equivalently fast code.

Most compilers will issue a warning message as: `warning: no previous prototype for 'add_ab'` for the preceding code, so it is a good idea to also put a prototype for the function in the file:

```
Datum add_ab(PG_FUNCTION_ARGS);
```

The usual place to put it, is just before the code line `PG_FUNCTION_INFO_V1(add_ab);`.

 While the prototype is not strictly required, it enables much cleaner compiles with no warnings.

Version 0 call conventions

There is an even simpler way to write PostgreSQL functions in C, called the **Version 0 calling conventions**. The preceding a + b function can be written as the following code:

```
int add_ab(int arg_a, int arg_b)
{
    return arg_a + arg_b;
}
```

Version 0 is shorter for very simple functions, but it is severely limited for most other usages—you can't do even some basic things such as checking if a pass by value argument is null, return a set of values, or write aggregate functions. Also, Version 0 does not automatically take care of hiding most differences of pass by value and pass by reference types that Version 1 does. Therefore, it is better to just write all your functions using Version 1 calling conventions and ignore the fact that Version 0 even exists.

From this point forward, we are only going to discuss Version 1 calling conventions for a C function.

 In case you are interested, there is some more information on Version 0 at `http://www.postgresql.org/docs/current/ static/xfunc-c.html#AEN50495`, in the section titled *35.9.3. Version 0 Calling Conventions.*

Makefile

The next step is compiling and linking the .c source file into a form that can be loaded into the PostgreSQL server. This can all be done as a series of commands defined in a Makefile function.

The PostgreSQL manual has a complete section about which flags and included paths you should pass on each of the supported platforms, and how to determine correct paths for including files and libraries.

Fortunately, all of this is also automated nicely for developers via the PostgreSQL extension building infrastructure—or PGXS for short—which makes this really easy for most modules.

 Depending on which version of PostgreSQL you have installed, you may need to add the development package for your platform. These are usually the -dev or -devel packages.

Now, let's create our Makefile function. It will look like the following code:

```
MODULES = add_func

PG_CONFIG = pg_config
PGXS := $(shell $(PG_CONFIG) --pgxs)
include $(PGXS)
```

And you can compile and link the module by simply running make:

```
$make
gcc ... -c -o add_func.o add_func.c
gcc ... -o add_func.so add_func.o
rm add_func.o
```

Here, "..." stands for quite some amount of flags, includes, and libraries added by PGXS.

This produces a dynamically loadable module in the current directory which can be used directly by PostgreSQL, if your server has access to this directory, which may be the case on a development server.

For a "standard" server, as installed by your package management system, you will need to put the module in a standard place. This can be done using the PGXS as well.

You simply execute `sudo make install` and everything will be copied to the right place, $`sudo make install`:

```
[sudo] password for hannu:
/bin/mkdir -p '/usr/lib/postgresql/9.3/lib'
/bin/sh /usr/lib/postgresql/9.3/lib/pgxs/src/makefiles/../../config/
install-sh -c -m 755  add_func.so '/usr/lib/postgresql/9.3/lib/'
```

CREATE FUNCTION add(int, int)

You are just one step away from being able to use this function in your database. You just need to introduce the module you just compiled to a PostgreSQL database using the CREATE FUNCTION statement.

If you followed the samples up to this point, the following statement is all that is needed, along with adjusting the path appropriately to where PostgreSQL is installed on your server:

```
hannu=# CREATE FUNCTION add(int, int)
hannu-#    RETURNS int
hannu-# AS '/usr/lib/postgresql/9.3/lib/add_func', 'add_ab_null'
hannu-# LANGUAGE C STRICT;
CREATE FUNCTION
```

And voilá — you have created your first PostgreSQL C-language extension function:

```
hannu=# select add(1,2);
 add
-----
   3
(1 row)
```

add_func.sql.in

While what we just covered is all that is needed to have a C function in your database, it is often more convenient to put the preceding CREATE FUNCTION statement in an SQL file.

You usually do not know the final path of where PostgreSQL is installed when writing the code, especially in the light of running on multiple versions of PostgreSQL and/or on multiple operation systems. Here also, PGXS can help.

You need to write a file called `add_funcs.sql.in` as follows:

```
CREATE FUNCTION add(int, int) RETURNS int
    AS 'MODULE_PATHNAME', 'add_ab'
    LANGUAGE C STRICT;
```

Then add the following line in your `Makefile` function right after the `MODULES=` ... line:

```
DATA_built = add_funcs.sql
```

Now, when running make, the `add_funcs.sql.in` is compiled into a file `add_funcs.sql` with `MODULE_PATHNAME` replaced by the real path where the module will be installed.

[add_func]$ make

sed 's,MODULE_PATHNAME,$libdir/add_func,g' add_func.sql.in >add_func.sql

Also, `sudo make install` will copy the generated `.sql` file into the directory with other `.sql` files for extensions, as shown:

$ sudo make install

/usr/bin/mkdir -p '/usr/lib/postgresql/9.3/share/contrib'

/usr/bin/mkdir -p '/usr/lib/postgresql/9.3/lib'

/bin/sh /usr/lib/postgresql/9.3/lib/pgxs/src/makefiles/../../config/ install-sh -c -m 644 add_func.sql '/usr/lib/postgresql/9.3/share/ contrib/'

/bin/sh /usr/lib/postgresql/9.3/lib/pgxs/src/makefiles/../../config/ install-sh -c -m 755 add_func.so '/usr/lib/postgresql/9.3/lib/'

After this, the introduction of your C functions to a PostgreSQL database is as simple as `hannu=# \i /usr/lib/postgresql/9.3/share/contrib/add_func.sql`:

```
CREATE FUNCTION
```

The path `/usr/lib/postgresql/9.3/share/contrib/` to `add_funcs.sql` needs to be looked up from the output of the `make install` command.

There is a much cleaner way to package up your code called **Extensions** where you don't need to look up for any paths and the preceding step would just be as follows:

```
CREATE EXTENSION chap8_add;
```

But it is relatively more complex to set up, so we are not explaining it here. *Chapter 13, Publishing Your Code as PostgreSQL Extensions* dedicated to extensions appears later in this book.

Summary for writing a C function

Writing a C function used in PostgreSQL is a straightforward process:

1. Write the C code in `modulename.c`.

2. Write the SQL code for `CREATE FUNCTION` in `modulename.sql.in`.

3. Write a `Makefile` function.

4. Run make to compile a C file and generate `modulename.sql`.

5. Run `sudo make install` to install the generated files.

6. Run the generated `modulename.sql` in your target database:

   ```
   hannu# \i /<path>/modulename.sql
   ```

> You must run the SQL code in any database you want to use your function. If you want all your new databases to have access to your newly generated function, add the function to your template database by running the `modulename.sql` file in database `template1` or any other database you are explicitly specifying in the `CREATE DATABASE` command.

You may have noticed that while creating the function, you specified the name of the loadable object file and the name of the C function. When the SQL function is called for the first time, the dynamic loader loads the object file in memory. If you would like some object files to be preloaded at server startup, you should specify them in the PostgreSQL `shared_preload_libraries` configuration parameter.

Adding functionality to add(int, int)

While our function works, it adds nothing in the preceding code just using `SELECT A + B`. But functions written in C are capable of so much more. So let's start adding some more functionality to our function.

Smart handling of NULL arguments

Notice the use of a `STRICT` keyword in the `CREATE FUNCTION add(int a, int b)` in the previously mentioned code. This means that the function will not be called if any of the arguments are `NULL`, but instead `NULL` is returned straightaway. This is similar to how most PostgreSQL operators work, including the + sign when adding two integers—if any of the arguments are `NULL` the complete result is `NULL` as well.

Next, we will extend our function to be smarter about NULL inputs and act like PostgreSQL's sum() aggregate function, which ignores NULL values in inputs and still produces the sum of all non-null values.

For this, we need to do two things:

- Make sure that the function is called when either of the arguments are NULL.
- Handle NULL arguments by effectively converting a NULL argument to 0 and returning NULL only in cases where both arguments are null.

The first one is easy — just leave out the STRICT keyword when declaring the function. The latter one also seems easy as we just leave out STRICT and let the function execute. For a function with int arguments, this almost seems to do the trick. All NULL values show up as 0s, and the only thing you miss will be returning NULL if both arguments are NULL.

Unfortunately, this only works by coincidence and is not guaranteed to work in future versions. Worse still, if you do it the same way for pass by reference types, it will cause PostgreSQL to crash on null pointer references.

Next, we show you how to do it properly. We need now to do two things: record if we have any non-null values and add all the non-null values we see:

```
PG_FUNCTION_INFO_V1(add_ab_null);
Datum
add_ab_null(PG_FUNCTION_ARGS)
{
    int32   not_null = 0;
    int32   sum = 0;
    if (!PG_ARGISNULL(0)) {
        sum += PG_GETARG_INT32(0);
        not_null = 1;
    }
    if (!PG_ARGISNULL(1)) {
        sum += PG_GETARG_INT32(1);
        not_null = 1;
    }
    if (not_null) {
        PG_RETURN_INT32(sum);
    }
    PG_RETURN_NULL();
}
```

This indeed does what we need:

```
hannu=# CREATE FUNCTION add(int, int) RETURNS int
    AS '$libdir/add_func', 'add_ab_null'
    LANGUAGE C;
CREATE FUNCTION
hannu=# SELECT add(NULL, NULL) as must_be_null, add(NULL, 1) as must_be_
one;
-[ RECORD 1 ]+--
must_be_null |
must_be_one  | 1
```

Achieving the same result using standard PostgreSQL statements, functions, and operators would be much more verbose:

```
hannu=# SELECT (case when (a is null) and (b is null)
hannu(#             then null
hannu(#             else coalesce(a,0) + coalesce(b,0)
hannu(#        end)
hannu-# FROM (select 1::int as a, null::int as b)s;
-[ RECORD 1 ]
case | 1
```

In addition to restructuring the code, we also introduced two new macros PG_ARGISNULL(<argnr>) for checking if the argument <argnr> is NULL and PG_RETURN_NULL() for returning NULL from a function.

> PG_RETURN_NULL() is different from PG_RETURN_VOID().
> The latter is for using functions which are declared to return
> pseudotype void or in other words, not to return anything.

Working with any number of arguments

After the rewrite to handle NULL values, it seems that with just a little more effort, we could make it work with any number of arguments. Just move the following code inside the for(;;) cycle over the arguments and we are done:

```
if (!PG_ARGISNULL(<N>)) {
       sum += PG_GETARG_INT32(<N>);
       not_null = 1;
   }
```

Actually, making the code use an array instead of a simple type is not that simple after all. To make things more difficult, there is no information or sample code on how to work with arrays in the official PostgreSQL manual for C-language extension functions. The line between "supported" and "unsupported" when writing C-language functions is quite blurred, and the programmer doing so is expected to be able to figure some things out independently.

The bright side is that the friendly folks at the PostgreSQL mailing lists are usually happy to help you out if they see that your question is a serious one and that you have made some effort to figure out the basic stuff yourself.

To see how arguments of array types are handled, you have to start digging around on the Internet and/or in the backend code. One place where you can find a sample is the contrib/hstore/ module in the PostgreSQL source code. The contrib modules are a great reference for examples of officially supported extension modules from PostgreSQL.

Though the code there does not do exactly what we need — it works on text [] and not int [] — it is close enough to figure out what is needed, by supplying the basic structure of array handling and sample usage of some utility macros and functions.

After some digging around in the backend code and doing some web searches, it is not very hard to come up with a code for integer arrays.

So, here is the C code for a function which sums all non-null elements in its argument array. The code should be added to add_func.c:

```c
#include "utils/array.h"   // array utility functions and macros
#include "catalog/pg_type.h" // for INT4OID

PG_MODULE_MAGIC;

Datum add_int32_array(PG_FUNCTION_ARGS);

PG_FUNCTION_INFO_V1(add_int32_array);

Datum
add_int32_array(PG_FUNCTION_ARGS)
{
    ArrayType   *input_array;

    int32   sum = 0;
    bool    not_null = false;
    // variables for "deconstructed" array
```

```
Datum        *datums;
bool         *nulls;
int           count;
// for loop counter
int           i;


input_array = PG_GETARG_ARRAYTYPE_P(0);
// check that we do indeed have a one-dimensional int array
Assert(ARR_ELEMTYPE(input_array) == INT4OID);

if (ARR_NDIM(input_array) > 1)
    ereport(ERROR,
            (errcode(ERRCODE_ARRAY_SUBSCRIPT_ERROR),
             errmsg("1-dimensional array needed")));

deconstruct_array(input_array,  // one-dimensional array
                  INT4OID,       // of integers
                  4,             // size of integer in bytes
                  true,          // int4 is pass-by value
                  'i',           // alignment type is 'i'
                  &datums, &nulls, &count); // result here

for(i=0;i<count;i++) {
    // first check and ignore null elements
    if ( nulls[i] )
        continue;
    // accumulate and remember there were non-null values
    sum += DatumGetInt32(datums[i]);
    not_null = true;
}

if (not_null)
    PG_RETURN_INT32(sum);
PG_RETURN_NULL();
}
```

So, what new things are needed for handling array types as arguments? First, you need to include definitions for array utility functions:

```
#include "utils/array.h"
```

Next, you need a pointer to your array:

```
ArrayType    *input_array;
```

Notice that there is no specific array-of-integers type but just a generic `ArrayType`, which is used for any array.

To initialize the array from the first argument, you use an already familiar looking macro:

```
input_array = PG_GETARG_ARRAYTYPE_P(0);
```

Except that instead of returning an `INT32` value, it returns an array pointer `ARRAYTYPE_P`.

After getting the array pointer, we perform a couple of checks:

```
Assert(ARR_ELEMTYPE(input_array) == INT4OID);
```

We assert that the element type of returned array is indeed an integer. (There are some inconsistencies in PostgreSQL code as the plain integer type can be called either `int32` or `int4` depending on where the definition comes from. But they both mean the same thing, except that one is based on the length in bits and the other in bytes.)

The type check is an assert and not a plain runtime check, because after you have your SQL definition part of the function in place, PostgreSQL itself takes care not to call the function with any other type of array.

The second check is for checking that the argument is really a one-dimensional array (PostgreSQL arrays can have 1 to *n* dimensions and still be of the same type), as shown:

```
if (ARR_NDIM(input_array) > 1)
    ereport(ERROR,
            (errcode(ERRCODE_ARRAY_SUBSCRIPT_ERROR),
             errmsg("use only one-dimensional arrays!")));
```

If the input array has more than one dimension, we raise an error. (We will discuss PostgreSQL's error reporting in C later, in its own section.)

If you need to work on arrays of an arbitrary number of dimensions, take a look at the source code of the `unnest()` SQL function which turns any array into a set of array elements.

The code is located in the `backend/utils/adt/arrayfuncs.c` file in the C function `array_unnest(...)`.

After we have done basic sanity checking on the argument, we are ready to start processing the array. As a PostgreSQL array can be quite a complex beast, with multiple dimensions and array elements starting at an arbitrary index, it is easiest to use a ready-made utility function for most tasks. So, here we use the deconstruct_ array(...) function to extract a PostgreSQL array in three separate C variables:

```
Datum      *datums;
bool       *nulls;
int        count;
```

The datums pointer will be set to point to an array filled with actual elements. The *nulls pointer will contain a pointer to an array of Booleans, which will be true if the corresponding array element was NULL, and count will be set to the number of elements found in the array, as shown:

```
deconstruct_array(input_array,   // one-dimensional array
                  INT4OID,       // of integers
                  4,             // size of integer in bytes
                  true,          // int4 is pass-by value
                  'i',           // alignment type is 'i'
                  &datums, &nulls, &count); // result here
```

The other arguments are as follows:

- input_array: This is the pointer to the PostgreSQL array
- INT4OID: This is the type of array element
- element size: This is the in-memory size of the element type
- true: This is the element pass-by-value
- element alignment id

The type OID for int4 (=23) is already conveniently defined as INT4OID. The others, you just have to look up.

The easiest way to get the values for type, size, passbyvalue, and alignment is to query these from the database:

```
c_samples=# select oid, typlen, typbyval, typalign from pg_type
c_samples-# where typname = 'int4';
-[ RECORD 1 ]
oid      | 23
typlen   | 4
typbyval | t
typalign | i
```

After the call to `deconstruct_array(...)` the rest is easy—just iterate over the value and null arrays and accumulate the sum:

```
for(i=0;i<count;i++) {
        // first check and ignore null elements
        if ( nulls[i] )
            continue;
        // accumulate and remember there were non-null values
        sum += DatumGetInt32(datums[i]);
        not_null = true;
    }
```

The only PostgreSQL-specific thing here is the use of the `DatumGetInt32(<datum>)` macro for converting the `Datum` to `integer`. The `DatumGetInt32(<datum>)` macro performs no checking of its argument to verify that it is indeed an integer (if you remember, this is C, so no type of info is available in the data itself), but using the `DatumGet*()` macro helps us to make the compiler happy.

We are almost done here, as returning the sum (or NULL in case all elements were NULL values) is exactly the same as in our previous function.

While this is all from the C side, we still need to teach PostgreSQL about this new function. The simplest way is to declare a function which takes an `int[]` argument:

```
CREATE OR REPLACE FUNCTION add_arr(int[]) RETURNS int
     AS '$libdir/add_func', 'add_int32_array'
     LANGUAGE C STRICT;
```

It works fine for any integer array you pass it for:

```
hannu=# SELECT add_arr('{1,2,3,4,5,6,7,8,9}');
-[ RECORD 1 ]
add_arr | 45


hannu=# SELECT add_arr(ARRAY[1,2,NULL]);
-[ RECORD 1 ]
add_arr | 3


hannu=# SELECT add_arr(ARRAY[NULL::int]);
-[ RECORD 1 ]
add_arr |
```

It even detects multidimensional arrays and errors out if it is passed one:

```
hannu=# select add_arr('{{1,2,3},{4,5,6}}');
ERROR:  1-dimensional array needed
```

What if we want to use it the same way as our two-argument add(a,b) function?

Since Version 8.4 of PostgreSQL, it is possible using support for VARIADIC functions, or functions taking a variable number of arguments.

Create the function as follows:

```
CREATE OR REPLACE FUNCTION add(VARIADIC a int[]) RETURNS int
    AS '$libdir/add_func', 'add_int32_array'
    LANGUAGE C  STRICT;
```

The previous calls to add_arr() can be rewritten as:

```
hannu=# select add(1,2,3,4,5,6,7,8,9);
-[ RECORD 1 ]
add | 45


hannu=# select add(NULL);
-[ RECORD 1 ]
add |


hannu=# select add(1,2,NULL);
-[ RECORD 1 ]
add | 3
```

Notice that you can't easily get ERROR: 1-dimensional array needed as VARIADIC always constructs a one-dimensional array from the arguments.

The only thing missing is that you can't have PostgreSQL's function overloading mechanism to distinguish between add(a int[]) and add(VARIADIC a int[]) — you simply can't declare both of these at the same time because for PostgreSQL they are the same function with only the initial argument detection done differently. That is why the array version of the function was named add_arr. In case you need to call one VARIADIC function from another, there is a way. You can call the VARIADIC version with an argument of the array type by prefixing the argument with VARIADIC on the call side as hannu=# select add(ARRAY[1,2,NULL]);:

```
ERROR:  function add(integer[]) does not exist
LINE 1: select add(ARRAY[1,2,NULL]);
```

```
HINT:   No function matches the given name and argument types. You might
need to add explicit type casts.
hannu=# select add(VARIADIC ARRAY[1,2,NULL]);
-[ RECORD 1 ]
add | 3
```

You can even smuggle in a multi dimensional array:

```
hannu=# select add(VARIADIC '{{1,2,3},{4,5,6}}');
ERROR:   1-dimensional array needed
```

This calling convention also means, that even when you create VARIADIC functions, you need to check the array dimensions.

Basic guidelines for writing C code

After having written our first function, let's look at some of the basic coding guidelines for PostgreSQL backend coding.

Memory allocation

One of the places you have to be extra careful when writing C code in general is memory management. For any non-trivial C program, you have to carefully design and implement your programs, so that all your allocated memory is freed when you are done with it, or else you will "leak memory" and will probably run out of memory at some point.

As this is also a common concern for PostgreSQL, it has its own solution – memory contexts. Let's take a deeper dive into them.

Use palloc() and pfree()

Most PostgreSQL memory allocations are done using PostgreSQL's memory allocation function palloc() and not standard C malloc(). What makes palloc() special is that it allocates the memory in the current context and the whole memory is freed in one go when the context is destroyed. For example, the transaction context – which is the current context when a user-defined function is called – is destroyed and memory allocated is freed at the end of transaction. This means that most times the programmers do not need to worry about tracking palloc() allocated memory and freeing it.

It is also easy to create your own memory contexts if you have some memory allocation needs with different life spans. For example, the functions for returning a set of rows (described in further detail later in this chapter) have a structure passed to them, where one of the members is reserved for a pointer to a temporary context specifically for keeping a function-level memory context.

Zero-fill the structures

Always make sure that new structures are zero-filled, either by using `memset` after allocating them or using `palloc0()`.

PostgreSQL sometimes relies on logically equivalent data items being also the same for bit-wise comparisons. Even when you set all the items in a structure, it is possible that some alignment issues leave garbage in the areas between structure elements if any alignment padding was done by the compiler.

If you don't do this, then hash indexes and hash joins of PostgreSQL may work inefficiently or even give wrong results. The planner's constant comparisons may also be wrong if constants which are logically the same are not the same via bit-wise equality, resulting in undesirable planning results.

Include files

Most of PostgreSQL internal types are declared in `postgres.h`, and the function manager interfaces (`PG_MODULE_MAGIC`, `PG_FUNCTION_INFO_V1`, `PG_FUNCTION_ARGS`, `PG_GETARG_<type>`, `PG_RETURN_<type>`, and so on) are in `fmgr.h`. Therefore, all your C extension modules need to include at least these two files. It is a good habit to include `postgres.h` first as it gives your code the best portability by (re)defining some platform dependent constants and macros. Including `postgres.h` also includes `utils/elog.h` and `utils/palloc.h` for you.

There are other useful include files in the `utils/` subdirectory which you also may need to include like `utils/array.h` used in the last example.

Another often used include directory is `catalog/` which gives you the initial (and by convention constant) part of most system tables, so you do not need to look up things like type identifier for the `int4` data type, but can use its predefined value `INT4OID` directly.

The values in `catalog/pg_*` include files are always in sync with what gets put into the database catalogs by virtue of being the definition of the structure and contents of the system catalog tables. The `.bki` files used when the `initdb` command sets up a new empty database cluster are generated from these `.h` files by the `genbki.pl` script.

Public symbol names

It is the programmer's task to make sure that any symbol names visible in the .so files do not conflict with those already present in the PostgreSQL backend, including those used by other dynamically loaded libraries. You will have to rename your functions or variables if you get messages to this effect. Pick sufficiently distinctive names for functions to avoid any such problems. Avoid short names that might be a source of potential conflict. This may be a bigger problem if the conflicts come from a third-party library your code is using. So test early in the development if you can link all the planned libraries to your PostgreSQL extension module.

Error reporting from C functions

One thing which went unexplained in the previous sample was the error reporting part:

```
if (ARR_NDIM(input_array) > 1)
    ereport(ERROR,
            (errcode(ERRCODE_ARRAY_SUBSCRIPT_ERROR),
            errmsg("use only one-dimensional arrays!")));
```

All error reporting and other off-channel messaging in PostgreSQL is done using the ereport(<errorlevel>, rest) macro whose main purpose is to make error reporting look like a function call.

The only parameter which is processed directly by ereport() is the first argument error level, or perhaps more exactly, the severity level or log level. All the other parameters are actually function calls which independently generate and store additional error information in the system to be written to logs and/or be sent to the client. Being placed in the argument list of the ereport() makes sure that these other functions are called before the actual error is reported. This is important because in the case of an error level being ERROR, FATAL, or PANIC the system cleans up all current transaction states and anything after the ereport() call will never get a chance to run. Error states the end of the transaction.

In case of ERROR, the system is returned to a clean state and it will be ready to accept new commands.

Error level FATAL will clean up the backend and exit the current session.

PANIC is the most destructive one and it will not only end the current connection, but will also cause all other connections to be terminated. PANIC means that shared state (shared memory) is potentially corrupted and it is not safe to continue. It is used automatically for things like core dumps or other "hard" crashes.

"Error" states that are not errors

WARNING is the highest non-error level. It means that something may be wrong and needs user/administrator attention. It is a good practice to periodically scan system logs for warnings. Use this only for unexpected conditions. See the next one for things happening on a regular basis. Warnings go to client and server logs by default.

NOTICE is for things which are likely of higher interest to users, like information about creating a primary key index or sequence for serial type (though these stopped to be NOTICE in the latest version of PostgreSQL). Like the previous one, NOTICE is sent both to client and server logs by default.

INFO is for things specifically requested by client, like VACUUM / ANALYSE VERBOSE. It is always sent to the client regardless of the client_min_messages GUC setting, but is not written to a server log when using default settings.

LOG and COMMERROR are for servers, operational messages, and by default are only written to the server log. The error level LOG can also be sent to the client if client_min_messages is set appropriately, but COMMERROR never is.

There are DEBUG1 to DEBUG5 in increasing order of verbosity. They are specifically meant for reporting debugging info and are not really useful in most other cases, except perhaps for curiosity. Setting higher DEBUGx levels is not recommended in production servers, as the amount logged or reported can be really huge.

When are messages sent to the client?

While most communication from the server to the client takes place after the command completes (or even after the transaction is committed in case of LISTEN/NOTIFY), everything emitted by ereport() is sent to the client immediately, thus the mention of off-channel messaging previously. This makes ereport() a useful tool for monitoring long-running commands such as VACUUM and also a simple debugging aid to print out useful debug info.

 You can read a much more detailed description of error reporting at http://www.postgresql.org/docs/current/static/error-message-reporting.html.

Running queries and calling PostgreSQL functions

Our next stop is running SQL queries inside the database. When you want to run a query against the database, you need to use something called **Server Programming Interface (SPI)**. SPI gives programmer the ability to run SQL queries via a set of interface functions for using PostgreSQL's parser, planner, and executor.

If the SQL statement you are running via SPI fails, the control is not returned to the caller, but instead the system reverts to a clean state via internal mechanisms for ROLLBACK. It is possible to catch SQL errors by establishing a sub-transaction around your calls. It is an involved process not yet officially declared "stable" and therefore, it is not present in the documentation on C extensions. If you need it, one good place to look at would be the source code for various pluggable languages (PL/python, PL/proxy, and so on) which do it and are likely to be maintained in good order if the interface changes.

In the PL/python source, the functions to examine are in the plpython/plpy_spi.c file and are appropriately named Ply_spi_ subtransaction_[begin|commit|abort]().

The SPI functions do return non-negative values for success, either directly via a return value or in a global variable SPI_result. Errors produce a negative value or Null.

A sample C function using SPI

Here is a sample function doing an SQL query via SPI_*() functions. It is a modified version of the sample from the standard documentation (it uses Version 1 calling conventions and outputs an extra bit of information). The .c, .sql.in, and Makefile functions for this sample are available in the spi_samples/ subdirectory.

```
Datum
count_returned_rows(PG_FUNCTION_ARGS)
{
    char *command;
    int cnt;
    int ret;
    int proc;

    /* get arguments, convert command to C string */
    command = text_to_cstring(PG_GETARG_TEXT_P(0));
```

```
cnt = PG_GETARG_INT32(1);

/* open internal connection */
SPI_connect();
/* run the SQL command */
ret = SPI_exec(command, cnt);
/* save the number of rows */
proc = SPI_processed;
/* If some rows were fetched, print them via elog(INFO). */
if (ret > 0 && SPI_tuptable != NULL)
{
    TupleDesc tupdesc = SPI_tuptable->tupdesc;
    SPITupleTable *tuptable = SPI_tuptable;
    char buf[8192];
    int i, j;

    for (j = 0; j < proc; j++)
    {
        HeapTuple tuple = tuptable->vals[j];
        // construct a string representing the tuple
        for (i = 1, buf[0] = 0; i <= tupdesc->natts; i++)
            snprintf(buf + strlen (buf),
                        sizeof(buf) - strlen(buf),
                        " %s(%s::%s)%s",
                        SPI_fname(tupdesc, i),
                        SPI_getvalue(tuple, tupdesc, i),
                        SPI_gettype(tupdesc, i),
                        (i == tupdesc->natts) ? " " : " |");
        ereport(INFO, (errmsg("ROW: %s", buf)));
    }
}

SPI_finish();
pfree(command);

PG_RETURN_INT32(proc);
}
```

After getting the arguments using the PG_GETARG_* macro, the first new thing shown is opening an internal connection via SPI_connect() which sets up the internal state for the following SPI_*() function calls. The next step is to execute a full SQL statement using SPI_exec(command, cnt).

The `SPI_exec()` function is a convenient variant of `SPI_execute(...)` with the `read_only` flag set to `false`. The `read_only` flag, if set to `true` means that only a read only command can be executed. There is also a third version of the execute at once SPI function, the `SPI_execute_with_args(...)`, which prepares the query, binds the passed-in arguments, and executes in a single call.

After the query is executed, we save the `SPI_processed` value for returning the number of rows processed at the end of the function. In this sample, it is not strictly necessary, but in general you need to save any `SPI_*` global variable because they could be overwritten by the next `SPI_*(...)` call.

To show what was returned by the query and also to show how to access fields returned by SPI functions, we next print out detailed info on any tuples returned by the query via the `ereport(INFO, ...)` call. We first checked that the `SPI_exec` call was successful (`ret > 0`) and that some tuples were returned (`SPI_tuptable != NULL`), and then for each returned tuple `for(j = 0; j < proc; ...)` we looped over the fields `for(i = 1; i <= tupdesc->natts;...)` formatting the fields info into a buffer. We get the string representations of the field name, value, and data type using SPI functions `SPI_fname()`, `SPI_getvalue()`, and `SPI_gettype()` and then send the row to the user using `ereport(INFO, ...)`. If you want to return the values from the function instead, see the next sections on returning the `SETOF` values and composite types.

Finally, we freed the SPI internal state using `SPI_finish();`. One can also free the space allocated for the command variable by the `text_to_cstring(<textarg>)` function, though it is not strictly necessary, thanks to the function call context being destroyed and memory allocated in it being freed anyway at the function exit.

Visibility of data changes

The visibility rules for data changes in PostgreSQL are that each command cannot see its own changes but usually can see changes made by commands which were started before it, even when the command is started by the outer command or query.

The exception is when the query is executed with a read-only flag set, in which case the changes made by outer commands are invisible to inner or called commands.

The visibility rules are described in the documentation at `http://www.postgresql.org/docs/current/static/spi-visibility.html` and may be quite complex to understand at first, but it may help to think of a read-only `SPI_execute()` call as being command-level, similar to the transaction isolation level serializable; and a read-write call similar to the read-committed isolation level.

This is further explained at `http://www.postgresql.org/docs/current/static/spi-examples.html` in the *Sample session* section.

More info on SPI_* functions

There is a lot more information on specific `SPI_*()` functions in the official documentation.

For PostgreSQL Version 9.3 functions, `http://www.postgresql.org/docs/current/static/spi.html` is the starting point for the SPI docs.

More sample code is also available in the PostgreSQL source in regression tests at `src/test/regress/regress.c` and in the `contrib/spi/` module.

Handling records as arguments or returned values

As our next exercise, let's write a function which takes a record of three integers a, b, and c as an argument and returns a set of different records—all permutations of a, b, and c with an extra field x computed as $a * b + c$.

First, this function is written in PL/python to make it easier to understand what we are trying to do:

```
hannu=# CREATE LANGUAGE plpythonu;
CREATE LANGUAGE
hannu=# CREATE TYPE abc AS (a int, b int, c int);
CREATE TYPE
hannu=# CREATE OR REPLACE FUNCTION
hannu-#     reverse_permutations(r abc)
hannu-#   RETURNS TABLE(c int, b int, a int, x int)
hannu-# AS $$
hannu$#     a,b,c = r['a'], r['b'], r['c']
hannu$#     yield a,b,c,a*b+c
hannu$#     yield a,c,b,a*c+b
hannu$#     yield b,a,c,b*b+c
hannu$#     yield b,c,a,b*c+a
hannu$#     yield c,a,b,c*a+b
hannu$#     yield c,b,a,c*b+a
hannu$# $$ LANGUAGE plpythonu;
CREATE FUNCTION
```

```
hannu=# SELECT * FROM reverse_permutations(row(2,7,13));
-[ RECORD 1 ]
c | 2
b | 7
a | 13
x | 27
-[ RECORD 2 ]
c | 2
b | 13
a | 7
x | 33
-[ RECORD 3 ]
c | 7
b | 2
a | 13
x | 62
-[ RECORD 4 ]
c | 7
b | 13
a | 2
x | 93
-[ RECORD 5 ]
c | 13
b | 2
a | 7
x | 33
-[ RECORD 6 ]
c | 13
b | 7
a | 2
x | 93
```

There are three new things that we are going to touch in the following C implementation of a similar function:

- How to fetch an element of RECORD passed as an argument
- How to construct a tuple to return a RECORD type
- How to return SETOF (also known as TABLE) of this RECORD

So let's dive into the C code for this right away (a sample can be found in the chap9/c_records/ directory).

For better clarity, we will explain this function in two parts: first, doing a simple reverse(a,b,c) function, which returns just a single record of (c,b,a,x=c*b+a), and then expanding it to return a set of permutations such as the sample PL/pythonu function.

Returning a single tuple of a complex type

The first step in constructing a version of the reverse permutations function in C is to start with simply being able to return a single record of type abc:

```
Datum
c_reverse_tuple(PG_FUNCTION_ARGS)
{
    HeapTupleHeader th;
    int32   a,b,c;
    bool    aisnull, bisnull, cisnull;

    TupleDesc resultTupleDesc;
    Oid resultTypeId;
    Datum retvals[4];
    bool  retnulls[4];
    HeapTuple rettuple;

    // get the tuple header of 1st argument
    th = PG_GETARG_HEAPTUPLEHEADER(0);
    // get argument Datum's and convert them to int32
    a = DatumGetInt32(GetAttributeByName(th, "a", &aisnull));
    b = DatumGetInt32(GetAttributeByName(th, "b", &bisnull));
    c = DatumGetInt32(GetAttributeByName(th, "c", &cisnull));

    // debug: report the extracted field values
```

```
    ereport(INFO,
            (errmsg("arg: (a: %d,b: %d, c: %d)", a, b, c)) );

    // set up tuple descriptor for result info
    get_call_result_type(fcinfo, &resultTypeId, &resultTupleDesc);
    // check that SQL function definition is set up to return arecord
    Assert(resultTypeId == TYPEFUNC_COMPOSITE);
    // make the tuple descriptor known to postgres as valid return
type
    BlessTupleDesc(resultTupleDesc);

    retvals[0] = Int32GetDatum(c);
    retvals[1] = Int32GetDatum(b);
    retvals[2] = Int32GetDatum(a);
    retvals[3] = Int32GetDatum(retvals[0]*retvals[1]+retvals[2]);

    retnulls[0] = aisnull;
    retnulls[1] = bisnull;
    retnulls[2] = cisnull;
    retnulls[3] = aisnull || bisnull || cisnull;

    rettuple = heap_form_tuple( resultTupleDesc, retvals, retnulls );

    PG_RETURN_DATUM( HeapTupleGetDatum( rettuple ) );
}
```

Extracting fields from an argument tuple

Getting the fields of an argument tuple is easy. First, you fetch the `HeapTupleHeader` file of the argument into the `th` variable using the `PG_GETARG_HEAPTUPLEHEADER(0)` macro, and then for each field you get the `Datum` (a generic type which can hold any field value in PostgreSQL) by the field name using the `GetAttributeByName()` function and then assign its value to a local variable after converting it to `int32` via `DatumGetInt32()`:

```
a = DatumGetInt32(GetAttributeByName(th, "a", &aisnull));
```

The third argument to `GetAttributeByName(...)` is an address of a `bool` which is set to `true` if the field was NULL.

There is also a companion function `GetAttributeByNum()` if you prefer to get the attributes by their numbers instead of names.

Constructing a return tuple

Constructing the return tuple(s) is almost as easy.

First, you get the called functions return type descriptor using the `get_call_result_type()` function:

```
get_call_result_type(fcinfo, &resultTypeId, &resultTupleDesc);
```

The first argument to this function is the `FunctionCallInfo` structure `fcinfo` which is used when calling the function you are currently writing (hidden behind the `PG_FUNCTION_ARGS` macro in the C function declaration). The other two arguments are addresses of the return type `Oid` and `TupleDesc` to receive the return tuple descriptor in case the function returns a record type.

Next, there is a safety assert for checking that the return type is really a record (or composite) type:

```
Assert(resultTypeId == TYPEFUNC_COMPOSITE);
```

This is to guard against errors in the CREATE FUNCTION declaration in SQL which tells PostgreSQL about this new function.

And there still remains one thing before we construct the tuple:

```
BlessTupleDesc(resultTupleDesc);
```

The purpose of `BlessTupleDesc()` is to fill in the missing parts of the structure, which are not needed for internal operations on the tuple, but are essential when the tuple is returned from the function.

So we are done with the tuple descriptor and finally, we can construct the tuple or record it to be returned.

The tuple is constructed using the `heap_form_tuple( resultTupleDesc, retvals, retnulls );` function which uses `TupleDesc` we just prepared. It also needs an array of `Datum` to be used as values in the return tuple, and an array of `bool`, which is used to determine if any field should be set to NULL instead of their corresponding `Datum` value. As all our fields are of type `int32`, their values in `retvals` are set using `Int32GetDatum(<localvar>)`. The array `retnull` is a simple array of `bool` and needs no special tricks to set its values.

Finally we return the constructed tuple:

```
PG_RETURN_DATUM( HeapTupleGetDatum( rettuple ) );
```

Here, we first construct `Datum` from the tuple we just constructed using `HeapTupleGetDatum()` and then use the `PG_RETURN_DATUM` macro.

Interlude – what is Datum?

In this chapter, we use something called `Datum` in several places. This calls for a bit of explanation about what a Datum is.

In short, a `Datum` is any data item the PostgreSQL processes and passes around. `Datum` itself does not contain any type information or info on whether the field is actually NULL. It is just a pointer to a memory. You always have to find out (or know beforehand) the type of any `Datum` you use and also how to find out if your data may be NULL instead of any real value.

In the preceding example, `GetAttributeByName(th, "b", &bisnull)` returns a `Datum`, and it can return something even when the field in the tuple is NULL, so always check for null-ness first. Also, the returned `Datum` itself cannot be used for much unless we convert it to some real type, as done in the next step using `DatumGetInt32()`, which simply converts the vague `Datum` to a real `int32` value basically doing a cast from a memory location of an undefined type to `int32`.

The definition of `Datum` in `postgresql.h` is `typedef Datum *DatumPtr;` that is anything pointed to by a `DatumPtr`. Even though `DatumPtr` is defined as `typedef uintptr_t Datum;` it may be easier to think of it as a (slightly restricted) `void *`.

Once more, any real substance is added to a `Datum` by converting it to a real type.

You can also go the other way, turning almost anything into a `Datum` as seen at the end of the function:

```
HeapTupleGetDatum( rettuple )
```

Again, for anything else in PostgreSQL to make use of such `Datum`, the type information must be available somewhere else, in our case the return type definitions of the function.

Returning a set of records

Next, we will modify our function to not just return a single record of reordered fields from an argument record, but to return all possible orderings. We will still add one extra field x as an example of how you can use the values you extracted from the argument.

For set-returning functions, PostgreSQL has a special calling mechanism where PostgreSQL's executor machinery will keep calling the function over and over again until it reports back that it does not have any more values to return. This return-and-continue behavior is very similar to how the `yield` keyword works in Python or JavaScript.

All calls to the set returning function get an argument a persistent structure maintained outside the function and made available to the function via macros: `SRF_FIRSTCALL_INIT()` for the first call and `SRF_PERCALL_SETUP()` for subsequent calls.

To further clarify the example, we provide a constant array of possible orderings to be used when permuting the values.

Also, we read argument fields `a`, `b`, and `c` only once at the beginning of the function and save the extracted values in a structure `c_reverse_tuple_args`, which we allocate and initialize at the first call. For the structure to survive through all calls, we allocate this structure in a special *memory context* which is maintained in the `funcctx -> multi_call_memory_ctx` and store the pointer to this structure in `funcctx -> user_fctx`. We also make use of `funcctx` fields: `call_cntr` and `max_calls`.

In the same code section run once at the first call, we also prepare the descriptor structure needed for returning the tuples. To do so, we fetch the return tuple descriptor by passing the address we get in `funcctx->tuple_desc` to the function `get_call_result_type(...)`, and we complete the preparation by calling `BlessTuple(...)` on it to fill in the missing bits needed for using it for returning values.

At the end of this section, we restore the memory context. While you usually do not need to `pfree()` the things you have `palloc()` allocated, you should always remember to restore the memory context when you are done using any context you have switched to, or else you risk messing up PostgreSQL in a way that can be hard to debug later!

The rest is something that gets done at each call, including the first one.

We start by checking that there is still something to do by comparing the current call to the max calls parameter. This is by no means the only way to determine if we have returned all values, but it is indeed the simplest way if you know ahead how many rows you are going to return. If there are no more rows to return, we signal this back using `SRF_RETURN_DONE()`.

The rest is very similar to what the previous single-tuple function did. We compute the `retvals` and `retnulls` arrays using the index permutations array `ips` and then construct a tuple to return using `heap_form_tuple(funcctx->tuple_desc, retvals, retnulls);`.

Finally, we return the tuple using macro `SRF_RETURN_NEXT(...)`, converting the tuple to `Datum`, as this is what the macro expects.

One more thing to note, all current versions of PostgreSQL will always keep calling your function until it returns `SRF_RETURN_DONE()`. There is currently no way to do an "early exit" from the callers side. This means that if your function returns 1 million rows and you do:

```
SELECT * FROM mymillionrowfunction() LIMIT 3;
```

The function will be called 1 million times internally, and all the results will be cached, and only after this, the first three rows will be returned and the remaining 9,99,997 rows are discarded. This is not a fundamental limitation, but just an implementation detail which is likely to change in some future version of PostgreSQL. Don't hold your breath though, this will only happen if somebody finds this valuable enough to implement.

The source with modifications described previously is as follows:

```
struct c_reverse_tuple_args {
    int32    argvals[3];
    bool     argnulls[3];
    bool     anyargnull;
};


Datum
c_permutations_x(PG_FUNCTION_ARGS)
{
    FuncCallContext      *funcctx;

    const char  *argnames[3] = {"a","b","c"};
    // 6 possible index permutations for 0,1,2
    const int    ips[6][3] = {{0,1,2},{0,2,1},
                              {1,0,2},{1,2,0},
                              {2,0,1},{2,1,0}};
    int i, call_nr;

    struct c_reverse_tuple_args* args;

    if(SRF_IS_FIRSTCALL())
    {
        HeapTupleHeader th = PG_GETARG_HEAPTUPLEHEADER(0);
        MemoryContext    oldcontext;
        /* create a function context for cross-call persistence */
        funcctx = SRF_FIRSTCALL_INIT();
```

```
        /* switch to memory context appropriate for multiple function
calls */
        oldcontext = MemoryContextSwitchTo(
                    funcctx->multi_call_memory_ctx
                    );
        /* allocate and zero-fill struct for persisting
           extracted arguments*/
        args = palloc0(sizeof(struct c_reverse_tuple_args));
        args->anyargnull = false;
        funcctx->user_fctx = args;
        /* total number of tuples to be returned */
        funcctx->max_calls = 6;
        // there are 6 permutations of 3 elements
        // extract argument values and NULL-ness
        for(i=0;i<3;i++){
            args->argvals[i] = DatumGetInt32(GetAttributeByName
               (th, argnames[i], &(args->argnulls[i])));
            if (args->argnulls[i])
                args->anyargnull = true;
        }
        // set up tuple for result info
        if (get_call_result_type(fcinfo, NULL, &funcctx->tuple_desc)
            != TYPEFUNC_COMPOSITE)
            ereport(ERROR,
                (errcode(ERRCODE_FEATURE_NOT_SUPPORTED),
                errmsg("function returning record called in context "
                        "that cannot accept type record")));
        BlessTupleDesc(funcctx->tuple_desc);
        // restore memory context
        MemoryContextSwitchTo(oldcontext);
    }

    funcctx = SRF_PERCALL_SETUP();
    args = funcctx->user_fctx;
    call_nr = funcctx->call_cntr;

    if (call_nr < funcctx->max_calls) {
        HeapTuple    rettuple;
        Datum        retvals[4];
```

```
        bool retnulls[4];

        for(i=0;i<3;i++){
            retvals[i] = Int32GetDatum(args->argvals[ips[call_nr][i]]);
            retnulls[i] = args->argnulls[ips[call_nr][i]];
        }
        retvals[3] = Int32GetDatum(args->argvals[ips[call_nr][0]]
                                 * args->argvals[ips[call_nr][1]]
                                 + args->argvals[ips[call_nr][2]]);
        retnulls[3] = args->anyargnull;

        rettuple = heap_form_tuple(funcctx->tuple_desc, retvals,
            retnulls);

        SRF_RETURN_NEXT(funcctx, HeapTupleGetDatum( rettuple ));
    }
    else    /* do when there is no more left */
    {
        SRF_RETURN_DONE(funcctx);
    }

}
```

Fast capturing of database changes

Some obvious things to code in C are logging or auditing triggers, which get called at each INSERT, UPDATE, or DELETE to a table. We have not set aside enough space in this book to explain everything needed for C triggers, but interested readers can look up the source code for the skytools package where you can find more than one way to write triggers in C.

The highly optimized C source for the two main triggers: logtriga and logutriga, includes everything you need to capture these changes to a table and also to detect table structure changes while the code is running.

The latest source code for skytools can be found at http://pgfoundry.org/projects/skytools.

Doing something at commit/rollback

As of this writing, there is no possibility to define a trigger function which is executed ON COMMIT or ON ROLLBACK. However, if you really need to have some code executed on these database events, you have a possibility to register a C-language function to be called on these events. Unfortunately, this registration cannot be done in a permanent way like triggers, but the registration function has to be called each time a new connection starts:

```
RegisterXactCallback(my_xact_callback, NULL);
```

Use grep -r RegisterXactCallback in the contrib/ directory of PostgreSQL's source code to find files with examples of actual callback functions.

Synchronizing between backends

All the preceding functions are designed to run in a single process/backend as if the other PostgreSQL processes did not exist.

But what if you want to log something to a single file from multiple backends?

Seems easy — just open the file and write what you want. Unfortunately, it is not that easy if you want to do it from multiple parallel processes and you do not overwrite or mix up the data with what other processes write.

To have more control over the writing order between backends, you need to have some kind of inter-process synchronization, and the easiest way to do this in PostgreSQL is to use *shared memory* and **light-weight locks** (**LWLocks**).

To allocate its own shared memory segment your .so file needs to be preloaded, that is, it should be one of the preloaded libraries given in the postgresql.conf variable shared_preload_libraries.

In the _PG_init() function of your module, you ask for the address of a name shared memory segment. If you are the first one asking for the segment, you are also responsible for initializing the shared structures; including, creating, and storing any LWLocks you wish to use in your module.

Writing functions in C++

It is a bad idea to mix PostgreSQL with C++ for a number of reasons. It is better to wrap your C++ code into C code behind extern C functions. This can be a problem if you heavily use templates and libraries like boost.

For more discussion on use of C++ read the PostgreSQL documentation here
`http://www.postgresql.org/docs/current/static/xfunc-c.html#EXTEND-CPP`.

Additional resources for C

In this chapter, we were able to only give you a very basic introduction to what is possible in C. Here is some advice on how to get more information.

First, there is of course the chapter *C-Language Functions* in the PostgreSQL manual. This can be found online at `http://www.postgresql.org/docs/current/static/xfunc-c.html` and as with most of the online PostgreSQL manuals, you usually can get to older versions if they exist.

The next one, surprisingly, is the PostgreSQL source code itself. However, you will usually not get very far by just opening the files or using `grep` to find what you need. If you are good with using `ctags` (`http://en.wikipedia.org/wiki/Ctags`) or another similar tool, it is definitely recommended.

Also, if you are new to these types of large-code exploration systems, then a really good resource for finding and examining PostgreSQL internals is maintained at `http://doxygen.postgresql.org/`. This points to the latest `git` master, so it may not be accurate for your version of PostgreSQL, but it is usually good enough and at least provides a nice starting point for digging around in the source code of your version.

Quite often, you will find something to base (parts of) your C source on in the `contrib/` directory in the source code. To get an idea of what lies there, read through the *Appendix F, Additional Supplied Modules* (`http://www.postgresql.org/docs/current/static/contrib.html`). It's entirely possible that somebody has already written what you need. There are many more modules in `http://pgfoundry.org` for you to examine and choose from. A word of warning though, while modules in `contrib/` are checked at least by one or two competent PostgreSQL core programmers, the things at `pgfoundry` can be of wildly varying quality. The top active projects are really good; however, so the main things to look at when determining if you can use them as a learning source are how active the project is and when was it last updated.

There is also a set of GUC parameters specifically for development and debugging which are usually left out of the sample `postgresql.conf` file. The descriptions and an explanation are available at `http://www.postgresql.org/docs/current/static/runtime-config-developer.html`.

Summary

As C is the language that PostgreSQL itself is written in, it is very hard to draw a distinction on what is an extension function using a defined API and what is hacking PostgreSQL itself.

Some of the topics that we did not touch at all were:

- Creating new installable types from scratch—see `contrib/hstore/` for a full implementation of a new type.

- Creating new index methods—download an older version of PostgreSQL to see how full text indexing support was provided as an add-on.

- Implementing a new `PL/*` language—search for `pl/lolcode` for a language, the sole purpose of which is to demonstrate how a PostgreSQL's `PL/*` language should be written (see `http://pgfoundry.org/projects/pllolcode/`). You may also want to check out the source code for PL/Proxy for a clean and well-maintained PL language. (The usage of PL/Proxy is described in the next chapter.)

Hopefully, this chapter gave you enough info to at least start writing PostgreSQL extension functions in C.

If you need more than what is available here or in the official PostgreSQL documentation, then remember that lots of PostgreSQL's backend developer documentation—often including answers to the questions How? and Why?—is in the source files. A lot of that can also be relevant to C extensions.

So remember—Use The Source, Luke!

In the next chapter we will discuss scaling the database using PL/Proxy.

10
Scaling Your Database with PL/Proxy

If you have followed the advice in the previous chapters for doing all your database access through functions, you are in a great position to scale your database by *horizontally* distributing the data over multiple servers, also known as **database sharding**. Horizontal distribution means that you keep just a portion of a table on each *partition* of the database, and that you have a method to automatically access the right database when accessing the data.

We will gently introduce the concepts leading to the PL/Proxy partitioning language, and then delve into the syntax and proper usage of the language itself. Let's start with writing a scalable application from scratch. First, we will write it to be as highly performing as possible on one server. Then, we will scale it by spreading it out on several servers. We will first get this implemented in PL/Pythonu and then in PL/Proxy.

 This approach is worth taking, only if you have (plans for) a really large database. For most databases, one server plus one or perhaps two hot standby servers should be more than enough.

Creating a simple single-server chat

Perhaps, the simplest application needing this kind of scalability is a messaging (or chat) application; so, let's write one.

The initial single-server implementation has the following specifications:

- There should be users and messages
- Each user has a username, password, e-mail, list of friends, and a flag to indicate if the user wants to get messages from only their friends, or from everybody
- For users, there are methods for:
    - Registering new users
    - Updating the list of friends
    - Logging in
- Each message has a sender, receiver, message body, and timestamps for sending and reading the message
- For messages, there are methods for:
    - Sending a message
    - Retrieving new messages

A minimalistic system implementing this, could look like the following:

Here, a web page opens a WebSocket (ws://) to a HUB (a message concentrator) which in turn talks to a database. On each new connection, the HUB logs in and on successful login opens a WebSocket connection to the web page. It then sends all new messages that have accumulated for the logged-in user since the last time they retrieved their messages. After that, the HUB waits for new messages and pushes them to the web page as they arrive.

The database part has two tables, the user_info table and message table. The following code will create the user_info table:

```
CREATE TABLE user_info (
    username text primary key,
    pwdhash text not null,   -- base64 encoded md5 hash of password
    email text,
    friend_list text[], -- list of buddies usernames
    friends_only boolean not null default false
);
```

The following code will create the message table:

```
CREATE TABLE message (
    from_user text not null references user_info(username),
    sent_at timestamp not null default current_timestamp,
    to_user text not null references user_info(username),
```

```
    read_at timestamp, -- when was this retrieved by to_user
    msg_body text not null,
    delivery_status text not null default 'outgoing' --  ('sent',
"failed")
    );
```

As this is still an *all-in-one database* implementation, the database functions corresponding to application methods are very simple.

The following code will create a user:

```
CREATE or REPLACE FUNCTION new_user(
    IN i_username text, IN i_pwdhash text, IN i_email text,
    OUT status int, OUT message text )
AS $$
BEGIN
    INSERT INTO user_info( username, pwdhash, email)
                VALUES ( i_username, i_pwdhash, i_email);
    status = 200;
    message = 'OK';
EXCEPTION WHEN unique_violation THEN
    status = 500;
    message = 'USER EXISTS';
END;
$$ LANGUAGE plpgsql SECURITY DEFINER;
```

This method just fails when the user is already defined. A more *real-life* function would propose a list of available usernames in this case.

The following method for login returns status 500 for failure and 200 or 201 for success. If the method returns 201, it means that there are unread messages for this user:

```
CREATE OR REPLACE FUNCTION login(
    IN i_username text, IN i_pwdhash text,
    OUT status int, OUT message text )
AS $$
BEGIN
    PERFORM 1 FROM user_info
    WHERE ( username, pwdhash) = ( i_username, i_pwdhash);
    IF NOT FOUND THEN
        status = 500;
        message = 'NOT FOUND';
      return;
    END IF;
    PERFORM 1 FROM  message
    WHERE  to_user =  i_username
      AND  read_at IS NULL;
```

```
IF FOUND THEN
    status = 201;
    message = 'OK. NEW MESSAGES';
ELSE
    status = 200;
    message = 'OK. NO MESSAGES';
END IF;
END;
$$ LANGUAGE plpgsql SECURITY DEFINER;
```

The following are the other two user methods for changing the friends, list and telling the system whether they want to receive mails that are only from friends. Error checking is omitted here for brevity:

```
CREATE or REPLACE FUNCTION set_friends_list(
    IN i_username text, IN i_friends_list text[],
    OUT status int, OUT message text )
AS $$
BEGIN
    UPDATE user_info
       SET  friend_list =  i_friends_list
    WHERE  username =  i_username;
    status = 200;
    message = 'OK';
END;
$$ LANGUAGE plpgsql SECURITY DEFINER;


CREATE or REPLACE FUNCTION msg_from_friends_only(
    IN i_username text, IN i_friends_only boolean,
     OUT status int, OUT message text )
AS $$
BEGIN
    UPDATE user_info SET  friends_only =   i_friends_only
    WHERE  username =  i_username;
    status = 200;
    message = 'OK';
END;
$$ LANGUAGE plpgsql SECURITY DEFINER;
```

The send_message() function is used for messaging, which simply sends messages, as shown in the following code:

```
CREATE or REPLACE FUNCTION send_message(
    IN i_from_user text, IN i_to_user text, IN i_message text,
    OUT status int, OUT message text )
```

```
AS $$
BEGIN
    PERFORM 1 FROM  user_info
    WHERE  username = i_to_user
      AND (NOT friends_only OR friend_list @> ARRAY[i_from_user]);
    IF NOT FOUND THEN
        status = 400;
        message = 'SENDING FAILED';
        RETURN;
    END IF;
    INSERT INTO message(from_user, to_user, msg_body,
      delivery_status)
    VALUES (i_from_user, i_to_user, i_message, 'sent');
    status = 200;
    message = 'OK';
EXCEPTION
    WHEN foreign_key_violation THEN
        status = 500;
        message = 'FAILED';
END;
$$ LANGUAGE plpgsql SECURITY DEFINER;
```

The function used for retrieving messages, is as follows:

```
CREATE or REPLACE FUNCTION get_new_messages(
    IN i_username text,
    OUT o_status int, OUT o_message_text text,
    OUT o_from_user text, OUT o_sent_at timestamp)
RETURNS SETOF RECORD
AS $$
BEGIN
    FOR o_status,  o_message_text, o_from_user,  o_sent_at IN
        UPDATE message
        SET read_at = CURRENT_TIMESTAMP,
            delivery_status = 'read'
        WHERE to_user =  i_username AND read_at IS NULL
        RETURNING 200, msg_body, from_user , sent_at
    LOOP
        RETURN NEXT;
    END LOOP;
END;
$$ LANGUAGE plpgsql SECURITY DEFINER;
```

We are almost done with the database part of our simple server. To finish it up, we need to do some initial performance tuning, and for that, we need some data in our tables. The easiest way is to use the `generate_series()` function to generate a list of numbers, which we will use as usernames. For our initial testing, names like 7 or 42 are as good as Bob, Mary, or Jill:

```
hannu=# SELECT new_user(generate_series::text, 'pwd', generate_
series::text || '@pg.org')
hannu-#   FROM generate_series(1,100000);

hannu=# WITH ns(n,len) AS (
hannu(#         SELECT *,(random() * 10)::int FROM
     generate_series(1,100000))
hannu-#             SELECT set_friends_list(ns.n::text,
hannu(#                 ARRAY( (SELECT (random() * 100000)::int
hannu(#                     FROM generate_series(1,len))
     )::text[]
hannu(# )
hannu-# FROM ns ;
```

Now, we have 100,000 users with 0 to 10 friends each, for a total of 501,900 friends.

```
hannu=# SELECT count(*) FROM (SELECT username,unnest(friend_list)
       FROM user_info) a;
-[ RECORD 1 ]-
count | 501900
```

Now, let's send each of the friends a message:

```
hannu=# SELECT send_message(username,unnest(friend_list),'hello
       friend!') FROM user_info;
```

Look how fast we can retrieve the messages:

```
hannu=# SELECT get_new_messages('50000');
                    get_new_messages
----------------------------------------------------------------
 (200,"hello friend!",49992,"2012-01-09 02:23:28.470979")
 (200,"hello friend!",49994,"2012-01-09 02:23:28.470979")
 (200,"hello friend!",49995,"2012-01-09 02:23:28.470979")
 (200,"hello friend!",49996,"2012-01-09 02:23:28.470979")
 (200,"hello friend!",49997,"2012-01-09 02:23:28.470979")
 (200,"hello friend!",49999,"2012-01-09 02:23:28.470979")
 (200,"hello friend!",50000,"2012-01-09 02:23:28.470979")
(7 rows)

Time: 763.513 ms
```

Spending almost a second getting seven messages seems slow, so we need to optimize a bit.

The first thing to do is to add indexes for retrieving the messages:

```
hannu=# CREATE INDEX message_from_user_ndx ON  message(from_user);
CREATE INDEX
Time: 4341.890 ms
hannu=# CREATE INDEX message_to_user_ndx ON  message(to_user);
CREATE INDEX
Time: 4340.841 ms
```

And check if this helped to solve our problem:

```
hannu=# SELECT get_new_messages('52000');
                      get_new_messages
-------------------------------------------------------------
 (200,"hello friend!",51993,"2012-01-09 02:23:28.470979")
 (200,"hello friend!",51994,"2012-01-09 02:23:28.470979")
 (200,"hello friend!",51996,"2012-01-09 02:23:28.470979")
 (200,"hello friend!",51997,"2012-01-09 02:23:28.470979")
 (200,"hello friend!",51998,"2012-01-09 02:23:28.470979")
 (200,"hello friend!",51999,"2012-01-09 02:23:28.470979")
 (200,"hello friend!",52000,"2012-01-09 02:23:28.470979")
(7 rows)
Time: 2.949 ms
```

Much better—indexed lookups are 300 times faster than sequential scans, and this difference will grow as tables get bigger!

As we are updating the messages and setting their status to read, it is also a good idea to set `fillfactor` to something less than 100 percent and this is shown in the following example:

> Fillfactor tells PostgreSQL not to fill up database pages completely, but to leave some space for HOT updates. When PostgreSQL updates a row, it only marks the old row for deletion and adds a new row to the data file. If the row that is updated only changes unindexed fields, and there is enough room in the page to store a second copy, a HOT update will be done instead. In this case, the copy can be found using original index pointers to the first copy, and no expensive index updates are done while updating. You can read more about the fillfactor at http://www.postgresql.org/docs/current/static/sql-createtable.html

```
hannu=# ALTER TABLE message SET (fillfactor = 90);
ALTER TABLE
Time: 75.729 ms
hannu=# CLUSTER message_from_user_ndx ON message;
CLUSTER
Time: 9797.639 ms

hannu=# SELECT get_new_messages('55022');
                      get_new_messages
-----------------------------------------------------------
 (200,"hello friend!",55014,"2012-01-09 02:23:28.470979")
 (200,"hello friend!",55016,"2012-01-09 02:23:28.470979")
 (200,"hello friend!",55017,"2012-01-09 02:23:28.470979")
 (200,"hello friend!",55019,"2012-01-09 02:23:28.470979")
 (200,"hello friend!",55020,"2012-01-09 02:23:28.470979")
 (200,"hello friend!",55021,"2012-01-09 02:23:28.470979")
 (200,"hello friend!",55022,"2012-01-09 02:23:28.470979")
(7 rows)

Time: 1.895 ms
```

Still better! The `fillfactor` made the `get_new_messages()` function another 20 to 30 percent faster, thanks to enabling the faster HOT updates!

Dealing with success – splitting tables over multiple databases

Now, let's roll forward a little in time and assume you have been successful enough to attract tens of thousands of users and your single database starts creaking under the load.

My general rule of thumb, is to start planning for a bigger machine, or splitting the database, when you are over 80 percent utilization at least for a few hours a day. It's good to have a plan earlier, but now you have to start doing something about really carrying out the plan.

What expansion plans work and when?

There are a couple of popular ways to grow database-backed systems. Depending on your use case, not all ways will work.

Moving to a bigger server

If you suspect that you are near your top load for the service or product, you can simply move to a more powerful server. This may not be the best long-time scaling solution if you are still in the middle, or even in the beginning of your growth. You will run out of *bigger* machines to buy long before you are done. Servers also become disproportionately more expensive as the size increases, and you will be left with at least one *different*, and thus not easily replaceable, server once you implement a proper scaling solution.

On the other hand, this will work for some time and is often the easiest way to get some headroom while implementing real scaling solutions.

Master-slave replication – moving reads to slave

Master-slave replication, either trigger-based or WAL-based, works reasonably well in cases where the large majority of the database accesses are reads. Some things that fall under this case, are website content managers, blogs, and other publishing systems.

As our chat system has more or less a 1:1 ratio of writes and reads, moving reads to a separate server will buy us nothing. The replication itself is more expensive than the possible win from reading from a second server.

Multimaster replication

Multi master replication is even worse than master-slave(s) when the problem is scaling a write-heavy workload. It has all the problems of master-slave, plus it introduces extra load via cross-partition locking or conflict resolution requirements, which further slows down the whole cluster.

Data partitioning across multiple servers

The obvious solution to scaling writes is to split them between several servers. Ideally you could have, for example, four servers and each of them getting exactly one fourth of the load.

In this case, each server would hold a quarter of users and messages, and serve a quarter of all requests.

To make the change transparent for database clients, we introduce a layer of proxy databases. These proxy databases can either reside on the same hosts as the partition databases or be on their own host. The role of the proxy databases is to pretend to be the database for clients, but in fact delegate the real work to partitions by calling the right function in the right partition database.

This client transparency is not terribly important if you have just one application accessing the database. If you did, you could then do the splitting in the client application. It becomes very handy as your system grows to have several applications, perhaps using many different platforms and frameworks on the client side.

Having a separate layer of proxy databases enables easy management of data splitting, so that the client applications don't need to know anything about the underlying data architecture. They just call the functions they need and that's all they need to know. In fact, you can switch out the whole database structure without the clients ever noticing anything, except the better performance from the new architecture.

More on how exactly the proxy works later. For now, let us tackle splitting the data.

Splitting the data

If we split the data, we need a simple and efficient way to determine which server stores each data row. If the data had an integer primary key, you could just go round-robin, store the first row on the first server, the second row on the second, and so on. This would give you a fairly even distribution, even when rows with certain IDs are missing.

The partitioning function for selecting between four servers would be simply:

```
partition_nr = id & 3
```

The partitioning mask 3 (binary 11) is for the first two bits. For eight partitions, you would use 7 (binary 111), and for 64 servers it would be 63 (00111111). It is not as easy with things like usernames, where putting all names starting with an A first, B second, and so on, does not produce an even distribution.

Turning the username into a fairly evenly distributed integer via the hash function solves this problem and can be used directly to select the partition.

```
partition_nr = hashtext(username) & 3
```

This would distribute the users in the following manner:

```
hannu=# SELECT username, hashtext(username) & 3 as partition_nr FROM
user_info;
-[ RECORD 1 ]+--------
username     | bob
partition_nr | 1
-[ RECORD 2 ]+--------
username     | jane
partition_nr | 2
-[ RECORD 3 ]+--------
```

```
username     | tom
partition_nr | 1
-[ RECORD 4 ]+--------
username     | mary
partition_nr | 3
-[ RECORD 5 ]+--------
username     | jill
partition_nr | 2
-[ RECORD 6 ]+--------
username     | abigail
partition_nr | 3
-[ RECORD 7 ]+--------
username     | ted
partition_nr | 3
-[ RECORD 8 ]+--------
username     | alfonso
partition_nr | 0
```

So, partition 0 gets user `alfonso`, partition 1 `bob` and `tom`, partition 2 `jane` and `jill`, and partition 3 gets `mary`, `abigail`, and `ted`. The distribution is not exactly one fourth to each partition; but as the number of partitions increase, it will be pretty close where this actually matters.

If we had no PL/Proxy language, we could write the partitioning functions in the most untrusted PL languages. For example, a simple login proxy function written in PL/Pythonu looks like this:

```
CREATE OR REPLACE FUNCTION pylogin(
    IN i_username text, IN i_pwdhash text,
    OUT status int, OUT message text )
AS $$
    import psycopg2
    partitions = [
        'dbname=chap10p0 port=5433',
        'dbname=chap10p1 port=5433',
        'dbname=chap10p2 port=5433',
        'dbname=chap10p3 port=5433',
    ]
    partition_nr = hash(i_username) & 3
    con = psycopg2.connect(partitions[partition_nr])
    cur = con.cursor()
    cur.execute('select * from login(%s,%s)', ( i_username,
    i_pwdhash))
    status, message = cur.fetchone()
```

```
        return (status, message)
$$ LANGUAGE plpythonu SECURITY DEFINER;
```

Here, we defined a set of four partition databases, given by their connect strings and stored as a list in variable `partitions`.

When executing the function, we first evaluate the hash function on the username argument (`hash(i_username)`) and extract two bits from it (`& 3`) to get an index into the partitions' list (the partition number) for executing each call.

Then, we open a connection to a partition database using the connect string selected by the partition number (`con=psycopg2.connect(partitions[partition_nr])`).

Finally, we execute a remote query in the partition database and return the results of this to the caller of this proxy function.

This works reasonably well, if implemented like this, but it also has at least two places where it is suboptimal:

- First, it opens a new database connection each time the function is called, which kills performance
- Second, it is a maintenance nightmare if you hard-wire the partition information in full, in all functions

The performance problem can be solved by caching the open connections, and the maintenance problem can be solved by having a single function returning the partition information. However, even when we do these changes and stay with PL/Pythonu for partitioning, we will still be doing a lot of copy and paste programming in each of our proxy functions.

Once we had reached the preceding conclusions, when growing our database systems at Skype, the next logical step was quite obvious. We needed a special partitioning language, which would do just this one thing – calling remote SQL functions, and then make it as fast as possible. And thus, the PL/Proxy database partitioning language was born.

PL/Proxy – the partitioning language

The rest of this chapter is devoted to the PL/Proxy language. First, we will install it. Then, we will look at its syntax and ways to configure the partitions for its use. Finally, we will discuss how to do the actual data migration from a single database to a partitioned one and then look at several usage examples.

Installing PL/Proxy

If you are on Debian, Ubuntu, or a Red Hat variant, installing the language is easy.

First, you have to install the required packages on your operating system:

```
sudo apt-get install postgresql-9.4-plproxy
```

Or:

```
sudo yum install plproxy94
```

If you need to install PL/Proxy from the source, you can download it from `http://pgfoundry.org/projects/plprox`, extract the sources in the `contrib` folder of your PostgreSQL source tree and run `make` and `make install`.

To install PL/Proxy you should run the `plproxy.sql` file, which is part of the source code or the package you installed.

The PL/Proxy language syntax

The PL/Proxy language itself is very simple. The purpose of a PL/Proxy function is to hand off the processing to another server, so that the language only needs six statements:

- `CONNECT` or `CLUSTER` and `RUN ON` for selecting the target database partition
- `SELECT` and `TARGET` for specifying the query to run
- `SPLIT` for splitting an `ARRAY` argument between several sub arrays for running on multiple partitions

CONNECT, CLUSTER, and RUN ON

The first group of statements handles the remote connectivity to the partitions. The help determines which database to run the query on. You specify the exact partition to run the query using `CONNECT`:

```
CONNECT 'connect string' ;
```

Here, `connect string` determines the database to run. `connect string` is the standard PostgreSQL connect string you would use to connect to the database from a client application, for example: `dbname=p0 port=5433 username=test host=localhost`.

Or, you can specify a name using CLUSTER:

```
CLUSTER 'usercluster';
```

Finally, you can specify a partition number using RUN ON:

```
RUN ON part_func(arg[, ...]) ;
```

part_func() can be any existing or user-defined PostgreSQL function returning an integer. PL/Proxy calls that function with the given arguments and then uses N lower bits from the result to select a connection to a cluster partition.

There are two more versions of the RUN ON statement:

```
RUN ON ANY;
```

This means that the function can be executed on any partition in a cluster. This can be used when all the required data for a function is present on all partitions.

The other version is:

```
RUN ON ALL;
```

This runs the statement on all partitions in parallel and then returns a concatenation of results from the partitions. This has at least three main uses:

- For cases when you don't know where the required data row is, like when getting data using non-partition keys. For example, getting a user by its e-mail when the table is partitioned by username.

- Running aggregate functions over larger subsets of data, say counting all users. For example, getting all the users who have a certain user in their friends' lists.

- Manipulating data that needs to be the same on all partitions. For example, when you have a price list that other functions are using, then one simple way to manage this price list is using a RUN ON ALL function.

SELECT and TARGET

The default behavior of a PL/Proxy function, if no SELECT or TARGET is present, is to call the function with the exact same signature as itself in the remote partition.

Suppose we have the function:

```
CREATE OR REPLACE FUNCTION login(
    IN i_username text, IN i_pwdhash text,
    OUT status int, OUT message text )
AS $$
```

```
      CONNECT 'dbname=chap10 host=10.10.10.1';
$$ LANGUAGE plproxy SECURITY DEFINER;
```

If it is defined in schema public, the following call `select * from login('bob', 'secret')` connects to the database `chap10` on host 10.10.10.1 and runs the following SQL statement there:

```
SELECT * FROM public.login('bob', 'secret')
```

This retrieves the result and returns it to its caller.

If you don't want to define a function inside the remote database, you can substitute the default `select * from <thisfunction>(<arg1>, ...)` call with your own by writing it in the function body of the PL/Proxy function:

```
CREATE OR REPLACE FUNCTION get_user_email(i_username text)
RETURNS SETOF text AS $$
    CONNECT 'dbname=chap10 host=10.10.10.1';
    SELECT email FROM user_info where username = i_username;
$$ LANGUAGE plproxy SECURITY DEFINER;
```

Only a single `SELECT` is supported; for any other, or more complex SQL statements, you have to write a remote function and call it.

The third option, is to still call a function similar to itself, but named differently. For example, if you have a proxy function defined not in a separate proxy database, but in a partition, you may want it to target the local database for some data:

```
CREATE OR REPLACE FUNCTION public.get_user_email(i_username text)
RETURNS SETOF text AS $$
    CLUSTER 'messaging';
    RUN ON hashtext(i_username);
    TARGET local.get_user_email;
$$ LANGUAGE plproxy SECURITY DEFINER;
```

In this setup, the local version of `get_user_email()` is in schema local on all partitions. Therefore, if one of the partitions connects back to the same database that it is defined in, it avoids circular calling.

SPLIT – distributing array elements over several partitions

The last PL/Proxy statement is for cases where you want some bigger chunk of work to be done in appropriate partitions.

For example, if you have a function to create several users in one call and you still want to be able to use it after partitioning, the SPLIT statement is a way to tell PL/Proxy to split the arrays between the partitions based on the partitioning function:

```
CREATE or REPLACE FUNCTION create_new_users(
    IN i_username text[], IN i_pwdhash text[], IN i_email text[],
    OUT status int, OUT message text )  RETURNS SETOF RECORD
AS $$
BEGIN
  FOR i IN 1..array_length(i_username,1) LOOP
      SELECT *
        INTO status, message
        FROM new_user(i_username[i], i_pwdhash[i], i_email[i]);
      RETURN NEXT;
  END LOOP;
END;
$$ LANGUAGE plpgsql SECURITY DEFINER;
```

The following PL/Proxy function definition, created on the proxy database, can be used to split the calls across the partitions:

```
CREATE or REPLACE FUNCTION create_new_users(
    IN i_username text[], IN i_pwdhash text[], IN i_email text[],
    OUT status int, OUT message text )  RETURNS SETOF RECORD
AS $$
  CLUSTER 'messaging';
  RUN ON hashtext(i_username);
  SPLIT  i_username,  i_pwdhash,  i_email;
$$ LANGUAGE plproxy SECURITY DEFINER;
```

It would be called by sending in three arrays to the function:

```
SELECT * FROM create_new_users(
    ARRAY['bob', 'jane', 'tom'],
    ARRAY[md5('bobs_pwd'), md5('janes_pwd'), md5('toms_pwd')],
    ARRAY['bob@mail.com', 'jane@mail.com', 'tom@mail.com']
);
```

It will result in two parallel calls to partitions 1 and 2 (as using hashtext(i_username) bob and tom map to partition 1 and mary to partition 2 of the total for the partitions, as explained earlier), with the following arguments for partition 1:

```
SELECT * FROM create_new_users(
    ARRAY['bob', 'tom'],
    ARRAY['6c6e5b564fb0b192f66b2a0a60c751bb',
        'edcc36c33f7529f430a1bc6eb7191dfe'],
    ARRAY['bob@mail.com','tom@mail.com']
);
```

And this for partition 2:

```
SELECT * FROM create_new_users(
    ARRAY['jane'],
    ARRAY['cbbf391d3ef4c60afd851d851bda2dc8'],
    ARRAY['jane@mail.com']
);
```

Then, it returns a concatenation of the results:

```
status | message
-------+---------
   200 | OK
   200 | OK
   200 | OK
(3 rows)
```

The distribution of data

First, what is a cluster in PL/Proxy? Well, the cluster is a set of partitions that make up the whole database. Each cluster consists of a number of partitions, as determined by the cluster configuration. Each partition is uniquely specified by its connect string. The list of connection strings is what makes up a cluster. The position of the partition in this list is what determines the partition number, so the first element in the list is partition 0, the second partition is 1, and so on.

The partition is selected by the output of the RUN ON function, and then masked by the right number of bits to map it on the partitions. So, if `hashtext(i_username)` returns 14 and there are four partitions (2 bits, mask binary 11 or 3 in decimal), the partition number will be 14 and 3 = 2, and the function will be called on partition 2 (starting from zero), which is the third element in the partition list.

The constraint that the number of partitions has to be a power of two may seem an unnecessary restriction at first, but it was done in order to make sure that it is, and will remain to be, easy to expand the number of partitions without the need to redistribute all the data.

For example, if you tried to move from three partitions to four, most likely three fourths of the data rows in partitions 0 to 2 have to be moved to new partitions to evenly cover 0 to 3. On the other hand, when moving from four to eight partitions, the data for partitions 0 and 1 is exactly the same that was previously on partition 0, 2-3 is the old 1 and so on. That is, your data does not need to be moved immediately, and half of the data does not need to be moved at all.

The actual configuration of the cluster, the definition of partitions, can be done in two ways, either by using a set of functions in schema `plproxy`, or you can take advantage of the SQL/MED connection management (SQL/MED is available starting at PostgreSQL 8.4 and above). You can read more about SQL/MED here `https://wiki.postgresql.org/wiki/SQL/MED`

Configuring the PL/Proxy cluster using functions

This is the original way to configure PL/Proxy, which works on all versions of PostgreSQL. When a query needs to be forwarded to a remote database, the function `plproxy.get_cluster_partitions(cluster)` is invoked by PL/Proxy to get the connection string to use for each partition.

The following function is an example, which returns information for a cluster with four partitions, p0 to p3:

```
CREATE OR REPLACE FUNCTION plproxy.get_cluster_partitions(cluster_name
text)
RETURNS SETOF text AS $$
BEGIN
    IF cluster_name = 'messaging' THEN
        RETURN NEXT 'dbname=p0';
        RETURN NEXT 'dbname=p1';
        RETURN NEXT 'dbname=p2';
        RETURN NEXT 'dbname=p3';
    ELSE
        RAISE EXCEPTION 'Unknown cluster';
    END IF;
END;
$$ LANGUAGE plpgsql;
```

A production application might query some configuration tables, or even read some configuration files to return the connection strings. Once again, the number of partitions returned must be a power of two. If you are absolutely sure that some partitions are never used, you can return empty strings for these.

We also need to define a `plproxy.get_cluster_version(cluster_name)` function. This is called on each request and if the cluster version has not changed, the output from a cached result from `plproxy.get_cluster_partitions` can be reused. So, it is best to make sure that this function is as fast as possible:

```
CREATE OR REPLACE FUNCTION plproxy.get_cluster_version(cluster_name
text)
RETURNS int4 AS $$
BEGIN
    IF cluster_name = 'messaging' THEN
        RETURN 1;
    ELSE
        RAISE EXCEPTION 'Unknown cluster';
    END IF;
END;
$$ LANGUAGE plpgsql;
```

The last function needed is `plproxy.get_cluster_config`, which enables you to configure the behavior of PL/Proxy. This sample will set the connection lifetime to 10 minutes:

```
CREATE OR REPLACE FUNCTION plproxy.get_cluster_config(
    in cluster_name text,
    out key text,
    out val text)
RETURNS SETOF record AS $$
BEGIN
    -- lets use same config for all clusters
    key := 'connection_lifetime';
    val := 10*60;
    RETURN NEXT;
    RETURN;
END;
$$ LANGUAGE plpgsql;
```

Configuring the PL/Proxy cluster using SQL/MED

Since version 8.4, PostgreSQL has support for an SQL standard for management of external data, usually referred to as SQL/MED. SQL/MED is simply a standard way to access a database. Using functions to configure partitions is arguably insecure, as any caller of `plproxy.get_cluster_partitions()` can learn connection strings for partitions that may contain sensitive info like passwords. PL/Proxy also provides a way to do the cluster configuration using SQL/MED, which follows the standard SQL security practices.

The same configuration, as discussed earlier, when done using SQL/MED, is as follows:

1. First, create a foreign data wrapper called `plproxy`:

   ```
   proxy1=# CREATE FOREIGN DATA WRAPPER plproxy;
   ```

2. Then, create an external server that defines both the connection options and the partitions:

   ```
   proxy1=# CREATE SERVER messaging FOREIGN DATA WRAPPER plproxy
   proxy1-# OPTIONS (connection_lifetime '1800',
   proxy1(#          p0 'dbname=p0',
   proxy1(#          p1 'dbname=p1',
   proxy1(#          p2 'dbname=p2',
   proxy1(#          p3 'dbname=p3'
   proxy1(# );
   CREATE SERVER
   ```

3. Then, grant usage on this server to either PUBLIC, so all users can use it:

   ```
   proxy1=# CREATE USER MAPPING FOR PUBLIC SERVER messaging;
   CREATE USER MAPPING
   ```

   Or, to some specific users or groups:

   ```
   proxy1=# CREATE USER MAPPING FOR bob SERVER  messaging
   proxy1-#   OPTIONS (user 'plproxy', password
              'very.secret');
   CREATE USER MAPPING
   ```

4. Finally, grant usage on the cluster to the users who need to use it:

   ```
   proxy1=# GRANT USAGE ON FOREIGN SERVER messaging TO bob;
   GRANT
   ```

More info on SQL/MED, as implemented in PostgreSQL, can be found at http://www.postgresql.org/docs/current/static/ sql-createforeigndatawrapper.html.

Moving data from the single to the partitioned database

If you can schedule some downtime and your new partition databases are as big as your original single database, the easiest way to partition the data is to make a full copy of each of the nodes and then simply delete the rows that do not belong to the partition:

```
pg_dump chap10 | psql p0
psql p0 -c 'delete from message where hashtext(to_user) & 3 <> 0'
psql p0 -c 'delete from user_info where hashtext(username) & 3 <> 0'
```

Repeat this for partitions p1 to p3, each time deleting rows which don't match the partition number (psql chap10p1 -c 'delete ... & 3 <> 1).

Remember to vacuum when you are finished deleting the rows. PostgreSQL will leave the dead rows in the data tables, so do a little maintenance while you have some downtime.

When trying to delete from user_info, you will notice that you can't do it without dropping a foreign key from message.from_user.

Here, we could decide that it is Okay to keep the messages on the receivers partition only, and if needed, that the sent messages can be retrieved using a RUN ON ALL function. So, we will drop the foreign key from messages.from_user.

```
psql p0 -c 'alter table message drop constraint
  message_from_user_fkey'
```

There are other options, when splitting the data, that require less disk space usage for a database system, if you are willing to do more manual work.

For example, you can copy over just the schema using pg_dump -s and then use COPY from an SQL statement to move over just the needed rows:

```
pg_dump -s chap10 | psql p0
psql chap10 -c "COPY (select * from message where hashtext(to_user) &
  3 = 0) TO stdout" | psql p0 -c 'COPY messages FROM stdin'
```

Or even set up a specially designed **Londiste replica** and do the switch from a single database to a partitioned cluster in only seconds, once the replica has reached a stable state.

Connection Pooling

PL/Proxy does not include a connection pooler and it is a good idea to use one like pgbouncer and pgpool. A connection pooler is a utility that helps you reduce the operating cost of database, when its large number of physical connections are pulling performance down.

PL/Proxy opens a connection to each partition from each backend process and a large number of connections can bring the performance of the server down. Using the connection pool will allow you to multiplex a lot of client connections over a small number of database connections. The pgbouncer is a recommended connection pooler because it's lightweight and very easy to setup. PL/Proxy attempts to connect to pgbouncer using the same database connection interface that it uses to connect to any PostgreSQL database. The client application supplies the IP address of the host running pgbouncer and the port number on which pgbouncer is listening for connections.

Summary

In this chapter, we have gone over the process of database sharding for databases that are too big to take the write load on a single host, or where you just want to have the added resilience of having a system where one host being down does not bring the whole system down.

In short, the process is:

- Decide which tables you want to split over multiple hosts
- Define a partitioning key
- Add the partition databases and move the data
- Set up the proxy functions for all the functions accessing those tables
- Watch for a little while that everything is working
- Relax

We also took a brief look at using PL/Proxy for simple remote queries to other PostgreSQL databases, which may be handy for some tasks, even after the new **Foreign Data Wrapper (FDW)** functionality in PostgreSQL replaced it for many uses.

While PL/Proxy is not for everyone, it may well save the day if you are suddenly faced with rapid database growth and have the need for an easy and clean way to spread the database over many hosts.

In the next chapter, we will look at the PL/Perl programming language.

11
PL/Perl – Perl Procedural Language

Perl is a feature-rich language, which has been around for a long time. PostgreSQL allows you to write Perl routines that are stored and executed inside the database. This ability is quite unique to PostgreSQL and allows you to do a lot of cool things, such as using Perl's text manipulation features inside a database. PL/Perl is one of the many languages that PostgreSQL supports for writing server-side routines.

As discussed in the earlier chapters, PostgreSQL supports trusted and untrusted languages. PL/Perl is available in both these flavors. The trusted version runs inside a safe container and, therefore, not the entire set of familiar native Perl operations is allowed.

In this chapter, we will cover the following topics:

- When to use PL/Perl
- How to install and write a basic function
- Passing arguments to and from PL/Perl functions
- Writing triggers in PL/Perl
- A brief introduction to untrusted PL/Perl

When to use PL/Perl

We will briefly discuss how to create Perl functions and use them in triggers. Some of you might ask when it is beneficial to use PL/Perl, since PostgreSQL supports a variety of languages that can be used to create triggers or write stored procedures/functions.

You might be more familiar with a language such as Perl than with Python or Tcl. This is a pretty good reason to choose a certain language over the other.

However, if the performance of the function is one of your considerations, then you might want to choose a language based on the nature of the code you want to write.

In general, PL/Perl will outperform PL/pgSQL, if the focus of the stored procedure is computational tasks, athematic, and string parsing and manipulation. However, PL/pgSQL will often be a clear winner if you need to access the database. PL/pgSQL is closely tied into the PostgreSQL execution engine and has a very low overhead of running a query, compared to other procedural languages.

Installing PL/Perl

PL/Perl is not installed by default if you used the standard source distribution to install PostgreSQL. If you compile PostgreSQL from the source, you need to configure the script with the `--with-perl` option.

If you used a binary distribution on your platform, you can normally install PL/Perl using your package manager. You can search for `postgresql-plperl`, or a similar package name, as it differs across the distributions. Once PostgreSQL is compiled with the correct option, or you have installed the appropriate package, you can create the PL language using the `createlang` utility or the `CREATE LANGUAGE` command, as shown here:

```
$ createlang plperl template1
```

Or the untrusted version, such as the following command:

```
$ createlang plperlu template1
```

hon

A simple PL/Perl function

Now, let's write our first simple Perl function to make sure that PL/Perl is installed correctly. We will use a sample function from the Perl FAQs, at `http://perldoc.perl.org/perlfaq5.html#How-can-I-output-my-numbers-with-commas-added%3f`, to write a PL/Perl function that adds commas to a number:

```
CREATE OR REPLACE FUNCTION commafy (integer) RETURNS text
AS $$
  local $_  = shift;
  1 while s/^([-+]?\d+)(\d{3})/$1,$2/;
  return $_;
$$ LANGUAGE plperl;
```

This function uses a smartly written regex to add commas to your numbers. Let's try and run it:

```
testdb=# SELECT commafy(1000000);
 commafy
-----------
 1,000,000
(1 row)
```

The code works and the function looks similar to other functions we have been writing in PL/pgSQL and PL/Python. The CREATE FUNCTION statement creates a function. It needs a name, function argument type list (you have to use parentheses, even if there are no arguments), a result type, and a language.

The function body is just an anonymous Perl subroutine. PostgreSQL passes this on to a Perl interpreter, in order to run this subroutine and return the results. Each function is compiled once per session. PL/Perl function arguments are stored in @_, just as in normal Perl subroutines and your code can handle them the same way.

The arguments passed to the PL/Perl function are converted to UTF-8 from the database encoding, and the return value is converted from UTF-8 back to the database encoding.

 Using UTF-8 for database encoding is encouraged as well. This will avoid the overhead of converting back and forth between encodings.

PL/Perl functions run in a scalar context and cannot return non-scalar types such as lists. You can return the non-scalar types, such as arrays, records, and sets, by returning a reference.

Passing and returning non-scalar types

If you pass array types as arguments to the PL/Perl function, they are passed as the blessed `ostgreSQL::InServer::ARRAY` objects. In Perl, `bless` associates an object with a class. This object can be treated as an array reference or as a string. If you have to return an array type, you must return an array by reference. Let's take a look at the following example:

```
CREATE OR REPLACE FUNCTION reverse(int[]) RETURNS int[]
AS $$
  my $arg = shift; # get the reference of the argument
```

```
  my @rev = reverse @{$arg}; # reverse the array
  return \@rev # return the array reference
$$ LANGUAGE plperl;

testdb=# select reverse(ARRAY[1,2,3,4]);
  reverse
-----------
 {4,3,2,1}
(1 row)
```

The preceding function reverses an integer array passed to the function using the reverse function of Perl. You can take a look at the comments in the code to understand it. First, we get the reference of the passed argument. We then reverse the array using a reference notation, @{$arg}, and store the result in an array called @rev. In the end, we return the reference of the array using the backslash. If you try to return the array directly, you will get an error.

Let's take a look at another function that concatenates two arrays and then reverses their order:

```
CREATE OR REPLACE FUNCTION concat_reverse_arrays(int[], int[]) RETURNS
int[]
AS $$
  my $arr1 = $_[0];
  my $arr2 = $_[1];

  push(@{$arr1}, @{$arr2});

  my @reverse = reverse @{$arr1};
  return \@reverse;
$$ LANGUAGE plperl;

testdb=# select concat_reverse_arrays(ARRAY[1,2,3],ARRAY[4,5,6]);
 concat_reverse_arrays
-----------------------
    {6,5,4,3,2,1}
```

Again, the code is quite simple. It takes two integer arrays as parameters, concatenates them into arr1, and reverses the order using standard Perl functions.

PL/Perl can take arguments of composite types and can also return composite types. The composite types are passed as a reference to hashes, and the keys of the hash are simply attribute names of the passed complex type. Let's take a look at an example:

```
CREATE TABLE item (item_name varchar, item_price int, discount int);

INSERT INTO item(item_name, item_price) VALUES('macbook',1200);
INSERT INTO item(item_name, item_price) VALUES('pen',5);
INSERT INTO item(item_name, item_price) VALUES('fridge',1000);


CREATE OR REPLACE FUNCTION add_discount(item) RETURNS item
AS $$
  my $item = shift;
  if ($item->{item_price} >= 1000) {
  $item->{discount} = 10;
  } else {
  $item->{discount} = 5;
  }

  return $item;
$$ LANGUAGE plperl;

testdb=# select add_discount(item.*) from item;
   add_discount
-------------------
 (macbook,1200,10)
 (pen,5,5)
 (fridge,1000,10)
(3 rows)
```

The preceding function is probably not the best use case for a complex type example, but it demonstrates the concepts sufficiently. First, we create a table and fill it up with some data, except the discount field. We then create a function that is passed an item type, and it fills up the discount field based on the price. You can see that since the complex types are passed as hash references, we need to use the $item->{discount} notation to access the keys, where each key corresponds to a field in the type.

You can also return the SETOF primitive and complex types from a PL/Perl function. In the next example, we will try to return a SETOF item type and also demonstrate how to run an SQL query in a PL/Perl function:

```
CREATE OR REPLACE FUNCTION set_dicounts() RETURNS SETOF item
AS $$
    my $rv = spi_exec_query('select * from item;');
    my $nrows = $rv->{processed};
```

```
    foreach my $rn (0 .. $nrows - 1) {
        my $item = $rv->{rows}[$rn];
            if ($item->{item_price} >= 1000) {
                $item->{discount} = 10;
            } else {
                $item->{discount} = 5;
            }
        return_next($item);
    }
    return undef;
$$ LANGUAGE plperl;

postgres=# select * from set_dicounts();
-[ RECORD 1 ]-------
item_name   | macbook
item_price  | 1200
discount    | 10
-[ RECORD 2 ]-------
item_name   | pen
item_price  | 5
discount    | 5
-[ RECORD 3 ]-------
item_name   | fridge
item_price  | 1000
discount    | 10
```

The first thing you notice about this function, is that it returns a SETOF item type. It uses `return_next` to build up the result set as it processes rows from the item table. The function is then terminated with a final `return undef` (you can also use just `return`). `spi_exec_query` executes SQL and returns the complete result set as a reference to an array of hash references. If you are dealing with a large number of rows, you may not want to use `spi_exec_query` as it returns all the rows at once, but you'd rather use the `spi_query` and `spi_fetch_row` functions, which allow you to iterate over the data like a cursor.

 You can read more about using data in a PL/Perl function in the PostgreSQL documentation at `http://www.postgresql.org/docs/current/static/plperl-builtins.html`.

Writing PL/Perl triggers

If you want to write trigger functions using Perl, then PL/Perl allows you to do all the good stuff that you have learned so far using PL/PgSQL. Let's rewrite an example we demonstrated in *Chapter 5, PL/pgSQL Trigger Functions*, in PL/Perl. Recall the simple, "Hey, I am called" trigger. The PL/Perl version of the example looks as shown in the following code. We probably don't need to provide a more complex example, as this simple example demonstrates the PL/Perl syntax in a sufficient way:

```
CREATE OR REPLACE FUNCTION notify_trigger_plperl() RETURNS TRIGGER
AS $$
   $result = sprintf('Hi, I got %s invoked FOR %s %s %s on %s',
                   $_TD->{name},
                   $_TD->{level},
                   $_TD->{when},
                   $_TD->{event},
                   $_TD->{table_name}
                   );
   if(($_TD->{event} cmp 'UPDATE') == 0){
      $result .= sprintf(' OLD = %s AND NEW=%s', $_TD->{old}{i},
$_TD->{new}{i});
      $_TD->{new}{i} = $_TD->{old}{i} + $_TD->{new}{i};
      elog(NOTICE, $result);
      return "MODIFY";
   } elsif(($_TD->{event} cmp 'DELETE') == 0){
      elog(NOTICE, "Skipping Delete");
      return "SKIP";
   }
   elog(NOTICE, $result);
$$ LANGUAGE plperl;

CREATE TABLE notify_test_plperl(i int);

CREATE  TRIGGER notify_insert_plperl_trigger
   BEFORE INSERT OR UPDATE OR DELETE ON notify_test_plperl
   FOR EACH ROW
EXECUTE PROCEDURE notify_trigger_plperl();
```

Let's try to run the INSERT, UPDATE, and DELETE commands:

```
testdb=# INSERT INTO notify_test_plperl VALUES(1);
NOTICE:  Hi, I got notify_insert_plperl_trigger invoked FOR ROW BEFORE
INSERT on notify_test_plperl
CONTEXT:  PL/Perl function "notify_trigger_plperl"
INSERT 0 1

testdb=# UPDATE notify_test_plperl SET i = 10;
NOTICE:  Hi, I got notify_insert_plperl_trigger invoked FOR ROW BEFORE
UPDATE on notify_test_plperl OLD = 1 AND NEW=10
CONTEXT:  PL/Perl function "notify_trigger_plperl"
UPDATE 1

testdb=# select * from notify_test_plperl;
  i
----
 11
(1 row)

postgres=# DELETE FROM notify_test_plperl;
NOTICE:  Skipping Delete
CONTEXT:  PL/Perl function "notify_trigger_plperl"
DELETE 0
```

Let's review what we have done so far. We have created a trigger function, a test table, and an actual trigger that runs before an INSERT, UPDATE, or DELETE for each row.

The trigger function uses a couple of things we have not discussed so far. In a PL/Perl trigger function, the hash reference $_TD contains information about the current trigger event. You can see the full list of keys in $_TD at http://www. postgresql.org/docs/current/static/plperl-triggers.html.

The triggers we have used in our example are explained in the following table:

Trigger name	Trigger description
$_TD->{name}	This denotes the name of the trigger. In our example, this will contain notify_trigger_plperl.
$_TD->{level}	This is a ROW or STATEMENT trigger. In our example, this will contain ROW.
$_TD->{when}	The BEFORE, AFTER, or INSTEAD OF trigger. In our example, this will contain BEFORE.

Trigger name	Trigger description
`$_TD->{event}`	The INSERT, UPDATE, DELETE, or TRUNCATE command. In our example, this will contain INSERT, UPDATE, or DELETE.
`$_TD->{table_name}`	This denotes the name of the table. In our example, this will contain notify_test_plperl.
`$_TD->{old}{i}`	This will contain the OLD value of the column i. In our example, this will contain 1.
`TD->{new}{i}`	This will contain the NEW value of the column i. In our example, this will contain 10.

We have also used a utility function called `elog()` in the trigger function. This function emits log messages. The level values that are possible are DEBUG, LOG, INFO, NOTICE, WARNING, and ERROR. The ERROR value propagates an error to the calling query and is similar to a Perl `die` command.

> You can view all the available built-ins and utility functions available in PL/Perl at http://www.postgresql.org/docs/current/static/ plperl-builtins.html.

Our trigger function returns the special values `"MODIFY"` and `"SKIP"` in the case of UPDATE and DELETE, respectively. If a PL/Perl trigger function returns `"MODIFY"`, it means that the NEW value has been modified by the trigger function. If a trigger function modifies a NEW value but does not return `"MODIFY"`, then the change done by the function will be discarded. The `"SKIP"` implies that the operation should not be executed.

Untrusted Perl

We discussed untrusted PL/PythonU in *Chapter 8, Using Unrestricted Languages*. PL/Perl is also available as an untrusted language. The trusted version runs inside a security context that does not allow interaction with the environment. Just like PL/Pythonu, we can bypass the security restrictions using PL/Perlu or the untrusted version. Let's rewrite the directory listing function `list_folder` from *Chapter 8, Listing directory contents* to a Perl equivalent:

```
CREATE OR REPLACE FUNCTION list_folder_plperl(directory VARCHAR)
RETURNS SETOF TEXT
AS $$
  my $d = shift;
  opendir(D, "$d") || elog (ERROR,'Cant open directory '.$d) ;
  my @list = readdir(D);
```

```
    closedir(D);

    foreach my $f (@list) {
      return_next($f);
    }
    return undef;
  $$ LANGUAGE plperlu;
```

Let's run our function, as shown here:

```
testdb=# SELECT list_folder_plperl('/usr/local/pgsql/bin');
      list_folder_plperl
  -------------------
    .
    ..
    clusterdb
    createdb
    createlang
    createuser
    dropdb
    droplang
    dropuser
    ecpg
    initdb
    pg_basebackup
    pg_config
    pg_controldata
    pg_ctl
    pg_dump
    pg_dumpall
    pg_isready
    pg_receivexlog
    pg_resetxlog
    pg_restore
    postgres
    postmaster
    psql
    reindexdb
    vacuumdb
  (26 rows)
```

If we try to create the preceding function as plperl instead of plperlu, we will get an error such as ERROR: 'opendir' trapped by operation mask at line 3 by the validator, because we are trying to access the host system.

Summary

The powerful Perl language is available in PostgreSQL as PL/Perl or PL/Perlu. This allows you to write stored procedures in Perl and to take advantage of all the cool features that Perl has to offer, such as a very large collection of modules available on CPAN. You can do almost everything you want with PL/pgSQL or PL/Python, including database access and writing triggers. The untrusted version of PL/Perl allows you to interact with the environment. PL/Perl will normally outperform PL/pgSQL in non-data intensive functions that focus more on string manipulation and computation.

In the next chapter, we will discuss another popular PL language called Pl/Tcl.

12
PL/Tcl – Tcl Procedural Language

Tools Command Language (Tcl), also commonly known as *tickle*, has been around for a long time. It was created by John Ousterhout in 1988 and got a lot of traction for rapid prototyping and scripted applications.

In this chapter, we will take a brief look at PL/Tcl. Between PL/Perl, PL/Python, and PL/pgSQL, you have very powerful languages available at your disposal that can do almost anything you need. For some other things, you have the option to write your functions in C. You might wonder why it is useful to discuss PL/Tcl. For a long time, in the early days of PostgreSQL, PL/Tclu (untrusted PL/Tcl) was the only way to do things *outside* PostgreSQL, such as interacting with the operating system. A lot of people still use it, and I personally think that it is so clean and powerful that it should not be overlooked.

PL/Tcl is available as a trusted and an untrusted language. This is achieved by providing two different Tcl interpreters. PL/Tclu uses the standard Tcl interpreter, while PL/Tcl uses a special *Safe Tcl* mechanism.

 You can read more about safe Tcl at http://www.tcl.tk/software/ plugin/safetcl.html.

In this chapter, we will cover the following topics:

- Installing PL/Tcl and writing a simple function
- Passing simple and complex parameters
- Accessing a database from a Pl/Tcl function
- Writing database triggers using Pl/Tcl

Installing PL/Tcl

PL/Tcl is not installed by default, if you've used the standard source distribution to install PostgreSQL. If you compiled PostgreSQL from the source, you need to run the configure script with the `--with-tcl` option.

If you've used a binary distribution on your platform, you can normally install PL/Tcl using your package manager. You can search for `postgresql-pltcl`, or a similar package name, as it differs across distributions. Once PostgreSQL is compiled with the correct option, or you have installed the appropriate package, you can create the language using the `createlang` utility or the `CREATE LANGUAGE` command:

```
$ createlang pltcl template1
```

You can use also use the untrusted version to create the language, as follows:

```
$ createlang pltclu template1
```

A simple PL/Tcl function

Now, let's write our first simple Tcl function to make sure that PL/Tcl is installed. We will write a simple factorial calculation function, as shown here:

```
CREATE OR REPLACE FUNCTION tcl_factorial(integer) RETURNS integer
AS $$
  set i 1; set fact 1
  while {$i <= $1} {
    set fact [expr $fact * $i]
    incr i
  }
  return $fact
$$ LANGUAGE pltcl  STRICT;
```

This function calculates the factorial of a number in an iterative way. Let's try and run it:

```
postgres=# SELECT tcl_factorial(5);
 tcl_factorial
---------------
           120
(1 row)
```

It works and the function looks similar to other functions we have been writing in PL/pgSQL and PL/Python. The `CREATE FUNCTION` statement creates a function. It needs a name, function argument type list (you have to use parentheses, even if there are no arguments), a result type, and a language.

The body of the function is just a Tcl script. PostgreSQL passes the body on to a Tcl interpreter to run this subroutine and return the results. The function arguments are passed on to the script as $1, $2,...$n.

Null checking with Strict functions

The STRICT keyword will save us from checking the null input parameters. If you have specified a function as STRICT and any of the input parameters are null, it results in the function not being called and a null result set is returned immediately:

```
postgres=# SELECT tcl_factorial(null);
 tcl_factorial
---------------

(1 row)
```

If you don't want to create a STRICT function, or you'd like to do the null checking yourself, you can rewrite the function, as shown in the following code snippet. This is useful if you have multiple parameters and you want to allow some parameters to be null:

```
CREATE OR REPLACE FUNCTION tcl_factorial_ns(integer) RETURNS integer
AS $$
    if {[argisnull 1]} {
        elog NOTICE "input is null"
        return -1
    }
    set i 1; set fact 1
    while {$i <= $1} {
        set fact [expr $fact * $i]
        incr i
    }
    return $fact
$$ LANGUAGE pltcl;
```

The argisnull function is used to check for null values. In the preceding example, the function returns -1 if the input argument is null, just to demonstrate that it works. If you want to return a null value from the function, you can use the built-in function return_null. In the preceding example, you can also see how to use the elog function in PL/Tcl:

```
postgres=# SELECT tcl_factorial_ns(null);
                          tcl_factorial_ns
------------------
                -1
(1 row)
```

The parameter format

All input parameters passed to PL/Tcl are converted to text. Within a PL/Tcl function, all values are text. When the function returns, another conversion is performed from the text string to the return type of the function, as long as the text being returned is an appropriate representation of the return type of the Pl/Tcl function; otherwise, the function will result in an error.

Passing and returning arrays

If you pass array types as an argument to the PL/Tcl function, they are passed as a string value, along with the brackets and the commas. Let's take a look at an example:

```
CREATE OR REPLACE FUNCTION tcl_array_test(integer[]) RETURNS int
AS $$
    set length [string length $1]
    return $length
$$ LANGUAGE pltcl;

testdb=# select tcl_array_test(ARRAY[1,2,3]);
 tcl_array_test
----------------
        7
    (1 row)
```

You are probably surprised at the return value of the preceding function. You passed an integer array to the function that is converted to a string value {1,2,3}, the length of which is indeed 7. If you want to process array values independently, you need a bit of string manipulation to extract the list out of the string, do the manipulation, and convert it back to the string format that you received it in.

Let's take a look at an example PL/Tcl function that will reverse an integer array and return the reversed integer array:

```
CREATE OR REPLACE FUNCTION tcl_reverse_array(integer[]) RETURNS
integer[]
AS $$
   set lst [regexp -all -inline {[0-9]} $1]
```

```
    set lst [join [lreverse $lst] ","]
    set lst  "{$lst}"
    return $lst
$$ LANGUAGE pltcl;

postgres=# select tcl_reverse_array(ARRAY[1,2,3]);
 tcl_reverse_array
-------------------
 {3,2,1}
(1 row)
```

The preceding function does the following:

1. The `tcl_reverse_array` function cleans up the input parameter by creating a list out of the string and removing the { and , characters. This is done using a regular expression and by only extracting numeric values out of the string.

2. It uses the `lreverse` function to reverse the contents of the list and then join the elements of the list back as an array, using the `join` function and using , as the join character.

3. Then, it adds brackets to the string before returning it. The return string is converted to an integer array as it is returned by the function.

Passing composite-type arguments

A composite-type, such as a table, or a user-defined type is passed to the PL/Tcl function as an associative array (Hash table). The attribute names of the composite-type are the element names in the array. Attributes with NULL values are not available in the Tcl array.

Let's take a look at an arbitrary example. We will create a function that takes a composite type as an argument and does some calculations based on the attribute values of the type. Let's create our type and the function:

```
CREATE TABLE orders(orderid int, num_people integer, order_amount
decimal);

INSERT INTO orders VALUES(1,1,23);
INSERT INTO orders VALUES(2,3,157);
INSERT INTO orders VALUES(3,5,567.25);
INSERT INTO orders VALUES(4,1,100);

CREATE OR REPLACE FUNCTION tip_calculator(orders, integer) RETURNS
decimal
AS $$
```

```
    if {$1(order_amount) > 0} {
      set tip [expr (double($1(order_amount) *
        $2)/100)/$1(num_people)]
      set tip [format "%.2f" $tip]
      return $tip
    }
    return 0;
  $$ LANGUAGE pltcl;
```

The orders table is quite simple to understand: it contains an order ID, the number of people in the orders table (num_people), and the total cost of the order (order_amount).

The function calculates the tip per person, based on the price of the meal (order_amount) and number of people. It takes an argument of the type orders and an integer value that represent the percentage of the tip that should be paid.

The function body calculates the tip and formats the result to two decimal places. If we run our function, this is what we should see:

```
postgres=# SELECT tip_calculator(orders.*,5) AS "tip per person" FROM
orders;
 tip per person
----------------
          1.15
          2.62
          5.67
          5.00
(4 rows)
```

You can see that all the attributes of the orders type can be accessed in the function as $1(order_amount), $1(num_people), and so on. This function gets called once for each row of the orders table and calculates the amount of the tip to be paid per person for each order, according to various parameters.

 You can see the full list of associative array commands in the official documentation for Tcl at http://www.tcl.tk/man/tcl8.5/tutorial/Tcl22.html.

At this moment, PL/Tcl functions don't allow the returning of a SETOF type, or composite type, from a function.

Accessing databases

PL/Tcl functions provide you with SPI functions to access the database and run DML/DDL statements.

The functions are the following:

- `spi_exec`: This executes a SQL statement
- `spi_prepare`: This prepares a SQL statement
- `spi_execp`: This executes a prepared statement

The `spi_exec` function has the following syntax:

```
spi_exec ?-count n? ?-array name? command ?loop-body?
```

The `spi_exec` function runs a SQL statement, and it takes some optional parameters, as follows:

- `-count`: This parameter allows you to specify the maximum number of rows processed by the command. If you provide the value 3, only 3 rows will be processed. This is similar to specifying FETCH [n] in a cursor.
- `-array`: If this parameter is specified, the column values are stored into a named associative array and the column names are used as array indexes. If this parameter is not specified, the result values are stored in the Tcl variables of the same name.

If there is a loop body specified, then it is treated as a script that is run for each row.

Let's take a look at an example of how to run SQL statements inside a PL/Tcl function. The following example, creates a function that loops over the rows in a table and updates a column in each row:

```
CREATE TABLE emp_sales(empid int PRIMARY KEY,
                       sales_amnt decimal,
                       comm_perc decimal,
                       comm_amnt decimal);

INSERT INTO emp_sales VALUES (1,32000, 5, NULL);
INSERT INTO emp_sales VALUES (2,5231.23, 3, NULL);
INSERT INTO emp_sales VALUES (3,64890, 7.5, NULL);


CREATE OR REPLACE FUNCTION tcl_calc_comm() RETURNS int
AS $$
  spi_exec -array C "SELECT * FROM emp_sales" {
```

```
    set camnt [ expr ($C(sales_amnt) * $C(comm_perc))/100 ]
        spi_exec "update emp_sales
        set comm_amnt = [format "%.2f" $camnt]
        where empid = $C(empid)"
}
$$ LANGUAGE pltcl;
```

The preceding example, does the following:

- It creates a table `emp_sales`, which contains the employee ID, how much sales the employee has made, and what is their commission percentage. The last column that represents the total commission to be paid to the employee based on his/her sales and his/her commission percentage is left blank intentionally, and it is filled by our function.

- It fills the table with some random data.

- Then, the function body runs a SQL statement using the `spi_exec` command, and the column values are returned in the associative array called `c`.

- Finally, the loop body calculates the commission value and updates the `comm_amnt` column for each row.

 You can read more about accessing the database in a PL/Tcl function at `http://www.postgresql.org/docs/current/interactive/pltcl-dbaccess.html`.

Writing PL/Tcl triggers

If you want to write trigger functions using Tcl, then PL/PTcl allows you to do all the good stuff that you have learned so far, using PL/pgSQL, PL/Perl, and PL/Python. Let's rewrite an example we demonstrated in *Chapter 5, PL/pgSQL Trigger Functions*. Recall the simple, "Hey, I am called" trigger. This is how the PL/Tcl version of the example looks:

```
CREATE OR REPLACE FUNCTION notify_trigger_pltcl() RETURNS TRIGGER
AS $$
    set result [format "Hi, I got %s invoked FOR %s %s %s on %s"
        $TG_name $TG_level $TG_when $TG_op $TG_table_name]
    if {$TG_op == "UPDATE"} {
        append result [format " OLD = %s AND NEW=%s" $OLD(i) $NEW(i)]
            set NEW(i) [expr $OLD(i) + $NEW(i)]
            elog NOTICE $result
            return [array get NEW]
    } elseif {$TG_op == "DELETE"} {
```

```
      elog NOTICE "DELETE"
      return SKIP
   } elog NOTICE $result
  return OK
$$ LANGUAGE pltcl;

CREATE TABLE notify_test_pltcl(i int);

CREATE  TRIGGER notify_insert_pltcl_trigger
  BEFORE INSERT OR UPDATE OR DELETE ON notify_test_pltcl
  FOR EACH ROW
EXECUTE PROCEDURE notify_trigger_pltcl();
```

The preceding code is almost a carbon copy of the one in *Chapter 11, PL/Perl – Perl Procedural Language,* but in the Tcl syntax. It demonstrates how to use TG variables, how to modify NEW values, and how to SKIP an operation.

It prints "Hey I got invoked" with different attributes of the trigger. In the case of an UPDATE, it also prints the NEW and OLD values, as well as modifies the NEW value and skips the DELETE operation. A PL/Tcl trigger function can return the following values:

- OK: This is the default value and implies that the operation executed by the user will proceed normally

- SKIP: This return value implies that the user-executed operation will be silently ignored

- LIST: This is returned by `array get` and implies that a modified version of the NEW array should be returned

- OLD and NEW: These values are available as associative arrays in a PL/Tcl trigger function, and the attributes of the table are the names of the elements in the array

Let's run INSERT, UPDATE, and DELETE to see the results:

```
postgres=# INSERT INTO notify_test_pltcl VALUES(1);
NOTICE:  Hi, I got notify_insert_pltcl_trigger invoked FOR ROW BEFORE
INSERT on notify_test_pltcl
INSERT 0 1
postgres=# UPDATE notify_test_pltcl SET i=10;
NOTICE:  Hi, I got notify_insert_pltcl_trigger invoked FOR ROW BEFORE
UPDATE on notify_test_pltcl OLD = 1 AND NEW=10
UPDATE 1
postgres=# DELETE FROM notify_test_pltcl;
NOTICE:  DELETE
DELETE 0
```

```
postgres=# SELECT * FROM notify_test_pltcl;
 i
----
 11
(1 row)
```

In a PL/Tcl trigger function, the $TG variables contain information about the current trigger event. You can see the full list of variables at http://www.postgresql.org/docs/current/interactive/pltcl-trigger.html.

The variables we have used in our example are explained in the following table:

Trigger name	Description
$TG_name	This denotes the name of the trigger. In our example, this will contain notify_trigger_pltcl.
$TG_level	This is a ROW or STATEMENT trigger. In our example, this will contain ROW.
$TG_when	This is a BEFORE, AFTER, or INSTEAD OF trigger. In our example, this will contain BEFORE.
$TG_op	This is an INSERT, UPDATE, DELETE, or TRUNCATE trigger. In our example, this will contain INSERT, UPDATE, or DELETE.
$TG_table_name	This denotes the name of the table. In our example, this will contain notify_test_pltcl.
$OLD(i)	This will contain the OLD value of the column i. In our example, this will contain 1.
$NEW(i)	This will contain the NEW value of the column i. In our example, this will contain 10.

Untrusted Tcl

Using untrusted Tcl (pltclu) is one of the oldest ways to do things outside the database. pltclu is executed using a normal Tcl interpreter and is pretty much free to do anything you'd like. Tcl has a lot of commands available to interact with the operating system and the environment. We will now take a look at a few simple examples.

The first example, reads the contents of the file and returns them as text, as shown in the following code:

```
CREATE OR REPLACE FUNCTION read_file(text) RETURNS text
AS $$
  set fptr [open $1]
  set file_data [read $fptr]
```

```
    close $fptr #close the file as it is already read
    return $file_data
$$ LANGUAGE pltclu;
```

The function is quite simple; it opens a file provided as a parameter, reads all its contents at once, and returns the text.

Let's run the preceding function:

```
postgres=# select
            read_file('/usr/local/pgsql/data/postmaster.pid');
        read_file
-----------------------
 61588                 +
 /usr/local/pgsql/data+
 1401041744            +
 5432                  +
 /tmp                  +
 localhost             +
    5432001    196608  +

(1 row)
```

Here is another function that does a directory listing, similar to the `plperlu` example in *Chapter 11, PL/Perl – Perl Procedural Language*. Since PL/Tcl does not support the returning of the SETOF text, we will simply return the complete directory listing as one string. As you can see in the following code, this can be done with a single line in Tcl:

```
CREATE OR REPLACE FUNCTION list_directory(text) RETURNS text
AS $$
    set dirList [glob -nocomplain -directory $1 *.*]
    return $dirList
$$ LANGUAGE pltclu;

testdb=# SELECT list_directory('/tmp');
                list_directory
-------------------------------------------------
 /tmp/lu84iont.tmp /tmp/unity_support_test.0
(1 row)
```

We read the contents of the file using Tcl's `glob` function and just returned the contents as a string.

Let's take a look at one last PL/Tclu function that will export the contents to a table as a `.csv` file:

```
CREATE OR REPLACE FUNCTION dump_table(text, text) RETURNS int
AS $$
```

```
    set filename $1
      set fileId [open $filename "w"]
    spi_exec -array emp "SELECT * FROM $2" {
      set row [format "%d,%.2f,%.2f,%.2f" $emp(empid)
        $emp(sales_amnt) $emp(comm_perc) $emp(comm_amnt)]
        puts $fileId $row
      }
      close $fileId
      return 0;
    $$ LANGUAGE pltclu STRICT;
```

Again, this function is quite simple and uses the concepts we have discussed before. It iterates over the table provided as the second parameter to this function and stores the data in a file named, as per the first parameter of this function. The file is written line by line as comma-separated values by iterating over the table data using spi_exec.

Let's run this function on the emp_sales table that we created earlier in this chapter:

```
postgres=# select dump_table('emp.txt','emp_sales');
 dump_table
------------
          0
(1 row)
```

This seems to work. We can verify this by running the read_file function we wrote earlier:

```
postgres=# select read_file('emp.txt');
        read_file
-------------------------
 1,32000.00,5.00,1600.00+
 2,5231.23,3.00,156.94  +
 3,64890.00,7.50,4866.75+

(1 row)
```

It seems that the function works, and we have a CSV dump of the table in no time.

Summary

The powerful, yet clean, Tcl language is available in PostgreSQL as PL/Tcl and the untrusted PL/Tclu. Both the languages use different Tcl interpreters. PL/Tclu is the oldest language used in PostgreSQL, to access things outside the database. It allows you to write stored procedures in Tcl and takes advantage of all the cool features that Tcl has to offer. You can do almost everything you can with other PL languages, including database access and writing triggers. The only major disadvantage of PL/Tcl is that it does not allow you to return composite types and sets from a function.

In the next chapter, we will explore how to publish your code as a PostgreSQL extension.

13
Publishing Your Code as PostgreSQL Extensions

If you are new to PostgreSQL, now is the time to dance for joy.

Now that you're done dancing, I'll tell you why. You have managed to avoid the "bad old days" of contrib modules. Contrib modules are the installation systems that were used to install related PostgreSQL objects prior to Version 9.1. They may be additional data types, enhanced management functions, or just really any type of module you want to add to PostgreSQL. They consist of any group of related functions, views, tables, operators, types, and indexes that were lumped into an installation file and committed to the database in one fell swoop. Unfortunately, contrib modules only provided for installation, and nothing else. In fact, they were not really an installation system at all. They were just some unrelated SQL scripts that happened to install everything that the author thought you needed.

PostgreSQL extensions provide many new services that a package management system should have. Well, at least the ones that module authors complained the most about not being present.

Some of the new features that you will be introduced to in this chapter include:

- Versioning
- Dependencies
- Updates
- Removal

When to create an extension

Well, first you have to understand that extensions are all about togetherness. Once the objects from a contrib module were installed, PostgreSQL provided no way to show a relationship between them. This led many developers to create their own (and at times rather ingenious) methods to version, update, upgrade, and uninstall all of the necessary "stuff" to get a feature to work.

So, the first question to ask yourself when contemplating a PostgreSQL extension as a way to publish your code is "How does all of the 'stuff' in my extension relate together?"

This question will help you make extensions that are as granular as reasonable. If the objective is to enhance PostgreSQL with the ability to provide an inventory management system, it might be better to start with an extension that provides a bill of materials data type first, and subsequently build additional extensions that are dependent upon that one. The moral of the story is to dream big, but create each extension with only the smallest number of related items that make sense.

A good example of an extension that provides a feature to PostgreSQL is OpenFTS. This extension provides full text searching capabilities to PostgreSQL by creating data types, indexes, and functions that are well related to each other.

Another type of extension is PostGIS, which provides a rich set of tools to deal with geographic information systems. Although this extension provides many more bits of functionality than OpenFTS, it is still as granular as possible by virtue of the fact that everything that is provided is necessary for geographic software development.

Possibly, you are a book author, and the only relationship that the objects in your extension have is that they need to be conveniently removed when your poor victim ...ahem...the reader is through with them. Welcome to the wonders of extensions.

For a list of very useful extensions that have gained some community popularity, you might want to take a look at this page fairly often: `http://www.postgresql.org/download/products/6/`.

You should also take a look at the PostgreSQL extension network at `http://www.pgxn.org`. Please note that installing extensions generally means running a script as a superuser; and nearly anyone can upload to pgxn, meaning that individuals really need to vet anything they get from pgxn very carefully.

To find out what objects can be packaged into an extension, look at the
ALTER EXTENSION ADD command in the PostgreSQL documentation:
`http://www.postgresql.org/docs/current/static/sql`
`-alterextension.html`

Unpackaged extensions

Starting with Version 9.1, PostgreSQL provides a convenient way to move from
the primordial ooze of unversioned contrib modules into the brave new world of
extensions. Basically, you provide a SQL file to show the relationship of the
objects to the extension. The contrib module's cube provides a good example of
this in `cube--unpackaged--1.0.sql`:

```
/* contrib/cube/cube--unpackaged--1.0.sql */

-- complain if script is sourced in psql, rather than via CREATE
EXTENSION
\echo Use "CREATE EXTENSION cube" to load this file. \quit

ALTER EXTENSION cube ADD type cube;
ALTER EXTENSION cube ADD function cube_in(cstring);
ALTER EXTENSION cube ADD function cube(double precision[],double
precision[]);
ALTER EXTENSION cube ADD function cube(double precision[]);
...
```

The code that provides multidimensional cubes for PostgreSQL has been stable for
quite some time. It is unlikely that a new version will be created any time soon. The
only reason for this module to be converted into an extension is to allow for easy
installation and removal.

You would then execute the command:

```
CREATE EXTENSION cube FROM unpackaged;
```

The unrelated items are now grouped together into the extension named cube. This
also makes it easier for the packaging maintainer on any platform to include your
extension into the repository. We'll show you how to make the packages to install
your extension in the *Building an extension* section.

Extension versions

The version mechanism for PostgreSQL extensions is simple. Name it whatever you want and give it whatever alphanumeric version number that suits your fancy. Easy, eh? Just name the files in this format:

```
extension--version.sql
```

If you want to provide an upgrade path from one version of your extension to another, you would provide the file:

```
extension--oldversion--newversion.sql
```

This simple mechanism allows PostgreSQL to update an extension that is already in place. Gone are the days of painful exporting and re-importing data just to change the definition of a data type. So, let's go ahead and update our example extension using the file `postal--1.0--1.1.sql`. This update is as easy as:

```
ALTER EXTENSION postal UPDATE TO '1.1';
```

> A note of caution: PostgreSQL does not have any concept of what your version number means. In this example, the extension was updated from Version 1.0 to 1.1 because we explicitly provided a script for that specific conversion. PostgreSQL did not deduce that 1.1 follows 1.0. We could have just as easily used the names of fruits or historical battleships for our version numbers and the result would have been the same.

PostgreSQL will use multiple update files if necessary to achieve the desired result. Given the following command:

```
ALTER EXTENSION postal UPDATE TO '1.4';
```

PostgreSQL will apply the files `postal--1.1--1.2.sql`, `postal--1.2--1.3.sql` and `postal--1.3--1.4.sql` in the correct order to achieve the desired version.

You may also use this technique to provide upgrade scripts that are in fact downgrade scripts, that is, they actually remove functionality. Be careful with this though. If a path to a desired version is to downgrade before an upgrade, PostgreSQL will take the shortest route. This may result in some unintended results, including data loss. My advice would be to not provide downgrade scripts. The risk just isn't worth it.

The .control file

Along with the extension installation script file, you must provide a `.control` file. The `.control` file for our example `postal.control` looks like this:

```
# postal address processing extension
comment = 'utilities for postal processing'
default_version = '1.0'
module_pathname = '$libdir/postal'
relocatable = true
requires = 'plpgsql'
```

The purpose of the `.control` file is to provide a description of your extension. This metadata may include `directory`, `default_version`, `comment`, `encoding`, `module_pathname`, `requires`, `superuser`, `relocatable`, and `schema`.

The main PostgreSQL documentation for this file is located at `http://www.postgresql.org/docs/current/static/extend-extensions.html`.

This example shows the `requires` configuration parameter. Our extension depends on the procedural language PL/pgSQL. On most platforms, it is installed by default. Unfortunately, it is not installed on all platforms, and nothing should be taken for granted.

Multiple dependencies can be indicated by separating them with commas. This comes in very handy when constructing a set of services based on multiple extensions.

As we mentioned in the previous section, PostgreSQL does not provide any interpretation of the version number of an extension. Versions can be names as well as numbers, so there is no way for PostgreSQL to interpret that `postal--lamb.sql` comes before `postal--sheep.sql`. This design limitation poses a problem to the extension developer, in that there is no way to specify that your extension depends on a specific version of another extension. I would love to see this configuration parameter enhanced with a syntax like `requires = postgis >= 1.3`, but alas, no such construction exists at the moment.

Building an extension

We have already covered the basics of creating a script file and a `.control` file. Actually, that is all that is necessary for a PostgreSQL extension. You may simply copy these files into the shared extension directory on your computer and execute the following command:

```
CREATE EXTENSION postal;
```

This will install your extension into the currently selected database.

The shared extension path is dependent on how PostgreSQL is installed, but for Ubuntu, it is `/usr/share/postgresql/9.2/extension`.

However, there is a much better way to do this that works with any package manager on any platform.

PostgreSQL provides an extension-building toolkit as a part of the server development package. To install this package on Ubuntu, you can type:

```
sudo apt-get install postgresql-dev-9.4
```

This will install all of the PostgreSQL source code necessary to create and install an extension. You would then create a file named `Makefile` in the same directory as the rest of your extension files. The content of this file looks like this:

```
EXTENSION = postal
DATA = postal--1.0.sql

PG_CONFIG = pg_config
PGXS := $(shell $(PG_CONFIG) --pgxs)
include $(PGXS)
```

This simple `Makefile` file will copy your extension script file and the `.control` file into the proper shared extension directory on any platform. Invoke it with this command:

```
sudo make install
```

You will see some output like this:

```
/bin/mkdir -p '/usr/share/postgresql/9.4/extension'
```
```
/bin/sh /usr/lib/postgresql/9.4/lib/pgxs/src/makefiles/../../config/
install-sh -c -m 644 ./postal.control '/usr/share/postgresql/9.4/
extension/'
```
```
/bin/sh /usr/lib/postgresql/9.4/lib/pgxs/src/makefiles/../../config/
install-sh -c -m 644 ./postal--1.0.sql  '/usr/share/postgresql/9.4/
extension/'
```

Your extension is now located in the proper directory for installation. You can install it into the current database with:

```
CREATE EXTENSION postal;
```

You will then see the confirmation text letting you know that you have now gone postal:

```
CREATE EXTENSION
```

Installing an extension

Extensions that have been packaged for you by your friendly distribution manager are very simple to install using the following command:

```
CREATE EXTENSION extension_name;
```

Most of the popular Linux distributions include a package called something like `postgresql-contrib-9.4`. This naming convention is left over from the contrib style installation of PostgreSQL objects. Don't worry, for PostgreSQL 9.4, this package will actually provide extensions rather than contrib modules.

To find out where the files were placed on Ubuntu Linux, you can execute the following command:

```
pg_config --sharedir
```

This will show you the installation directory of shared components:

```
/usr/share/postgresql/9.4
```

The extensions will be located in a directory called `extension`, immediately below the shared directory. This will then be named `/usr/share/postgresql/9.2/extension`.

To see what extensions are available for you to install, try this command:

```
ls $(pg_config -sharedir)/extension/*.control
```

You can also see the list of installed extensions using the plsql meta-command `\dx`.

This will show you all the extensions that have been made available to you by your Linux distribution's package management system.

For extensions that you have created yourself, you must copy your SQL script file and the `.control` file to the shared extension directory before invoking CREATE EXTENSION in PostgreSQL.

```
cp postal.control postal--1.0.sql $(pg_config --sharedir)/extension
```

To see the procedure for doing this reliably on any target platform, refer to the *Building an Extension* section.

Viewing extensions

Querying the `pg_extension` system view or using the meta-command `\dx` will show the extensions currently installed in the database.

```
postgres=# \dx
List of installed extensions
-[ RECORD 1 ]---------------------------
Name        | pgcrypto
Version     | 1.0
Schema      | public
Description | cryptographic functions
-[ RECORD 2 ]---------------------------
Name        | plperl
Version     | 1.0
Schema      | pg_catalog
Description | PL/Perl procedural language
-[ RECORD 3 ]---------------------------
Name        | plpgsql
Version     | 1.0
Schema      | pg_catalog
Description | PL/pgSQL procedural language
```

The extensions that are ready to be installed can be viewed from the `pg_available_extensions` or `pg_available_extension_versions` system views.

Publishing your extension

Thank you for contributing to the PostgreSQL community! Your support will not go unnoticed in this gathering of like-minded individuals who are all slightly smarter than each other. Your work will be seen by dozens of developers looking for community solutions to common problems. You have indeed made the open source world a better place.

Since we are talking about publication, you should consider the licensing model for your extension. The publication methods that we are about to describe assume that the extension will be made available to the general public. As such, please consider the PostgreSQL license for your extension. You can find the current one here:

```
http://www.postgresql.org/about/licence/
```

Introduction to PostgreSQL Extension Network

When you want to publish your module, you could start writing packaging scripts for each of the distribution systems for every operating system. This is the way the PostgreSQL extensions have been distributed in the past. That distribution system has not been very friendly to the open source community, or very well received. In an effort to make extension publication more palatable, a group of open source writers and backing companies got together and founded the **PostgreSQL Extension Network (PGXN)**.

The PostgreSQL Extension Network `http://pgxn.org/` provides a central repository for your open source extensions. By the kindness of the maintainers, it also provides installation scripts for your extensions that will work on most of the popular PostgreSQL deployment operating systems.

Signing up to publish your extension

To sign up to publish your extension, perform the following steps:

1. Start by requesting an account on the management page: `http://manager.pgxn.org`.

2. Click on **Request Account** and fill in your personal information. The PostgreSQL Extension Network folks will get back to you via e-mail. Enrollment requests are currently processed by an actual human, so the e-mail response will not be immediate .

3. Click on the provided link in the e-mail to confirm your account and set a new password on the PGXN website:

Subject:	Welcome to PGXN!
From:	"PGXN Admins" <pgxn@pgexperts.com>
Date:	Tue, March 6, 2012 10:20 am
To:	"bithead" <kirk@webfinish.com>
Priority:	Normal
Options:	View Full Header I View Printable Version I Download this as a file

```
What up, bithead.

Your PGXN account request has been approved. Ready to get started?
Great! Just click this link to set your password and get going:

    https://manager.pgxn.org/account/reset/nvrmG

Best,

PGXN Management
```

4. You will then be prompted to create a password for your account:

5. Set a password that you will remember, and confirm by typing it again. Click on **Change** and you will be welcomed to the site:

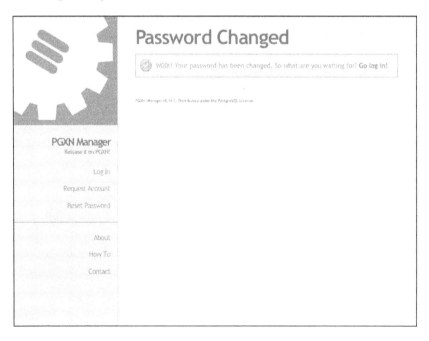

That is all there is to getting signed up. Once you have your new account set up, you can do a few things that will make PostgreSQL extension programming much more painless.

Creating an extension project the easy way

First, let's install some utility packages that will create a lot of boilerplate files that we have already described in earlier sections. The commands below are for a Debian/Ubuntu system:

```
apt-get install ruby
apt-get install rubygems
apt-get install ruby1.8-dev
apt-get install libopenssl-ruby1.8
gem install rubygems-update
/var/lib/gems/1.8/bin/update_rubygems
gem install pgxn_utils
```

You will now find that you have a utility installed named `pgxn-utils`. This utility makes it super simple to create an extension project.

```
pgxn-utils skeleton myextension
      create  myextension
      create  myextension/myextension.control
      create  myextension/META.json
      create  myextension/Makefile
      create  myextension/README.md
      create  myextension/doc/myextension.md
      create  myextension/sql/myextension.sql
      create  myextension/sql/uninstall_myextension.sql
      create  myextension/test/expected/base.out
      create  myextension/test/sql/base.sql
```

Wow! All of the files that we have mentioned so far just got created in a single step. Several files also got created to support the old contrib style of deployment. The next few sections will show which ones are important to you for extension development.

This package management system has one notable restriction. In contrast to PostgreSQL, which allows version numbers to be any alphanumeric text, this package management requires version numbers to follow the rules of semantic versioning.

This version format includes major version, minor version, and release number in the format `major.minor.release`. This is to assist the package manager in installing your package on multiple operating system platforms. Just go with it, you'll thank us later.

Providing the metadata about the extension

There are three files used to provide data about the extension. The PostgreSQL Extension Network uses one of them on the website, `META.json`, for search criteria and description text for the extension. `META.json` will be located in `myextension/META.json`.

Here is an example:

```
{
    "name": "myextension",
    "abstract": "A short description",
    "description": "A long description",
    "version": "0.0.1",
    "maintainer": "The maintainer's name",
    "license": "postgresql",
    "provides": {
        "myextension": {
            "abstract": "A short description",
            "file": "sql/myextension.sql",
            "docfile": "doc/myextension.md",
            "version": "0.0.1"
        }
    },
    "release_status": "unstable",

    "generated_by": "The maintainer's name",


    "meta-spec": {
        "version": "1.0.0",
        "url": "http://pgxn.org/meta/spec.txt"
    }
}
```

You should add some sections to it to describe your keywords and any additional resources that you make available to the user. These sections would look like this:

```
"tags": [
  "cures cancer",
  "myextension",
```

```
        "creates world peace"
    ],
    "resources": {
        "bugtracker":
            {"web": "https://github.com/myaccount/myextension/issues/"},
        "repository": {
            "type": "git",
            "url": "git://github.com/myaccount/myextension.git",
            "web": "https://github.com/myaccount/myextension/"
        }
    }
}
```

The complete file would then look like this:

```
{
    "name": "myextension",
    "abstract": "A short description",
    "description": "A long description",
    "version": "0.0.1",
    "maintainer": "The maintainer's name",
    "license": "postgresql",
    "provides": {
        "myextension": {
            "abstract": "A short description",
            "file": "sql/myextension.sql",
            "docfile": "doc/myextension.md",
            "version": "0.0.1"
        }
    },
    "release_status": "unstable",

    "generated_by": "The maintainer's name",


    "meta-spec": {
        "version": "1.0.0",
        "url": "http://pgxn.org/meta/spec.txt"
    }
    "tags": [
        "cures cancer",
        "myextension",
        "creates world peace"
    ],
    "resources": {
        "bugtracker":
```

```
        {"web": "https://github.com/myaccount/myextension/issues/"},
      "repository": {
       "type": "git",
       "url": "git://github.com/myaccount/myextension.git",
       "web": "https://github.com/myaccount/myextension/"
    }
  }
}
```

The next file that you will need to modify is README.md. This file is located in myextension/README.md. An example is provided with the code that accompanies this book. Due to the length, it will not be reproduced here. This file is distributed along with your extension. It is a markdown syntax file that is meant for human consumption. Describe anything you like in it. Mine includes a recipe for Döner Kebabs. Quite tasty! But most importantly, put a nice long description of the benefits and ease of use of your extension. Finally, we come to doc/myextension.md. This file is used by the PostgreSQL Extension Network to provide a very nice landing page for your extension. It will look something like this:

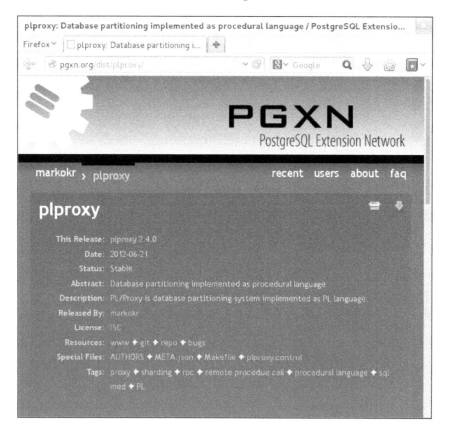

This file is formatted with markdown. You may use several different markup syntaxes here. A discussion of wiki markup is beyond the scope of this description, but the formatting that is in the example is likely to be all you will ever need anyway.

Here is an example of the content of the file:

```
myextension
===========

Synopsis
--------

    Show a brief synopsis of the extension.

Description
-----------

A long description

Usage
-----

    Show usage.

Support
-------

    There is issues tracker? Github? Put this information here.

Author
------

[The maintainer's name]

Copyright and License
---------------------

Copyright (c) 2012 The maintainer's name.
```

Fill out the file with some descriptive narrative about your extension. Add anything that you think might be relevant to the user that is evaluating your extension before making a decision to install it. This is your chance to impress the masses of PostgreSQL developers. So don't be shy here.

Writing your extension code

Put your SQL code in the file that was provided for you in `myextension/sql/`
`myextension.sql`. This file should contain all of the objects that make up
your extension.

```
/* myextension.sql */

-- complain if script is sourced in psql, rather than via CREATE
EXTENSION
\echo Use "CREATE EXTENSION myextension" to load this file. \quit

CREATE FUNCTION feed_the_hungry() ...
```

You can provide any additional SQL files in the same directory for maintaining
versions as described in the *Extension versions* section. Anything named `*.sql`
that is located in this directory will be included in the distribution.

Creating the package

To ultimately submit our extension to the PostgreSQL Extension Network, we
need to package all the files into a single `.zip` file. Assuming we're following good
practices, and we're keeping all of our source code in a handy Git repository, we can
create the package through a simple Git command. Try this one on for size:

```
git archive --format zip --prefix=myextension-0.0.1/ \
    --output ~/Desktop/myextension-0.0.1.zip master
```

This command will create a package for you that is suitable for submission to the
PostgreSQL Extension Network. All we need to do now is submit it.

Submitting the package to PGXN

Now that you have a nice ZIP file in hand, you can go to the PostgreSQL Extension
Network and make your accomplishment available to the community.

1. Start by going to `http://www.pgxn.org`:

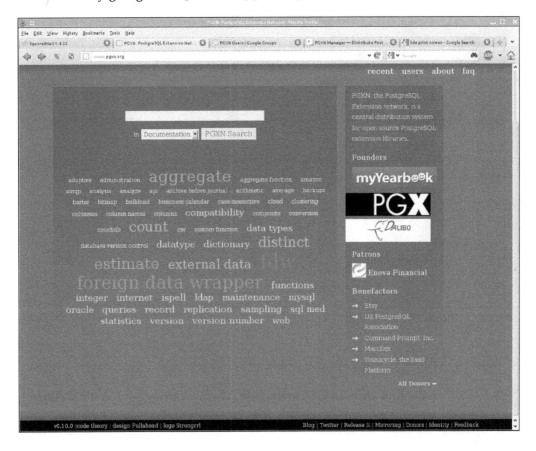

2. At the bottom of the page is a link named **Release It**. Click on the link and you will be taken to the PGXN Manager where you should log in with the username and password that you created in the first section:

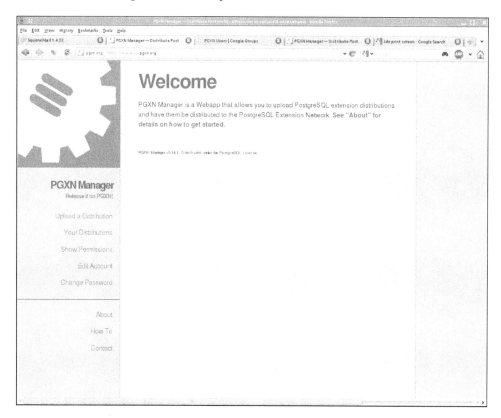

3. Click on the link **Upload a Distribution**. This will bring you to the screen where you can upload the ZIP file that you created in the *Creating the package* section:

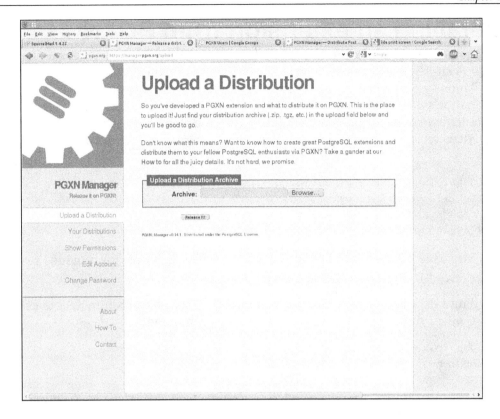

4. Browse your computer for the ZIP file and upload it to the PostgreSQL Extension Network.

That's it. Thanks again for contributing to the PostgreSQL community.

Installing an extension from PGXN

The PostgreSQL Extension Network provides a platform-independent tool to install PostgreSQL extensions. This tool is written in Python, and uses the Python installation system for distributing itself. This is handy because the Python distribution system exists virtually on every PostgreSQL supportable platform and makes it very simple to get PostgreSQL extensions distributed to the community. The extension installer works with a single set of instructions on all targets:

```
easy_install pgxnclient
Installing pgxncli.py script to /usr/local/bin
Installing pgxn script to /usr/local/bin
Processing dependencies for pgxnclient
Finished processing dependencies for pgxnclient
```

Now you have the tools installed to manage PostgreSQL extensions provided by the PostgreSQL Extension Network.

Installing extensions is really simple. For example, if we had a requirement to use a new `tinyint` data type, we could add it with this command:

```
pgxn install tinyint
INFO: best version: tinyint 0.1.1
INFO: saving /tmp/tmpKvr0kM/tinyint-0.1.1.zip
INFO: unpacking: /tmp/tmpKvr0kM/tinyint-0.1.1.zip
INFO: building extension
...
```

The extension is now available in the shared extensions directory on your machine. To activate it for any database, you would use the command that we started the chapter with:

```
CREATE EXTENSION tinyint;
```

You will then see the confirmation text letting you know that `tinyint` has been added:

```
CREATE EXTENSION
```

You now have the extension available for use in your local database. Enjoy!

Summary

Wow, this has been a long hard road toward getting an extension configured and installed. We have used programming skills, system administrative skills, database administrative skills, and wiki editing. Along the way, we saw some Ruby, Python, shell scripting, PL/pgSQL, and MediaWiki.

Believe it or not, this is the simplified process. Hard to imagine, eh? Well, continuous work is being done on the PostgreSQL Extension Network to further simplify this catastrophe of a development system. My thanks go out to David E. Wheeler and crew for making this new system available. As the framework now exists to help with the task, there will be dramatic improvements coming in the months and years ahead.

Now that I'm done complaining about it, this extension system is actually revolutionary. I say this because no other database platform provides any such framework at all. PostgreSQL leads the pack when it comes to the ability to make changes to the basic functionality of the product. The fact that extensions can be installed and removed from the product is an indicator of how inviting PostgreSQL is to the open source community.

Extend it to do whatever you want, and they'll give you the tools to do it. This makes a PostgreSQL server the perfect framework to use for your data processing needs.

In the next chapter, we will learn more about PostgreSQL as an extensible database and look at how to create user-defined data types and operators.

14
PostgreSQL as an Extensible RDBMS

PostgreSQL is an extensible database. I hope you've learned this much by now.
It is extensible by virtue of the design that it has. As discussed before, PostgreSQL
uses a catalog-driven design. In fact, PostgreSQL is more catalog-driven than most
of the traditional relational databases. The key benefit here is that the catalogs can
be changed or added to, in order to modify or extend the database functionality.
PostgreSQL also supports dynamic loading, that is, a user-written code can be
provided as a shared library, and PostgreSQL will load it as required.

Extensibility is critical for many businesses, which have needs that are specific to
that business or industry. Sometimes, the tools provided by the traditional database
systems do not fulfill those needs. People in those businesses know best how to solve
their particular problems, but they are not experts in database internals. It is often
not possible for them to cook up their own database kernel or modify the core or
customize it according to their needs. A truly extensible database will then allow you
to do the following:

- Solve domain-specific problems in a seamless way, like a native solution
- Build complete features without modifying the core database engine
- Extend the database without interrupting availability

PostgreSQL not only allows you to do all of the preceding things, but also does these,
and more with utmost ease. In terms of extensibility, you can do the following things
in a PostgreSQL database:

1. Create your own data types
2. Create your own functions
3. Create your own aggregates

4. Create your own operators

5. Create your own index access methods (operator classes)

6. Create your own server programming language

7. Create foreign data wrappers (SQL/MED) and foreign tables

So far in this book, you learned to create functions and triggers in various programming languages available in PostgreSQL, as well as create user-defined types. You also learned how to use these functions in triggers and rules. As you can see, there are many more types of extensions you can do to the database, and this provides you with all the tools you need to customize and extend the database to suit your business needs. Before we discuss the previously mentioned cases briefly, let's take a look at what you can't extend in PostgreSQL.

What can't be extended?

Although PostgreSQL is an extensible platform, there are certain things that you can't do or change without explicitly doing a fork, as follows:

1. You can't change or plug in a new storage engine. If you are coming from the MySQL world, this might annoy you a little. However, PostgreSQL's storage engine is tightly coupled with its executor and the rest of the system, which has its own benefits.

2. You can't plug in your own planner/parser. One can argue for and against the ability to do that, but at the moment, the planner, parser, optimizer, and so on are baked into the system and there is no possibility of replacing them. There has been some talk on this topic, and if you are of the curious kind, you can read some of the discussion at `http://bit.ly/1yRMkK7`.

3. We will now briefly discuss some more of the extensibility capabilities of PostgreSQL. We will not dive deep into the topics, but we will point you to the appropriate link where more information can be found. The chapter material will serve as an easy-to-understand introductory tutorial on the subject matter. It is by no means a comprehensive discussion of the topics.

Creating a new operator

Now, let's take look at how we can add a new operator in PostgreSQL. Adding new operators is not too different from adding new functions. In fact, an operator is syntactically just a different way to use an existing function. For example, the + operator calls a built-in function called `numeric_add` and passes it the two arguments.

When you define a new operator, you must define the data types that the operator expects as arguments and define which function is to be called.

Let's take a look at how to define a simple operator. You have to use the CREATE OPERATOR command to create an operator.

In *Chapter 2, Server Programming Environments*, we wrote a function to calculate the Fibonacci number of a given integer. Let's use that function to create a new Fibonacci operator, ##, which will have an integer on its left-hand side:

```
CREATE OPERATOR ## (PROCEDURE=fib, LEFTARG=integer);
```

Now, you can use this operator in your SQL to calculate a Fibonacci number:

```
testdb=# SELECT 12##;
?column?
----------
      144
(1 row)
```

Note that we defined that the operator will have an integer on the left-hand side. If you try to put a value on the right-hand side of the operator, you will get an error:

```
postgres=# SELECT ##12;
ERROR:  operator does not exist: ## integer at character 8
HINT:  No operator matches the given name and argument type(s). You
might need to add explicit type casts.
STATEMENT:  select ##12;
ERROR:  operator does not exist: ## integer
LINE 1: select ##12;
               ^

HINT:  No operator matches the given name and argument type(s). You
might need to add explicit type casts.
```

Overloading an operator

Operators can be overloaded in the same way as functions. This means, that an operator can have the same name as an existing operator but with a different set of argument types. More than one operator can have the same name, but two operators can't share the same name if they accept the same types and positions of the arguments. As long as there is a function that accepts the same kind and number of arguments that an operator defines, it can be overloaded.

Let's override the ## operator we defined in the last example, and also add the ability to provide an integer on the right-hand side of the operator:

```
CREATE OPERATOR ## (PROCEDURE=fib, RIGHTARG=integer);
```

Now, running the same SQL, which resulted in an error last time, should succeed, as shown here:

```
testdb=# SELECT ##12;
 ?column?
----------
     144
(1 row)
```

You can drop the operator using the DROP OPERATOR command.

> You can read more about creating and overloading new operators in the PostgreSQL documentation at http://www.postgresql.org/docs/current/static/sql-createoperator.html and http://www.postgresql.org/docs/current/static/xoper.html.

There are several optional clauses in the operator definition that can optimize the execution time of the operators by providing information about operator behavior. For example, you can specify the commutator and the negator of an operator that help the planner use the operators in index scans. You can read more about these optional clauses at http://www.postgresql.org/docs/current/static/xoper-optimization.html.

Since this chapter is just an introduction to the additional extensibility capabilities of PostgreSQL, we will just introduce a couple of optimization options; any serious production quality operator definitions should include these optimization clauses, if applicable.

Optimizing operators

The optional clauses tell the PostgreSQL server about how the operators behave. These options can result in considerable speedups in the execution of queries that use the operator. However, if you provide these options incorrectly, it can result in a slowdown of the queries. Let's take a look at two optimization clauses called **commutator** and **negator**.

COMMUTATOR

This clause defines the commuter of the operator. An operator A is a commutator of operator B if it fulfils the following condition:

```
x A y = y B x.
```

It is important to provide this information for the operators that will be used in indexes and joins. As an example, the commutator for > is <, and the commutator of = is = itself.

This helps the optimizer to flip the operator in order to use an index. For example, consider the following query:

```
SELECT * FROM employee WHERE new_salary > salary;
```

If the index is defined on the salary column, then PostgreSQL can rewrite the preceding query as shown:

```
SELECT * from employee WHERE salary < new_salary
```

This allows PostgreSQL to use a range scan on the index column salary. For a user-defined operator, the optimizer can only do this flip around if the commutator of a user-defined operator is defined:

```
CREATE OPERATOR > (LEFTARG=integer, RIGHTARG=integer, PROCEDURE=comp,
COMMUTATOR = <)
```

NEGATOR

The negator clause defines the negator of the operator. For example, <> is a negator of =. Consider the following query:

```
SELECT * FROM employee WHERE NOT (dept = 10);
```

Since <> is defined as a negator of =, the optimizer can simplify the preceding query as follows:

```
SELECT * FROM employee WHERE dept <> 10;
```

You can even verify that using the EXPLAIN command:

```
postgres=# EXPLAIN SELECT * FROM employee WHERE NOT
            dept = 'WATER MGMNT';
                        QUERY PLAN
-------------------------------------------------------
 Foreign Scan on employee  (cost=0.00..1.10 rows=1 width=160)
   Filter: ((dept)::text <> 'WATER MGMNT'::text)
```

```
    Foreign File: /Users/usamadar/testdata.csv
    Foreign File Size: 197
(4 rows)
```

Creating index access methods

So far in this book, you came across examples of creating new data types or user-defined types and operators. What we haven't discussed so far is how to index these types. In PostgreSQL, an index is more of a framework that can be extended or customized for using different strategies. In order to create new index access methods, we have to create an operator class. Let's take a look at a simple example.

Let's consider a scenario where you have to store some special data such as an ID or a social security number in the database. The number may contain non-numeric characters, so it is defined as a text type:

```
CREATE TABLE test_ssn (ssn text);

INSERT INTO test_ssn VALUES ('222-11-020878');
INSERT INTO test_ssn VALUES ('111-11-020978');
```

Let's assume that the correct order for this data is such that it should be sorted on the last six digits and not the ASCII value of the string.

The fact that these numbers need a unique sort order presents a challenge when it comes to indexing the data. This is where PostgreSQL operator classes are useful. An operator allows a user to create a custom indexing strategy.

Creating an indexing strategy is about creating your own operators and using them alongside a normal B-tree.

Let's start by writing a function that changes the order of digits in the value and also gets rid of the non-numeric characters in the string to be able to compare them better:

```
CREATE OR REPLACE FUNCTION fix_ssn(text)
 RETURNS text AS $$
 BEGIN

        RETURN substring($1,8) || replace(substring($1,1,7),'-','');

 END;
$$LANGUAGE 'plpgsql' IMMUTABLE;
```

Let's run the function and verify that it works:

```
testdb=# SELECT fix_ssn(ssn) FROM test_ssn;
  fix_ssn
-------------
 02087822211
 02097811111
(2 rows)
```

Before an index can be used with a new strategy, we may have to define some more functions depending on the type of index. In our case, we are planning to use a simple B-tree, so we need a comparison function:

```
CREATE OR REPLACE FUNCTION ssn_compareTo(text, text)
RETURNS int AS
$$
  BEGIN
     IF fix_ssn($1) < fix_ssn($2)
     THEN
           RETURN -1;
     ELSIF fix_ssn($1) > fix_ssn($2)
     THEN
           RETURN +1;
       ELSE
             RETURN 0;
      END IF;
END;
$$ LANGUAGE 'plpgsql' IMMUTABLE;
```

It's now time to create our operator class:

```
CREATE OPERATOR CLASS ssn_ops
FOR TYPE text USING btree
AS
OPERATOR        1          <  ,
OPERATOR        2          <= ,
OPERATOR        3          =  ,
OPERATOR        4          >= ,
OPERATOR        5          >  ,
FUNCTION        1          ssn_compareTo(text, text);
```

You can also overload the comparison operators if you need to compare the values in a special way, and use the functions in the compareTo function as well as provide them in the CREATE OPERATOR CLASS command.

We will now create our first index using our brand new operator class:

```
CREATE INDEX idx_ssn ON test_ssn (ssn ssn_ops);
```

We can check whether the optimizer is willing to use our special index, as follows:

```
testdb=# SET enable_seqscan=off;
testdb=# EXPLAIN SELECT * FROM test_ssn WHERE ssn = '02087822211';
                             QUERY PLAN
-----------------------------------------------------------------
 Index Only Scan using idx_ssn on test_ssn  (cost=0.13..8.14 rows=1
width=32)
    Index Cond: (ssn = '02087822211'::text)
(2 rows)
```

Therefore, we can confirm that the optimizer is able to use our new index.

You can read about index access methods in the PostgreSQL documentation at `http://www.postgresql.org/docs/current/static/xindex.html`.

Creating user-defined aggregates

User-defined aggregate functions are probably a unique PostgreSQL feature, yet they are quite obscure and perhaps not many people know how to create them. However, once you are able to create this function, you will wonder how you have lived for so long without using this feature.

This functionality can be incredibly useful, because it allows you to perform custom aggregates inside the database, instead of querying all the data from the client and doing a custom aggregate in your application code, that is, the number of hits on your website per minute from a specific country.

PostgreSQL has a very simple process for defining aggregates. Aggregates can be defined using any functions and in any languages that are installed in the database. Here are the basic steps to building an aggregate function in PostgreSQL:

1. Define a start function that will take in the values of a result set; this function can be defined in any PL language you want.

2. Define an end function that will do something with the final output of the start function. This can be in any PL language you want.

3. Define the aggregate using the CREATE AGGREGATE command, providing the start and end functions you just created.

Let's steal an example from the PostgreSQL wiki at `http://wiki.postgresql.org/wiki/Aggregate_Median`.

In this example, we will calculate the statistical median of a set of data. For this purpose, we will define start and end aggregate functions.

Let's define the end function first, which takes an array as a parameter and calculates the median. We are assuming here that our start function will pass an array to the following end function:

```
CREATE FUNCTION _final_median(anyarray) RETURNS float8 AS $$
  WITH q AS
  (
     SELECT val
     FROM unnest($1) val
     WHERE VAL IS NOT NULL
     ORDER BY 1
  ),
  cnt AS
  (
     SELECT COUNT(*) AS c FROM q
  )
  SELECT AVG(val)::float8
  FROM
  (
     SELECT val FROM q
     LIMIT  2 - MOD((SELECT c FROM cnt), 2)
     OFFSET GREATEST(CEIL((SELECT c FROM cnt) / 2.0) - 1,0)
  ) q2;
$$ LANGUAGE sql IMMUTABLE;
```

Now, we create the aggregate as shown in the following code:

```
CREATE AGGREGATE median(anyelement) (
  SFUNC=array_append,
  STYPE=anyarray,
  FINALFUNC=_final_median,
  INITCOND='{}'
);
```

The `array_append` start function is already defined in PostgreSQL. This function appends an element to the end of an array.

In our example, the start function takes all the column values and creates an intermediate array. This array is passed on to the end function, which calculates the median.

Now, let's create a table and some test data to run our function:

```
testdb=# CREATE TABLE median_test(t integer);
CREATE TABLE
```

```
testdb=# INSERT INTO median_test SELECT generate_series(1,10);
INSERT 0 10
```

The `generate_series` function is a set returning function that generates a series of values, from start to stop with a step size of one.

Now, we are all set to test the function:

```
testdb=# SELECT median(t) FROM median_test;
 median
--------
    5.5
(1 row)
```

The mechanics of the preceding example are quite easy to understand. When you run the aggregate, the start function is used to append all the table data from column t into an array using the `append_array` PostgreSQL built-in. This array is passed on to the final function, `_final_median`, which calculates the median of the array and returns the result in the same data type as the input parameter. This process is done transparently to the user of the function who simply has a convenient aggregate function available to them.

You can read more about the user-defined aggregates in the PostgreSQL documentation in much more detail at `http://www.postgresql.org/docs/current/static/xaggr.html`.

Using foreign data wrappers

PostgreSQL **foreign data wrappers** (**FDW**) are an implementation of **SQL Management of External Data** (**SQL/MED**), which is a standard added to SQL in 2013.

FDWs are drivers that allow PostgreSQL database users to read and write data to other external data sources, such as other relational databases, NoSQL data sources, files, JSON, LDAP, and even Twitter.

You can query the foreign data sources using SQL and create joins across different systems or even across different data sources.

There are several different types of data wrappers developed by different developers and not all of them are production quality. You can see a select list of wrappers on the PostgreSQL wiki at `http://wiki.postgresql.org/wiki/Foreign_data_wrappers`.

Another list of FDWs can be found on PGXN at `http://pgxn.org/tag/fdw/`.

Let's take look at a small example of using `file_fdw` to access data in a CSV file.

First, you need to install the `file_fdw` extension. If you compiled PostgreSQL from the source, you will need to install the `file_fdw` contrib module that is distributed with the source. You can do this by going into the `contrib/file_fdw` folder and running `make` and `make install`. If you used an installer or a package for your platform, this module might have been installed automatically.

Once the `file_fdw` module is installed, you will need to create the extension in the database:

```
postgres=# CREATE EXTENSION file_fdw;
CREATE EXTENSION
```

Let's now create a sample CSV file that uses the pipe, |, as a separator and contains some employee data:

```
$ cat testdata.csv
AARON, ELVIA J|WATER RATE TAKER|WATER MGMNT|81000.00|73862.00
AARON, JEFFERY M|POLICE OFFICER|POLICE|74628.00|74628.00
AARON, KIMBERLEI R|CHIEF CONTRACT EXPEDITER|FLEET
MANAGEMNT|77280.00|70174.00
```

Now, we should create a foreign server that is pretty much a formality because the file is on the same server. A foreign server normally contains the connection information that a foreign data wrapper uses to access an external data resource. The server needs to be unique within the database:

```
CREATE SERVER file_server FOREIGN DATA WRAPPER file_fdw;
```

The next step, is to create a foreign table that encapsulates our CSV file:

```
CREATE FOREIGN TABLE employee (
     emp_name       VARCHAR,
     job_title        VARCHAR,
     dept           VARCHAR,
     salary           NUMERIC,
     sal_after_tax    NUMERIC
) SERVER file_server
OPTIONS (format 'csv',header 'false' , filename '/home/pgbook/14/
testdata.csv', delimiter '|', null '');'');
```

The `CREATE FOREIGN TABLE` command creates a foreign table and the specifications of the file are provided in the `OPTIONS` section of the preceding code. You can provide the format, and if the first line of the file is a header (`header 'false'`), in our case there is no file header.

We then provide the name and path of the file and the delimiter used in the file, which in our case is the pipe symbol |. In this example, we also specify that the null values should be represented as an empty string.

Let's run a SQL command on our foreign table:

```
postgres=# select * from employee;
-[ RECORD 1 ]-+-------------------------
emp_name      | AARON, ELVIA J
job_title     | WATER RATE TAKER
dept          | WATER MGMNT
salary        | 81000.00
sal_after_tax | 73862.00
-[ RECORD 2 ]-+-------------------------
emp_name      | AARON, JEFFERY M
job_title     | POLICE OFFICER
dept          | POLICE
salary        | 74628.00
sal_after_tax | 74628.00
-[ RECORD 3 ]-+-------------------------
emp_name      | AARON, KIMBERLEI R
job_title     | CHIEF CONTRACT EXPEDITER
dept          | FLEET MANAGEMNT
salary        | 77280.00
sal_after_tax | 70174.00
```

Great, looks like our data is successfully loaded from the file.

You can also use the \d meta command to see the structure of the employee table:

```
postgres=# \d employee;

               Foreign table "public.employee"
    Column     |        Type        | Modifiers | FDW Options
---------------+--------------------+-----------+-------------
 emp_name      | character varying  |           |
 job_title     | character varying  |           |
 dept          | character varying  |           |
 salary        | numeric            |           |
 sal_after_tax | numeric            |           |
Server: file_server
FDW Options: (format 'csv', header 'false',
    filename '/home/pg_book/14/testdata.csv', delimiter '|',
      "null" '')
```

You can run explain on the query to understand what is going on when you run a query on the foreign table:

```
postgres=# EXPLAIN SELECT * FROM employee WHERE salary > 5000;
                        QUERY PLAN
--------------------------------------------------------
 Foreign Scan on employee  (cost=0.00..1.10 rows=1 width=160)
   Filter: (salary > 5000::numeric)
   Foreign File: /home/pgbook/14/testdata.csv
   Foreign File Size: 197
(4 rows)
```

The ALTER FOREIGN TABLE command can be used to modify the options.

 More information about the file_fdw is available at http://www.postgresql.org/docs/current/static/file-fdw.html.

You can take a look at the CREATE SERVER and CREATE FOREIGN TABLE commands in the PostgreSQL documentation for more information on the many options available. Each of the foreign data wrappers comes with its own documentation about how to use the wrapper. Make sure that an extension is stable enough before it is used in production. The PostgreSQL core development group does not support most of the FDW extensions.

If you want to create your own data wrappers, you can find the documentation at http://www.postgresql.org/docs/current/static/fdwhandler.html as an excellent starting point. The best way to learn, however, is to read the code of other available extensions.

Summary

PostgreSQL can be extended in many more ways than what we have discussed so far in the book. This includes the ability to add new operators, new index access methods, and create your own aggregates. You can access foreign data sources, such as other databases, files, and web services using PostgreSQL foreign data wrappers. These wrappers are provided as extensions and should be used with caution, as most of them are not officially supported.

Even though PostgreSQL is very extensible, you can't plug in a new storage engine or change the parser/planner and executor interfaces. These components are very tightly coupled with each other and are, therefore, highly optimized and mature.

Index

K

keep it simple stupid (KISS) 28
k nearest neighbor (KNN) 31

L

licensing 38
light-weight locks (LWLocks) 202
log trigger 154-157
looping syntax
  URL 61
loops
  statement, terminating 62
  with counters 60, 61

M

Makefile function 173
Master-slave replication 213
metadata
  providing, for extension 266-269
Multi-master replication 213
Multiversion Concurrency Control
    (MVCC) 116

N

NEGATOR clause 281
NEW record
  modifying 111
NULL arguments
  handling 176-178

O

operator
  new operator, creating 278, 279
  optimizing 280
  overloading 279, 280
  PostgreSQL documentation, URL 280
  used, for data comparisons 15
operator, optimizing
  COMMUTATOR 281
  NEGATOR 281
optional clauses
  URL 280

os.walk()
  URL 168
OUT parameters
  about 81
  and records 80
  no predefined structure, returning
      with 84, 85
  records, returning 81, 82
  RETURNS TABLE, using 83
  SETOF ANY, returning 85-87
  variadic argument lists 87, 88

P

package
  creating 270
  submitting, to PGXN 271-273
palloc()
  using 186
parameters 49
Pentaho data integration (kettle) 41
Pentaho Report Server 41
PERFORM command
  versus SELECT command 64
Perl 229
pfree()
  using 186
pgAdmin3 41
  installing 135
pgfoundry
  URL 203
PGXN
  about 263
  extension, installing from 274
  FDWs URL 286
  package, submitting 271-273
  URL 271
php5-postgresql 41
pl/lolcode
  URL 204
PL/Perl
  function 230, 231
  function, URL 230-237
  installing 230
  non-scalar types, passing 231-234
  non-scalar types, returning 231-234
  triggers, writing 235-237

Thank you for buying
PostgreSQL Server Programming
Second Edition

About Packt Publishing

Packt, pronounced 'packed', published its first book, *Mastering phpMyAdmin for Effective MySQL Management*, in April 2004, and subsequently continued to specialize in publishing highly focused books on specific technologies and solutions.

Our books and publications share the experiences of your fellow IT professionals in adapting and customizing today's systems, applications, and frameworks. Our solution-based books give you the knowledge and power to customize the software and technologies you're using to get the job done. Packt books are more specific and less general than the IT books you have seen in the past. Our unique business model allows us to bring you more focused information, giving you more of what you need to know, and less of what you don't.

Packt is a modern yet unique publishing company that focuses on producing quality, cutting-edge books for communities of developers, administrators, and newbies alike. For more information, please visit our website at www.packtpub.com.

About Packt Open Source

In 2010, Packt launched two new brands, Packt Open Source and Packt Enterprise, in order to continue its focus on specialization. This book is part of the Packt Open Source brand, home to books published on software built around open source licenses, and offering information to anybody from advanced developers to budding web designers. The Open Source brand also runs Packt's Open Source Royalty Scheme, by which Packt gives a royalty to each open source project about whose software a book is sold.

Writing for Packt

We welcome all inquiries from people who are interested in authoring. Book proposals should be sent to author@packtpub.com. If your book idea is still at an early stage and you would like to discuss it first before writing a formal book proposal, then please contact us; one of our commissioning editors will get in touch with you.

We're not just looking for published authors; if you have strong technical skills but no writing experience, our experienced editors can help you develop a writing career, or simply get some additional reward for your expertise.

PostgreSQL 9 High Availability Cookbook

ISBN: 978-1-84951-696-9   Paperback: 398 pages

Over 100 recipes to design and implement a highly available server with the advanced features of PostgreSQL

1. Create a PostgreSQL cluster that stays online even when disaster strikes.

2. Avoid costly downtime and data loss that can ruin your business.

3. Perform data replication and monitor your data with hands-on industry-driven recipes and detailed step-by-step explanations.

PostgreSQL Cookbook

ISBN: 978-1-78355-533-8   Paperback: 286 pages

Over 90 hands-on recipes to effectively manage, administer, and design solutions using PostgreSQL

1. Implement a highly available PostgreSQL database server and perform administrative and development functions with PostgreSQL.

2. Perform database operations in PostgreSQL using Perl and Python.

3. Step-by-step recipes focusing on providing real-world Postgresql solutions.

Please check **www.PacktPub.com** for information on our titles

PostgreSQL Server Programming

ISBN: 978-1-84951-698-3   Paperback: 264 pages

Extend PostgreSQL and integrate the database layer into your development framework

1. Understand the extension framework of PostgreSQL, and leverage it in ways that you haven't even invented yet.

2. Write functions, create your own data types, all in your favourite programming language.

3. Step-by-step tutorial with plenty of tips and tricks to kick-start server programming.

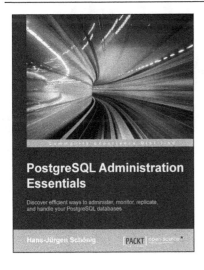

PostgreSQL Administration Essentials

ISBN: 978-1-78398-898-3   Paperback: 142 pages

Discover efficient ways to administer, monitor, replicate, and handle your PostgreSQL databases

1. Learn how to detect bottlenecks and make sure your database systems offer superior performance to your end users.

2. Replicate your databases to achieve full redundancy and create backups quickly and easily.

3. Optimize PostgreSQL configuration parameters and turn your database server into a high-performance machine capable of fulfilling your needs.

Please check **www.PacktPub.com** for information on our titles

www.ingramcontent.com/pod-product-compliance
Lightning Source LLC
Chambersburg PA
CBHW062106050326
40690CB00016B/3224